Irene B.

ROSES, FOUNTAINS, AND GOLD

Roses, Fountains, and Gold

The Virgin Mary in History, Art, and Apparition

BY
JOHN MARTIN

IGNATIUS PRESS   SAN FRANCISCO

Cover art: *The Mystic Nativity* (detail),
Sandro Botticelli
The National Gallery, London
Art Resource, New York

Cover design by Roxanne Mei Lum

ISBN 0–89870–680–7
Library of Congress catalogue number 97–76858
Printed in the United States of America ∞

To Mary Gehringer,
  who pointed the way,
and to Peter Kreeft,
  who made straight the path

The Church cannot insist too much on the true position of Mary, for it is a strong hedge round the doctrine of the Incarnation. Every grace of Mary's, every prerogative, every dignity she has, is hers simply because she is the Mother of Christ; and it is wholly for His sake that we honor her, nor do we give her any honor which does not in consequence redound to Him of necessity.

— Abbot Chapman, *Bishop Gore and the Catholic Claims*

Hear and let it penetrate into your heart, my dear little son: let nothing discourage you, nothing depress you. Let nothing alter your heart or your countenance. Also, do not fear any illness or vexation, anxiety or pain. Am I not here who am your Mother? Are you not under my shadow and protection? Am I not your fountain of life? Are you not in the crossing of my arms?

— The Blessed Virgin speaking to Juan Diego,
a converted Aztec Christian, on Tepeyac Hill
(December 1531)

CONTENTS

I

THE BEAUTIFUL LADY WHO
KEEPS APPEARING

Kings' daughters were among thy honorable women; upon thy
right hand did stand the queen in gold of Ophir.
—Psalm 45 (King James Version)

Like that tower of David to which she is sometimes compared,
the Blessed Virgin Mary still points beyond the temporal stars
from an eternal hill in Jerusalem. And by the infinitely generous
will of the Creator, the human Mother of the divine Christ is
somehow not only there but everywhere—a loving and life-
giving presence who bestrides our narrow world like an angelic
colossus, joining heaven's grace to the prayers of earth. To know
her story in all its depth and richness is to penetrate to the very
heart of the great mystery—indeed, to the *sacred* heart of the
great mystery. To be ignorant of her story, on the other hand, is
to be like Tolstoy's modern historian: a deaf man answering
questions that no one has put to him. This book, then, is an
attempt to answer the *right* questions and thus provide the
Marian knowledge that will make the reader ask, half in indignation and half in wonder: "How can I have gone through life
without knowing these things? How can anyone else?"

Even looked at superficially, the life of Mary should give us
pause. After all, not only have numberless sinners down the centuries and throughout the nations found in her both an

inspiring example and a gracious advocate, but Western civilization itself bears her stamp: the greatest works of art in the history of the world—Europe's Gothic cathedrals—rose in her
honor; Michelangelo exalted her in marble; Leonardo captured
her in paint; Schubert immortalized her in song; and artists
both great and various have made Madonna and Child a permanent possession of the normal heart.

Yet to get any deep and lasting sense of this endearingly human and eternally sacred young woman, we need to range all
over the globe—to return to ancient Ephesus, to hear the words
of great Marian scholars, to see her influence in the history of
Mexico and France, to understand why both Rome and Constantinople have endlessly glorified her in shrine, basilica, ikon,
pilgrimage, and prayer, to see why all generations have not only
called her blessed but referred to her by that stupendous title:
Theotokos, Mater Dei, the Mother of God.

We also need to see her through the eyes of those who have
been privileged to behold her in apparition—such visionaries,
for example, as Bernadette Soubirous, the saintly young peasant
girl eternally identified with Lourdes and all its wonders. Indeed, we need to look with special care at Mary's appearances
over the last seven of those eighty generations that have called
her blessed, because they have great things to tell us not only
about the Maid of Nazareth but also about what heaven re-
quires of the children of earth if they are to be spared the fire
both here and hereafter.

To be sure, Marian apparitions are nothing new. They have
been reported numerous times through the Christian centuries,
and perhaps the most significant one of all took place on a hill
in Mexico in 1531—as we shall see. Yet the eight that began in
France shortly after the death of Napoleon Bonaparte in 1821
and ended in Belgium in 1933, just as Hitler was coming to
power next door in Germany, deserve particular attention. As
with Guadalupe, they have a claim on us for three special

reasons: (1) They illuminate Mary's many-faceted role in an unforgettably personal way; (2) they speak to us with a whole new intensity about truth, salvation, time, and danger; and (3) they were all laboriously authenticated: far from being imagined by hysterics or invented by charlatans, they happened. Though we will be looking at them in detail in later chapters, here is a brief summary:

- In July 1830, Mary appeared to the devout twenty-four-year-old Catherine Labouré in the Paris chapel of the Daughters of Charity. In the most astonishing of a series of visions, one that lasted a full two hours, the Virgin appeared all in white with her feet resting on a globe and her gemmed fingers emitting dazzling rays. "The ball that you see", she explained, "represents the whole world, especially France, and each person in particular. The rays are the symbols of the graces I shed upon those who ask for them."

- In September 1846, she appeared to two young cowherds at a ravine high in the French Alps near the village of La Salette. She wore a long white dress, a crown edged with roses, an apron of gold, and a blazing crucifix. "If my Son is not to cast you off," she said to France through the children, "I am obliged to entreat him without ceasing." As a sign to the doubters, she caused water to flow from a dried-up stream—with stupendous healing miracles soon to follow.

- In February 1858, she appeared to Bernadette Soubirous, a fourteen-year-old asthmatic shepherdess, at a grotto near Lourdes, in the French Pyrenees. This time she wore a white veil and gown, with a blue sash at her waist, and carried a large rosary. On each of her bare feet was a yellow rose. During the course of eighteen apparitions spread over a period of five months, she pointed, on one memorable occasion, to a spot in the earth where, when Bernadette dug, a stream appeared—in fact, a healing stream, like the one at La Salette. When her sceptical pastor asked Bernadette to find out the Lady's name, Bernadette returned with the sensational news that the Lady had identified herself by proclaiming in the local dialect: "Que soy era Immaculado Conceptiou" (I am the Immaculate Conception).

- In January 1871, she appeared in Pontmain, a small town in the north of France. The first two witnesses were young boys, who saw in the sky a "Lady" dressed in a blue robe sprinkled with stars. Their disbelieving parents, seeing nothing, summoned the nuns in charge of the local school. The nuns saw no more than had the parents, but two little girls they had brought along did see and confirm the description given by the young boys—a beautiful Lady wearing a star-studded blue robe and a gold crown. Later, the Lady gave them a message about her Son in gold letters on a white banner, following which they saw a large red crucifix surmounted by a placard inscribed in bright red letters: JESUS CHRIST.

- In August 1879, she appeared in the remote Irish hillside town of Knock—as the central figure in a remarkable tableau that also included Saint John the Evangelist (holding a large, open book) and an altar on which rested a cross and a young lamb. The vision lasted for more than two hours, as villagers summoned their friends that they too might look on at that west-country wonder.

- In May 1917, she appeared to three young shepherd children at the Cova da Iria, a wild bit of country near Fatima, a Portuguese village ninety miles north of Lisbon. The children described her as so dazzling as to seem made of light and reported that she wore a simple tunic and a mantle whose border seemed to glitter like gold. Remarkably, she spoke of the dangers of an evil not yet apparent—the atheism that would arrive with the October Revolution that year and submerge Russia in a latter-day Babylonian Captivity (1917–1987) exactly as long—seventy years—as the one under which the Jews had suffered twenty-five centuries earlier.

- In November 1932, she appeared to five young children in the Belgian town of Beauraing, sixty miles southeast of Brussels. She wore a heavily pleated white gown that reflected a blue light, and she had a rosary draped over her right arm. Starting with the sixth of her thirty-three showings there, she appeared under a hawthorn tree, announcing, "I will convert sinners." On the last day of the year she gave the children a breathtaking vision of her heart as a heart of gold, surrounded by glittering rays—undoubtedly an echo of Fatima, where she had emphasized her Immaculate Heart.

- In January 1933, less than a month after the last Beauraing vision, she appeared to Mariette Beco, a twelve-year-old farm girl in Banneux, Belgium. As always, Mary's costume was slightly different from its predecessors. This time her right foot was crowned with a single golden rose, and on her right arm was a rosary with a golden chain and cross. As at Lourdes, she wore a white dress with a blue sash. And now she had yet another message for the world: "I am the Virgin of the poor." In a reprise of La Salette and Lourdes, she revealed the presence of a then unknown spring and asked that a chapel be built nearby.

These eight appearances constitute perhaps the most remarkable hundred years of heaven-to-earth dialogue since the first century A.D. Indeed, in all of them, the very tone and heraldry of Paradise can be felt quite apart from Mary's words, and not merely in such obvious signs as the crown she wore at La Salette or the stars on her gown at Pontmain. It can be felt especially in the repetition of what might be called "themes"—the celestial blue and white of her garments, her Christlike concern for children and the poor, and her identification with those symbols of earthly beauty and heavenly favor that inspired the title of this book: roses, fountains, and gold.

Roses, whether in the Virgin's crown at La Salette, on her forehead at Knock, or on her feet at Lourdes and Banneux, not only symbolize love but recall that mystical passage in the Song of Solomon: "I am the rose of Sharon and the lily of the valleys." Fountains, as at La Salette, Lourdes, and Banneux, remind us not only of baptism and Revelation's river of life flowing out of the throne of God but also Jesus' words to the woman of Samaria about "a well of water springing up into everlasting life". And gold, as in the gold apron at La Salette, the gold-bordered mantle at Fatima, the heart of gold at Beauraing, and the gold rosary at Banneux, speaks both for permanence and for the pure gold of the heavenly Jerusalem.

Thus, even if the Virgin had said nothing in any of these eight apparitions—and she spoke in all but two—her appearance would have been a language in its own right. Indeed, perhaps the most eloquent aspect of Mary in apparition is the dazzling light in which she so often appears—that light that never was on land or sea except by the illumination of heaven on great occasions. When Moses came down from Mount Sinai with the tablets of the Law, "the skin of his face shone, and they were afraid to come near him." When Jesus was transfigured on a high mountain, "his face did shine as the sun and his raiment was white as the light." Mary's transfiguration-like appearance at Fatima not only recalls those supernatural visions but can be testified to by a witness still living in 1998—ninety-one-year-old Carmelite Sister Lucia Abóbora, a child of ten when she first saw the Virgin.

Whether in word or image, then, Mary said things in those eight apparitions that need to be looked at in detail—as they later will be. One thing makes them especially compelling, however, and that is their central message, which echoes that concise command in the first chapter of Mark: "Repent and believe the Gospel." If the 116 years from 1337 to 1453 are conveniently labeled the Hundred Years' War, the 103 years from Catherine Labouré's vision in 1830 to Mariette Beco's last sight of the Virgin in 1933 could be called the Hundred Years' Warning. Among other things, the Virgin was saying what prophets have been saying since Moses burned the golden calf: Unless sinners straighten out and look up, divine anger will break forth and crash down.

At Fatima especially, with a seventy-year darkness soon to engulf Russia, did the beautiful Lady in the sun-bright robe speak not only to sin in general but to what the socially conscious nineteenth-century Russian intellectuals called the "accursed questions": How should we live? Why are we here? What must we do? Because those questions were about to be ruthlessly answered by the *wrong* sort of Russian intellectuals—Lenin and his Bolsheviks—and because Mary knew that, she spoke of "converting" a Russia that had not yet been lost. And knowing other things that earthlings do not, she spoke of converting it, not by dazzling power plays and diplomatic finesse, but by a prayer life centered on the fifty-nine beads and fifteen mysteries of the rosary. Alas, although with many exceptions, her recipe for deliverance was ignored while Lenin's was enthusiastically followed.

Fatima, of course, did not represent the Virgin's last word. Beauraing and Banneux were yet to come, and in these latter days, especially in the last thirty years or so, there have been reports of Marian apparitions all around the world—Argentina, Ireland, Japan, Korea, and Venezuela, among many others. Are these—if they are in fact authentic—simply a geographical broadening, a kind of booster-shot warning to a world reluctant to listen, or is there some other explanation? Some of the messages, in any case, have been both highly specific and ominously accurate and will later be carefully considered.

Yet ever since that summer night in 1830 when Catherine Labouré heard the Virgin say, "My child, the good God wishes to charge you with a mission", what has towered above any single appearance or set of appearances has been the growing sense that the Creator has been speaking through Mary to the tribes of earth as once he spoke through Moses to the tribes of Israel. Indeed, with both "natural" and man-made devastation so obviously intensifying, from Chernobyl to the horrific earthquakes in Japan and the Philippines, the question inevitably raised is one that most of us would probably rather not think about: Are Mary's words of apocalyptic warning even now being confirmed?

Yet before we look at the Virgin in the light of what is yet to come, it is essential to look at her in the light of what she was from the very first. And that means going all the way back to the conception we call immaculate.

2

THE IMMACULATE CONCEPTION AND THE IMMACULATE COMPLETION

For as a virgin she conceived, as a virgin she gave birth, a virgin she remained.

—Saint Augustine, *Sermons*, 51

Like the poor, misconceptions about the Immaculate Conception have always been with us. Fortunately, the most common one, unlike the situation with the poor, can be cleared up without noisy debates in Hyde Park and the utopian master plans of the New World Order. Very simply, the term applies, not to the conception of Jesus in the womb of Mary, but to the conception of Mary in the womb of *her* mother, Saint Anne.

Jesus' conception was also immaculate, of course, but in the divine plan, *that* immaculate conception required the prior one. If Mary had not been permanently free of any trace of the sin that the two citizens of Eden brought into the world, then Jesus, the all-perfect second Person of the Holy Trinity, true God and true Man, would have received his blood, bone, and sinew from the flesh of a woman who had not at every second of her life been immaculate. While that was unacceptable to divinity, it was not quite unthinkable to humanity, and it would be many centuries before what had always been known in heaven was declared on earth. That great truth would be established once and for all only in the nineteenth century with the Blessed Virgin's revelations to Catherine Labouré and Bernadette Soubirous and a papal declaration proclaiming the Immaculate Conception an article of faith (see chapter 14).

And there is a related question not to be overlooked: Did this singularly exalted young woman later take up a more "normal" life as the mother of other, quite ordinary children, or did she complete her existence in the same immaculate and virginal way in which she began it? That is the question of what might be called "the immaculate completion", and it will be dealt with as soon as we have looked carefully at the Immaculate Conception. Perhaps the most helpful non-divine authority on *that* subject is John Henry Cardinal Newman (1801–1890), Oxford scholar and Catholic theologian, and I gratefully quote and paraphrase him in the paragraphs that follow.

As Newman explains it, the Immaculate Conception means that Mary was conceived in the womb of her mother, not with a different nature from ordinary human beings, but rather with the divine grace that preserved her from sin from the first moment of her being. Thus, he points out, she was the second woman in history to be without original sin from the instant she was created—Eve, her later transgression notwithstanding, having been the first. On the male side, Adam shared the distinction, and another who came close to doing so was John the Baptist, who was filled with the Holy Spirit from the moment he leaped for joy in his mother's womb.

"Does the objector not believe", Newman asks, "that Saint John the Baptist had the grace of God—that is, was regenerated, even before his birth? What do we believe of Mary, but that grace was given her at a still earlier period? . . . A more abundant gift of grace made her what she was from the first."

Again, he asks, did the great honor bestowed on Mary so exalt her that she did not require the salvation provided by the death of her Son? "Just the contrary", says Newman. "We say that she, of all mere children of Adam, is in the truest sense the fruit and purchase of His passion. He has done for her more than for anyone else. To others He gives grace and regeneration at a *point* in their earthly existence; to her from the very beginning."

Newman, by the way, had far more than an academic interest in the subject. Whether by chance or the design of Providence, he was privileged to be living and writing in those exciting 1850s when Pope Pius IX was declaring what a fourteen-year-old shepherdess would confirm when she rushed from the grotto at Lourdes to the office of her pastor to quote the Virgin's astounding words: "I am the Immaculate Conception." (Again, chapter 14 gives a fuller historical perspective and an appreciation of the great drama surrounding this doctrine.)

Let us now move on to the question of the immaculate completion. After all, there are those who, while they do not exactly raise the question of sin, do raise the question of whether or not Mary, far from remaining a virgin, ultimately became the wife of Joseph in every sense and as a result gave birth to additional children. If she in fact did, that would seem to be a difficult reality to reconcile with the idea of the Virgin as a divinely created Holy of Holies, reserved for God alone. After all, even Israel's Holy of Holies could be entered by man in the person of the High Priest just once a year. Yet here we would have God's own *sanctum sanctorum* entered by man in the person of Mary's spouse whenever he chose to assert his marital rights—a most difficult idea to harmonize with Mary's virginal role in general and the forty-fourth chapter of Ezekiel in particular. That chapter, by the way, is the source of one of Mary's many titles, the Gate of Heaven:

> Then said the Lord unto me: This gate shall be shut, it shall not be opened, and no man shall enter in by it; because the Lord, the God of Israel, hath entered in by it, therefore it shall be shut. It is for the prince; the prince, he shall sit in it to eat bread before the Lord; he shall enter by the way of the porch of that gate, and shall go out by way of the same.

Yet, the sceptical reader may well ask, whether or not this passage symbolically refers to Mary, does the New Testament not clearly indicate that Jesus had brothers and sisters? And to be sure, there are those verses in Matthew 12:47–50, beginning, "Behold, thy mother, and thy brethren stand without, desiring to speak with thee", and ending with Jesus indicating his disciples and saying, "Behold my mother and my brethren: For whosoever shall do the will of my Father, which is in heaven, the same is my brother, and sister, and mother."

No matter what anyone's first impressions may be, however, three distinct interpretations are possible:

1. The "brethren" referred to were indeed Mary's children, fathered by Joseph.

2. The "brethren" were not Mary's children but her stepchildren, having been fathered by Joseph in a previous marriage—or alternatively, children the couple had adopted.

3. The "brethren" were not *immediate* family. ("Brethren" was a general term, one that could apply not only to brothers and sisters but also to kinsmen.)

If the third is the correct explanation—and as we shall see, there are very good reasons for thinking it is—this would be an accurate paraphrase of what Jesus was saying: "You say my relatives are waiting outside. Well, then, let me make a point. These people in here may not be my relatives, but if they do the will of my father, they will be as close to me as if they were my own brother, sister, or mother." Is he saying he *has* a brother and sister? No, he is simply using family terms for emphasis and would naturally use those that express the deepest blood relation. Would not his original words lose all their force if he said, "For whosoever shall do the will of my Father, which is in heaven, the same is my nephew, aunt, and brother-in-law"?

The great difficulty here is that Hebrew and Aramaic, the languages spoken by Jesus, had no exclusive word for cousin. Understandably, then, this caused serious confusion in the New

Testament, which was written chiefly in Greek. It even caused confusion in the Old Testament, since the Hebrew word *ah* (brother) was also used for "kinsman". In the Greek of the New Testament, in any case, the word *ah* is rendered as *adelphos*, even though *adelphos* means a blood brother.

In fact, *adelphos* is used not only for "kinsman" but also for people who are not blood relatives at all, as in the following: Christ "appeared to more than five hundred brothers [*adelphoi*, plural] at one time" (1 Cor 15:6), "that he might be the first born among many brothers" (Rom 8:29), and Silvanus, "a faithful brother" (1 Pet 5:2). If *adelphos*, the Greek word for blood brother, then, can be used to describe not only secondary relatives but even people who are not relatives at all, how can anyone state with any confidence that Jesus had brothers and that Mary was their mother as well?

Be all that as it may, let us consider the other two possibilities, starting with the second: Did Joseph have children of his own? Quite possibly he did, but if so, why do we never hear of them until Jesus, already over thirty years old, has begun his public ministry? The Gospels make no mention of them either on the Herod-escaping journey to Egypt or on the return to Judea, or, for that matter, at any other point in the early life of Jesus.

That leaves the first possibility: Did Joseph have other children by Mary? If not, how can we explain that seemingly explicit passage (Mt 13:55) where Jesus' fellow Nazarenes, indignant at the authority he displays in his teaching, ask in a belittling way: "Is not this the carpenter's son? Is not his mother called Mary? and his brethren James and Joseph, and Simon and Judas? and his sisters, are they not all with us?"

The first point to note is that the problem with the word "sister" is much the same as the problem with "brother": it can also mean cousin or close relative. The second point to note is that Mary had a sister (or at least a close relative) also named Mary—Mary the wife of Cleophas (see Jn 19:25). Now, and this

is crucial, in Matthew 27:56, Mary the wife of Cleophas is specifically referred to as the mother of the aforementioned James
and Joseph. They would therefore not be the brothers of Jesus
but his cousins or even his second cousins.

Whether the other two "brothers" and the "sisters" referred
to are also the children of Mary the wife of Cleophas it would
be impossible to say. Yet to be aware that a passage referring to
James and Joseph as the *adelphoi* brothers of Jesus when they are
in fact *not* his blood brothers is to be aware that any passage
dealing with the relatives of Jesus must be looked at with ex-
treme care. Again, if James, Joseph, Simon, and Judas and the
nameless sisters really were members of Jesus' immediate family,
one can only marvel at the way they all stayed out of sight so
much of the time. Consider some of the occasions on which we
would reasonably expect to hear about them and consider instead what we do hear:

1. The feast of the Passover when Jesus was twelve years old (Lk
   2:41–50). The passage is puzzling enough as it is, leaving us
   to wonder how, on leaving Jerusalem, Joseph and Mary
   would simply assume that their twelve-year-old son was "in
   the company" of their fellow Nazarene pilgrims and thus
   would go "a day's journey" before turning back to look for
   him. But it is even more difficult to imagine that their other
   children, if other children they had, would not have been
   mentioned at some point in this, the only recorded episode
   in Jesus' youth.

2. The marriage in Cana of Galilee (Jn 2:1–11). Note the list of
   those attending: ". . . and the mother of Jesus was there: and
   both Jesus was called, and his disciples to the marriage." At a
   wedding in a village only five miles or so from Nazareth, it
   seems more than a little odd that Jesus, Mary, and the disciples were invited, but none of Mary's other children. Some
   bitter feelings there, one would think!

3. At the Cross (Jn 19:25–27). This is where the absence of

those "brothers" and "sisters" becomes truly astonishing. Here we have four and only four "insiders" present: the Virgin; her sister (or close relative) Mary, the wife of Cleophas; Mary Magdalen; and the apostle John. Now, here is what the passage tells us: "When Jesus therefore saw his mother, and the disciple standing by whom he loved, he saith unto his mother, Woman, behold thy son! Then saith he to the disciple, Behold thy Mother! And from that hour that disciple took her unto his home." Amazing! Mary has presumably lavished her affection on these other children of hers time out of mind, and now they not only fail to put in an appearance at the Cross, they leave their widowed mother to be cared for by someone who is not even a blood relative! What did Saint Paul say (1 Tim 5:8)? "If any provide not for his own, and specially for those of his own house, he hath denied the faith, and is worse than an infidel."

With that in mind, consider what is reported as happening in the upper room on the day of Pentecost. Here we are, only fifty-two days after the Crucifixion, and yet we read that among those gathering in the upper room with the apostles are Mary the mother of Jesus and his *brethren*. How is that again? Some or all of those brothers and sisters who failed to show up at the Cross and who left their mother to be cared for by an outsider have now suddenly joined the other 114 close followers of Jesus and are praying in one accord with them? Not an easy thing to believe.

Meanwhile, there is yet another mention of a "brother" of Jesus that needs to be looked at, since there are those who use it to argue that Jesus had a brother in James every bit as much as Wilbur Wright had a brother in Orville. If anything, it shows once again how misleading the generalized use of *adelphos* can be. In Galatians 1:19, Saint Paul refers to the apostle James as the "brother" of the Lord. What *apostle* James could this be? Certainly not James the son of Joseph and Mary. As the Gospels make clear, the only two apostles named James are James the son of Zebedee and James the son of Alphaeus. Neither, then, could have been the *blood* brother of Jesus. Nor, for that matter, is Mary anywhere called the mother of anyone except Jesus.

Further, Mary's perpetual virginity is one of the staunchest traditions of the Church, not some doubtful question debated by councils and theologians and after long and heated argument decided in Mary's favor. From the ancient Church Fathers to the most recent pronouncements of the Second Vatican Council, the Church has been of one mind and has spoken with one voice in this tender and tremendous matter—the voice of Saint Augustine's "a virgin ever virgin". It might also be pointed out that if Mary's role has greatly expanded since the days of that fledgling Church led by Peter and Paul, so has the confirmation of her heaven-granted powers. In the historical fulfillment of Nicea and Ephesus, Guadalupe and Lepanto, Lourdes and Fatima, we see that the Church that declared Mary ever virgin has also had the incomparable blessing of having her ever present.

To sum up, then, it would seem that to that noble band of illustrious phantoms—the Flying Dutchman, the Wandering Jew, the Legion of the Lost, and the eighty thousand Russians whose ghostly snow-topped railway carriages passed through England on their way to the Western Front in 1916—we must add the Lost Brothers and Sisters of Jesus.

Finally, it seems only fitting that Mary herself should have the last word. She uttered it in 1933, standing under that hawthorn tree in Beauraing, Belgium. Seventy-five years before, she had said at Lourdes, "I am the Immaculate Conception." Now, at Beauraing, she announced that she was also what we might very well call the Immaculate Completion, for she spoke in the tense reserved for eternity, the present perpetual: "I am the Immaculate Virgin." So she was, so she is, and so she shall remain.

3

MOTHER OF GOD AND
MOTHER OF ALL LIVING

All of us who are united with Christ and are, as the apostle says,
*Members of His body, made from His body, made from His flesh, and
from His bones* (Ephesians 5:30), have come forth from the
womb of Mary as a body united to its head. Hence, in a spiritual and mystical sense, we are called children of Mary; and she
is the mother of us all.
—Pope Saint Pius X, *Ad diem illum*, February 2, 1904

A sure way to miss the historical significance of Mary is to think
of her as a kind of late-blooming flower who, like pilgrimages
and unicorns, became truly popular only when the symbols and
superstitions of the Middle Ages had reached flood tide. The
reality is that she was a surpassingly important presence from the
very early Christian generations. Not only do we see her glorified with her infant Son in paintings on catacomb walls, we find
her sung and celebrated in the writings of the first Fathers of the
Church—by all those great names that still ring out like a roll call
of heroes from some transcendent Christian Valhalla: Irenaeus,
Justin Martyr, Tertullian, Athanasius, Jerome, Augustine.

And to be sure, why would Mary not have been saluted as
reverently by those mighty figures as she had earlier been by the
angel Gabriel? After all, as she herself prophesied, *all* generations would call her blessed; there was to be no going through a
period of eclipse, as so many famous artists do, and then being

thumpingly rediscovered. As the human temple in whom God himself had spent his first nine months on earth, she was too important for that, and her importance, like her blessedness, is unending.

Consider this: In the same year (1846) that Mary appeared to the two young cowherds on that Alpine meadow near La Salette, the great German-Jewish poet and wit Heinrich Heine, several hundred miles away in Paris, was delighting his friend Balzac with this sly epigram: "I have observed that to beget a child, a man and a woman are needed, particularly a woman." Though Mary did not, as far as we know, appear to Heinrich Heine, I like to think that if she had done so, he would have bowed low and thanked her for demonstrating just how truly he had spoken. After all, without any help whatsoever from a man, Mary had begotten not only a child but the most important Child of all time—the mighty God, the Son of the everlasting Father, the Prince of Peace. And meanwhile, even as she did so, she was beginning to fulfill yet another great role, having been destined from all eternity to restore by grace what the first woman had destroyed by sin—to become, in fact, the second Eve, "the mother of all living".

It may be objected that this additional momentous role is not mentioned by Saint Paul or any of the other New Testament writers, and while that is true, there is every reason why they did not mention it. Since Saint Paul and his evangelical brethren knew only the still-living earthly Mary and believed in the imminent return of her Son, they could hardly be expected to delve into a matter that would have seemed of little urgency in a world where their first duty was to go and baptize all nations as quickly as they knew how.

Nor should we wonder why Mary plays so small a part in the history of the very early Church as recorded in the Acts of the Apostles. Her role in the divine scheme of things, after all, was not to be a missionary, a prophet, or even the leader of a charismatic prayer group: it was to bring Christ into the world and, only after she had left this green footstool behind, to assume in heaven her maternal office on behalf of the children of earth. Apart from the fact that Christianity insisted on an all-male priesthood, as did Judaism, the role of a mere deacon or bishop would have been an inconceivable reduction in rank for someone who, among other things, had clothed, fed, and taught the Author of the Universe his first words in Hebrew and Aramaic.

And even that incomparable honor was only the beginning. As it was with Jesus and John the Baptist—"He must increase but I must decrease"—so was it with the apostles and Mary: they were great and did their greatest work while they lived; Mary was great and became even greater after she left this earth—even as the Church's understanding of her role increased.

In fact, that deepening appreciation has a parallel in art—in the exaltation of Mary first expressed by those early muralists in pagan Rome and enriched and magnified all down the centuries. But useful as this development in artistic expression may be as a parallel, perhaps it is to look at the question the wrong way around, for in fact Mary did far more for art than art could ever do for her.

As no one needs to be reminded, the God of the Old Testament ("For there shall no man see me and live") looked askance at the making of images, knowing well the perverted devotion to which the Israelites (and all other human tribes) were prone. Yet because Mary's sinless humanity made possible the Incarnation, when man could at last see God and live, all of us can say what Saint Paul said in his Second Letter to the Corinthians (4:6): We see "the glory of God in the face of Jesus Christ". That face had now not only been seen, it could be represented—as it was in those early centuries and as it has been ever since. And with what other face could it more fittingly be portrayed than the face of Jesus' only human parent—she whose very features were reflected in his own?

But tributes to Mary deeper far than sacred art were being uttered in those early centuries by the thunderous voice of the Spirit-guided Church, and one of the greatest had to do with her part in the reconciling of humanity to God, a reconciliation necessitated by the disobedience in the Garden. Eve had opened the door to human catastrophe, and Adam had walked through it. In the birth at Bethlehem and the drama at Jerusalem, that catastrophe would be swallowed up in the life, death, and victory of the second Adam, who is Christ (1 Cor 15:45). And of vital importance to that victory was Mary, she whom the Fathers insisted was the second Eve.

It was during the great postapostolic period of the early Church that the inspired Christian commentators began pointing out a deep and, so to speak, ripening truth. It was this: The three great figures involved in the drama of Eden—the serpent, the woman, and the man—were destined to meet again (first in Bethlehem, Nazareth, and Jerusalem and later throughout the rest of the world), but with very different results. The serpent would be the same evil being as always, of course, but there was to be a new and triumphant Adam in Jesus and a new and triumphant Eve in Mary—and it had all been prophetically spelled out in Genesis 3:15: "I will put enmity between thee and the woman, and thy seed and her seed; she shall crush thy head, and thou shalt lie in wait for her heel."

This, at least, was the time-honored translation, although there has long been disagreement concerning the precise pronouns to be used. While the Douay Bible (1609), based on Saint Jerome's Latin Vulgate, renders the passage, "She shall crush thy head but thou shalt lie in wait for her heel," the 1914 edition carries this instructive footnote:

> *She shall crush. Ipsa* (she) the woman; so divers of the fathers read this place, conformably to the Latin: others read it *ipsum,* that is, the seed. The sense is the same: for it is by her seed, Jesus Christ, that the woman crushes the serpent's head. . . . The

Hebrew text, as Bellarmine observes, is ambiguous: He mentions one copy that had *ipsa* instead of *ipsum*, and so it is even printed in the Hebrew interlineary edition, 1572. . . . The fathers who have cited the old Italic version, taken from the Septuagint [a translation of the Old Testament into Greek by Hebrew scholars at some point between 250 and 100 B.C.] agree with the Vulgate, which is followed by almost all the Latins; and hence we may argue with probability that the Septuagint and the Hebrew formerly acknowledged *ipsa*, which now moves the indignation of Protestants so much, as if we intended by it to give any divine honor to the Blessed Virgin. . . . We know that all the power of the Mother of God is derived from the merits of her Son. . . . Christ crushed the serpent's head by his death, suffering himself to be wounded in the heel. His blessed mother crushed him likewise, by her co-operation to the mystery of the Incarnation; and by rejecting with horror, the very first suggestions of the enemy to commit even the smallest sin.

On the other hand, *A Catholic Commentary on Holy Scripture* (CCHS, 1953) says flatly that "it can hardly be doubted that the feminine pronoun had its origin in the error of an early Vulgate copyist", who mistranslated the feminine *ipsa* where he should have used the masculine *ipse*. The commentator points out that Jerome, in one of his works, "quotes the old Latin version of this text with the masculine *ipse* and translates the Hebrew with the same. . . . It is therefore highly improbable that he translated *ipsa* here."

In any case, to paraphrase Ira Gershwin, whether you say *ipse* and I say *ipsa* is of little consequence. If the woman does not directly crush the serpent's head, she does so indirectly through her Son and seed, Jesus. Above all, if in the second meeting among the three figures of Eden, Jesus is understood as the second Adam, Mary is, by a similar analogy, the second Eve.

Of all the early commentators who take up this question, the one with the most impressive credentials is Saint Irenaeus (125–202), bishop of Lyons. Irenaeus had been taught by the great bishop and martyr Saint Polycarp (70–155), who, incredibly enough, had been a disciple of Saint John—and of course John was not only a great apostle and the author of the Fourth Gospel, he was Mary's host, companion, and adopted son. So when we listen to Irenaeus, we should be aware he writes as one no farther away from the late-life reminiscences of the venerable John than those living in the 1990s are from the late-life reminiscences of Dwight D. Eisenhower. If Irenaeus sounds assured, he has good reason: he was a bishop who had been taught his faith by a bishop who had been taught *his* faith by one of the twelve *original* bishops, that same beloved disciple who had received Christ's Body and Blood at the Last Supper, stood with Mary at the foot of the Cross, eaten a fish meal with Jesus by the Sea of Tiberias following the Resurrection, and witnessed the tongues of fire on the Day of Pentecost. In a sense, then, it is not only Irenaeus but the Apostolic Succession itself that seems to speak:

> As Eve by the speech of an angel was seduced, so as to flee God, transgressing His word, so also Mary received the good tidings by means of the angel's speech, so as to bear God within her, being obedient to His word. And, though the one had disobeyed God, yet the other was drawn to obey God; that of the virgin Eve the Virgin Mary might become the advocate. And, as by a virgin the human race had been bound to death, by a virgin it is saved, the balance being preserved, a virgin's disobedience by a virgin's obedience.

Irenaeus' impeccable apostolic bloodlines aside, he was just one of three great voices in his own century expressing the same thought from far distant outposts of the Empire. Irenaeus wrote from the heart of what is now France; Justin Martyr (born in 120, five years earlier than Irenaeus) from Asia Minor (present-day Turkey); and Tertullian (160–240) from the North African side of the Mediterranean—Carthage. What that kinship of thought on three separate continents almost certainly establishes is that, far from venturing a new interpretation of

Mary's role, they were simply putting a long-standing interpretation into their own words.

Clearly, then, these teachings about Mary's enormous importance in the scheme of things are not some capricious invention of the later Church; rather it is we latter-day sceptics who have capriciously denied to Mary the honor that was rightfully hers from the beginning. In any case, let us look at what these two other great figures had to say, starting with Justin Martyr, a Palestinian Greek who, though a layman, is considered the most important Christian apologist of the second century. Like Saint Paul, he was beheaded in Rome, martyred because he refused to sacrifice to the Roman gods. His last words were unforgettable: "No right-minded man forsakes truth for falsehood." This was his idea of not forsaking the truth as it concerned the "second Eve":

> We know that He . . . by means of the Virgin became man, that by that way the disobedience arising from the serpent had its beginning, by that way also it might have an undoing. For Eve, being a virgin and undefiled, conceiving the word that was from the serpent, brought forth disobedience and death; but the Virgin Mary, taking faith and joy, when the Angel told her the good tidings . . . answered, "Be it to me according to Thy word."

And Tertullian, a Roman born and bred in Africa, like Augustine after him, put the case every bit as strongly as his theological think-alikes in France and Asia Minor:

> God recovered His image and likeness, which the devil had seized, by a rival operation. For into Eve, as yet a virgin, had crept the word which was the framer of death. Equally into a virgin was to be introduced the Word of God which was the builder-up of life; that, what by that sex had gone into perdition, by the same sex might be brought back to salvation. Eve had believed the serpent; Mary believed Gabriel; the fault which the one committed by believing, the other by believing has blotted out.

And far from being the last word on the subject, these arguments on behalf of Mary's role continued to be made by the Church Fathers of the third, fourth, and fifth centuries—including those two extraordinary saints and scholars Jerome (331–420) and Augustine (354–430). Jerome put it all into a nutshell: "Death by Eve, life by Mary." Augustine, meanwhile, not only commented approvingly on the words of his fellow bishop Irenaeus, he added his own:

> It is a great sacrament that, whereas through woman death became our portion, so life was born to us by woman; that, in the case of both sexes, male and female, the baffled devil should be tormented, when on the overthrow of both sexes he was rejoicing; whose punishment would have been small, if both sexes had been liberated in us, without our being liberated through both.

And if the title "second Eve", paralleling as it does Jesus' title of the "second Adam", seems an astounding verbal garland, Mary was given an even greater at the Council of Ephesus in 431. The term was *Theotokos*, or God-bearer. Actually, orthodox theologians had been using the title unofficially for quite some time—and long before anyone got around to making a serious objection to it. Origen (185–254) was the first sacred writer in whose work it appears, but his writing makes it clear it was in use even before *his* time. Among other pre-Ephesus users of the term was Athanasius (295–373), that great champion of orthodoxy, who used it often and emphatically. When, finally, the objection came, it came with considerable force: the objector was no modest and retiring figure but Nestorius, the newly appointed patriarch of Constantinople. A monk, scholar, ambitious churchman, and zealous opponent of heresy, real or imagined, he very publicly objected to calling the virgin the Mother of God, insisting that she bore Jesus, not as God, but as man.

In the theological donnybrook that followed, it was Nestorius' misfortune to be pitted against Cyril of Alexandria, a bishop as fierce as any who ever pulled on the miter. The patri-archs of Alexandria, and Cyril was a patriarch's patriarch, had become the richest and most powerful in the Roman Empire, not to mention what remained of the Egyptian. While they styled themselves the successors of Saint Mark, they could not help but be aware they were also heirs of the glory that was Thebes and the grandeur that was Karnak and, thus, successors of the high priests of Amen Ra and all those pyramid-building pharaohs. And indeed, to his critics, Cyril must have seemed less like a successor to that other famous bishop of Alexandria, Athanasius, than to Ramses the Great.

Cyril was born about 380, seven years after the death of Athanasius, and by 412 he was bishop, having succeeded his uncle Theophilus. Even without an influential relative, he would almost certainly have risen to command: he was ex-tremely well educated, steeped not only in theology but in the Greek classics, and a born debater and orator. He was also a brilliant writer, often compared to Saint Augustine, and indeed Pope Leo XIII thought so highly of his work that in 1882 he named him a doctor of the Church. Still, there was that other side. Though he showed himself a great friend of the poor and was so forgiving in spirit as to write "There is no sin that cannot be remitted" and "He wills Iscariot to be saved as well as Peter", he was also the one-man religious army who shut the churches of the Novationist schismatics, broke the power of Alexandria's Jewish bankers, and now and again stirred up the monks against the civil authorities. And though he was not himself involved, he reportedly expressed no regret when a mob of his more fren-zied supporters murdered Hypatia, a philosopher celebrated for her beauty, learning, and eloquence but who had the bad luck to be at least the friend and perhaps the lover of the imperial pre-fect, Orestes, with whom Cyril had quarreled.

This, then, was the implacable foe Nestorius would face in the year following the death of the great Saint Augustine in

430. Clearly, the time had come to resolve a question that had not been fully answered in Christianity's first four centuries. To be sure, the theologians of the time accepted the teaching of the Church that Christ was both divine and human. Yet the interrelationship of the Godhood and the Manhood was yet to be officially defined. Cyril argued that the two natures were so closely united that the Mother who gave birth in Bethlehem could be called not only the Mother of Jesus but the Bearer of God. Nestorius insisted that the two natures were so distinct that Mary could be termed Christ-bearer and nothing more. Thus, when a Roman synod declared that correct Christology required the use of *Theotokos* and asked Nestorius to disown his errors, Nestorius instead persuaded the Emperor (Theodosius II) to convene a general council—the Council of Ephesus.

And so, with the issue blazing and the fire alarms going off in Constantinople and Alexandria, Cyril pulled on the asbestos suit of the Spirit and headed straight for the flames. First, he talked most of the Eastern monks into backing him; and second, and even more important, he won the support of Pope Celestine I, thus getting himself authorized to act as Rome's representative in the East. That was all the mandate he needed, and in 430 at a synod in Alexandria, demonstrating none of the shuffling professional courtesy so typical of our modern bishops, he condemned and anathematized Nestorius with enough *odium theologicum* to empty a seminary.

Then, in 431, Cyril presided at that decisive general council in Ephesus. Nestorius was both condemned and deposed, and Mary was officially acclaimed as the Mother of God. Yet, while Rome recognized, confirmed, and even celebrated the decree of the Council, the imperial government did not. After all, the authorities contended, Cyril had gone ahead without waiting for the arrival of some forty-three bishops sympathetic to the Nestorian position. And, since there was a very thin wall in those days between Church and state, Cyril was put in an Asia

Minor prison and remained there for two months before escaping to Alexandria, there to reign supreme once again. Nestorius, meanwhile, deposed from his see, languished for five years in his old monastery near Antioch. Then, in 436, he was exiled to Upper Egypt, there to die in 451. One thinks of W. H. Auden's celebrated line, "History to the defeated may say Alas, but cannot help nor pardon."

Yet whatever the tactics used by Cyril and whatever the pain inflicted on Nestorius, the ultimate decision reached by the Council was of momentous significance. It powerfully reinforced the great orthodox tradition that Christ incarnate has two natures, human and divine, inseparably united in one Person, or "hypostasis" (Greek for "something that underlies something else"), and therefore called the hypostatic union. Nestorianism, on the contrary, so stressed the independence of the two natures as to suggest that they were in effect two persons or hypostases loosely joined by a moral union. In the orthodox view, that was unthinkable because it identified Christ as a God-inspired man rather than as God-made-man and thus denied the reality of the Incarnation.

Cyril, and the Church on whose behalf he spoke, therefore condemned the view of anyone who asserted that "the man assumed" (that is, the human nature) in Christ is to be co-worshiped along with God the Word. No, the proper response was to worship the Word-made-flesh with a single, indivisible worship, as—thanks to this long-ago victory—virtually all Christians have done ever since. They believe, and so say we all, that Christ is a single Person, at once wholly human and wholly divine. And this was guaranteed and made possible because Mary—can it be denied?—carried in her womb and gave birth, not merely to the possessor of one of those natures, but to the God-made-man in whom they were indissolubly joined from the moment of conception. *Theotokos* she was indeed.

Significantly, Mary received that greatest of her titles in the city where tradition says she spent her last earthly years, that city in which Christianity, no doubt with her help, had long since supplanted a deeply rooted goddess religion: the city of Ephesus. And what better place for the perfect Mother to triumph than in a city that had once exalted a very different kind of female: the goddess Diana, worshiped in festivals, images, and in the splendor of a red and gold temple celebrated as one of the Seven Wonders of the Ancient World. "Great is Diana of the Ephesians!" had been the cry of those who wanted the head of Saint Paul for spoiling the trade in goddess objects with this new thing called Christianity. Now, a greater than Diana was there. (We will be looking at Ephesus more fully in our next chapter.)

☙

"Mother of God", "Second Eve"—this honoring of Mary with sublime titles is not the only "later Church" practice that goes back to the early days. Even that phenomenon which seems to belong almost exclusively to more recent centuries—the Marian apparition—is reported on good authority to have taken place as early as the third century. Saint Gregory of Nyssa, writing a century later, related that it was through an especially dramatic apparition that Saint Gregory Thaumaturgus ("Wonder Worker", 213–270, bishop of Neocaesarea) received a still extant Creed.

As she would in the tiny Irish village of Knock sixteen hundred years later, Mary appeared to Gregory in the company of Saint John and asked the Apostle to disclose to the young man "the mystery of godliness". Gregory, not yet called to the priesthood, had been pondering theological doctrine through a dark night of the soul and was no doubt delighted when the Apostle, answering that he was ready "to comply with the wish of the Mother of the Lord", set forth "a formulary, well-turned and complete, and so vanished". For the record, that apparition-sent

Creed began with the beautiful opening line, "There is One God, Father of a Living Word."

Still another "recent" part of the Marian picture, the dogma of the Assumption—the taking up of Mary into heaven in a kind of simultaneous resurrection and ascension—even that turns out to have a venerable tradition. While to many outside and even inside the faith, the doctrine seemed to come from religious left field when Pope Pius XII officially defined it in 1950, once again it was a case of a "modern" doctrine rooted in antiquity. Far from being novel, it had been mentioned in Church writings as early as the sixth century and in all likelihood had simply been common knowledge from the time it occurred. As John Henry Newman commented a century ago:

> If her body was not taken into heaven, where is it? . . . Why do we not hear of her tomb as being here or there? Why are pilgrimages not made to it? Why are relics not producible of her, as of the saints in general? . . . St. Peter speaks of the sepulchre of David as known in his day, though he had died many hundred years before. . . . Such too had been the honor already paid to St. John the Baptist, his tomb being spoken of by St. Mark as generally known. Christians from the earliest times went from other countries to Jerusalem to see the holy places. And, when the time of persecution was over, they paid still more attention to the bodies of the saints, as of St. Stephen, St. Mark, St. Barnabas, St. Peter, St. Paul and other Apostles and Martyrs. These were transported to great cities, and portions of them sent to this place or that. Thus, from the first to this day it has been a great feature and characteristic of the Church to be most tender and reverent towards the bodies of the saints. Now if there was anyone who more than all would be preciously taken care of it would be Our Lady. Why, then, do we hear nothing of the Blessed Virgin's body and its separate relics? . . . Plainly because that sacred body is in heaven, not on earth.

That, of course, is merely the deductive logic of the case. For those who insist on documentation, it must be conceded that no one has yet discovered in the records of the old Ephesus

Courthouse a signed Certificate of Departure declaring that one Mary of Nazareth, mother and widow, had left this earth body and soul for another place of domicile. But again, the voice of ancient tradition and, as Newman so forcefully points out, the absence of relics and a tomb are powerful arguments that the Assumption of Mary is no mere assumption by man.

From the standpoint of documentation, in any case, the first *recorded* affirmation of belief in Mary's bodily presence in heaven that we possess was set down by Theoteknos, bishop of Livias, writing in the year 550. And only a century later, in 650, the feast of the Assumption (August 15) was celebrated in Rome. Soon after, perhaps the most beautiful of all summations of the meaning of the Assumption was written by John of Damascus (675–749), theologian and monk, while living at the monastery of Mar Saba between Jerusalem and the Dead Sea:

> It was fitting that she, who had kept her virginity intact in childbirth, should keep her own body free from all corruption even after death. It was fitting that the spouse, whom the Father had taken to Himself, should live in the Divine Mansions. It was fitting that she, who had seen her son upon the Cross which she had escaped in the act of giving birth to Him, should look upon Him as He sits with the Father. It was fitting that God's Mother should possess what belongs to her Son, and that she should be honored by every creature as the Mother and as the handmaid of God.

And such profound reverence was nothing new. Perhaps the most electrifying evidence of Marian devotion in the Church's early history is a document from ancient Egypt, discovered in 1917 and now in the John Rylands Library at the University of Manchester. Referred to as the *Sub Tuum* (short for *Sub tuum praesidium confugimus*—"We fly to thy protection"), it is a third-century papyrus written in Greek, and it contains what may well be the original version of the famous prayer still said by Catholics today:

We fly to your patronage,
O holy Mother of God;
despise not our petitions in our necessities,
but deliver us always from all danger,
O glorious and blessed Virgin.

Sometime, then, in the 200s, or, for all we know, even before, and certainly long before the canonical books of the New Testament had been sorted out and more than a millennium before Luther began insisting on the principle of the Bible and nothing but the Bible, the Spirit-guided early Church was praying, as the older Church prays now, to Mary as intercessor. And this was going on, let us not forget, in the days of the Roman amphitheater and the savage persecutions, in the days we lovingly think of as early Christianity—from the sign of the fish in the marketplace to the pre-dawn assembling in the catacombs.

To sum up, then, Marian devotion was and is something at once ancient, widespread, and profoundly satisfying to human nature, and not the outgrowth of idolatry, papal whim, nostalgia for a goddess figure, or a behind-the-scenes campaign by early feminists. On the contrary, it almost certainly was and is the result of something quite different: the will and plan of God. He clearly wanted all generations to call Mary blessed—indeed, he inspired her to make the bold prediction that they would—and so, by outer signs and inner promptings to his followers, he saw to it that she was not only *called* blessed, but *treated* as blessed.

Yet, it will inevitably be asked, "Why so much attention? Why so *many* devotions?" No one can say for sure, of course, but it may well be simply because God has in part used Mary to create within the Church the right sort of male and female balance. He did so, we may assume, because he did not want a Christian version of Sparta, where all the heroes would be male and all the virtues masculine, where the highest ideal would be

the pillar saint, living year after year twenty feet above the
ground in the open air, ignoring toothache and hail and crying
through his tears and malnutrition, "I have overcome!" Rather,
it seems clear he wanted a woman to play a mighty and continuing role in the household of faith—inspiring gallantry and
tenderness and providing a permanent example of dovelike
purity, motherly concern, and family solidarity—and so he not
only tolerated the many special devotions to Mary, he encouraged them.

Possessing, as he does, an intelligence even greater than that
of some of our Swiss and Dutch theologians, the Almighty understood that not only would Mary not create a spiritual diver-
sion, taking away the glory that belongs only to the Creator, but
would instead increase that glory. And we see the evidence of
that on all sides. Those who say the rosary tend to keep the faith
of Christ. Those who meditate on Mary's Immaculate Heart
also adore Christ's sacred one. Those who say "Hail, Mary" also
say "Our Father". And those who say the former do not say,
"Hail, Goddess" or "Hail, Favored of Zeus". They say what the
awestruck angel Gabriel said two thousand years ago: "Hail, full
of grace, the Lord is with thee."

We know we have a Father in heaven, infinite beyond all
imagining. But it is no small consolation to realize we also have
a Mother up there—great, but *not* beyond all imagining. And
those who ignore her, that Mother of God and Mother of All
Living, inevitably miss a great part of the depth and beauty of
the full Christian faith.

4

MARY AND THE FIRST THOUSAND YEARS

If thou seekest the dread throne of God on earth,
Marvel at the sight of the virgin's temple
For she beareth God in her arms. . . .
When the barbarians were attacking the city,
They saw her leading the army in the field,
And straightaway bent their unbending necks.
—Greek Anthology I, 120

(Constantinople underwent a famous siege by the Avars and Persians
under the Emperor Heraclius in 626 and was allegedly saved by the
miraculous intervention of Our Lady of Blackernae; the patriarch
Sergius was active in organizing the supplications.)

If the history of the early Church sometimes reads like a Graham Greene thriller, where the pursuit never ceases and the
hunted walk on the razor's edge from morning to night, perhaps that explains why from so early a time the Virgin was
called on by those in peril from the state's various forms of
capital punishment: sword, fire, cross, and amphitheater. The
woman who "beareth God in her arms", it was no doubt felt,
could also protect the endangered here on earth. There were at
least six major state-sponsored persecutions in the first three
Christian centuries, and that evil night when Nero lighted
Rome's amphitheater with the flaming bodies of believers tied
to pillars was only the most picturesque of the numberless
horrors inflicted.

Nor were the worst of the persecutions confined to the capital or to the earliest days. The greatest of the great, Peter (crucified) and Paul (beheaded), were of course martyred in first-century Rome, but to take just a few other random examples, the aged and saintly Polycarp was burned alive in 155 at Smyrna (on the Aegean coast of present-day Turkey), while third-century Carthage saw both the martyrdom of the brilliant Cyprian (beheaded) in 258, and, earlier, in 203, the heroic amphitheater witness of the young women Perpetua and Felicity, exhorting each other to ever greater levels of courage through successive attacks by a leopard, a bear, and a wild boar.

The primary source of the danger, of course, was the power wielded all across the vast Roman Empire by the not-to-be-challenged state—which was considered no mere government but a kind of god, personified in the divinity of the emperor. It tolerated any number of *outré* cults even in imperial Rome itself—including Mithraism, the highly popular Persian import, with its baptism in the warm blood of a sacrificed bull—but it would tolerate no religion that it thought promoted bad citizenship or disloyalty. And not only was Christianity seemingly doing just that, it was growing with alarming speed. Oscar Wilde summed it up with his usual irresistible humor, but of course it was no joke:

> You know, Nero was obliged to do something. They were making him ridiculous. What he thought was: "Here everything was going on very well, when one day two incredible creatures arrived from somewhere in the provinces. They are called Peter and Paul, or some unheard-of names like that. Since they are here, life in Rome has become impossible. They collect crowds and block the traffic with their miracles. It is really intolerable. I, the Emperor, have no peace. When I get up in the morning and look out of the window, the first thing I see is a miracle going on in the back garden."

The response to this sort of perceived impudence was typically Roman and straightforward: bring in the suspects and insist that they burn incense while saying the appropriate reverent words before a portrait of the emperor. If they did so, they would receive a *libellus*, a written document attesting to loyal citizenship. If they refused, they could start preparing for a prompt and interesting death.

What is perhaps surprising is that the persecutions were as likely to take place under an "enlightened" emperor as they were under a degenerate like Nero. Nero's murderous campaign started in A.D. 64 and made him seem the fulfillment of everything horrible the Christians had been warned about in the person of the Antichrist. Yet a hundred years later things were almost as bad under Marcus Aurelius, the benevolent emperor/ philosopher who in his classic *Meditations* had written the blameless words, "In this life one thing only is of precious worth: to live out one's days in truthfulness and fair dealing, and in charity even with the false and unjust."

Justin Martyr, the great second-century apologist (who, as we saw in chapter 3, championed Mary as the second Eve), not only tried to reconcile all that was best in Roman thought with Christian teaching, he went so far as to dedicate his *Apology* to his fellow author, the emperor. How Marcus responded we are not told, but it is safe to say he would have admired Justin's last words: "No right-minded man forsakes truth for falsehood."

And great were the numbers of right-minded men and women refusing to make that exchange, because the periodic rounding up and putting to death of Christians went on for the greater part of three hundred years. Nero (54–68) and Domitian (81–96) conducted the chief persecutions in the first century; Marcus Aurelius (161–180) and his dissolute son Commodus (180–193) in the second; Maximinus (235–238) and Diocletian (284–305) in the third. Incidentally, the Pax Romana (27 B.C. to A.D. 180), the longest span without a major war in the history of Western civilization, was in no sense a Pax Christiana. Of the first thirty bishops of Rome, twenty-nine suffered martyrdom.

Perhaps the most savage persecution was the one conducted by the emperor Maximinus, a Thracian soldier risen from the ranks who had become emperor in the Macbeth fashion—by murdering his predecessor. That took place in 235, and in that same year, partly to acquire new wealth and partly to make scapegoats of the Christians, he issued an edict calling for the arrest of all Christian leaders, the confiscation of their goods, and the burning of all their buildings—a kind of Roman forerunner of the Nazis' 1938 *Kristallnacht*, when countless Jewish businesses were destroyed, hundreds of synagogues were burned, and thirty thousand Jews were carted off to concentration camps. Under Maximinus, the more fortunate Christian leaders were put to death; the less fortunate were shipped off to the lead mines in Sardinia, where they were permanently manacled, branded on the forehead, had the left eye gouged out and the left foot crippled, and were expected to work a twenty-hour day on undersized rations. (Fortunately, no one survived this demonic nightmare for longer than fourteen months.)

These, then, were the days of angelic faith and fiendish persecution, the three centuries during which orthodox Christianity succeeded in establishing itself—three centuries of heroic evangelism, dramatic martyrdom, and patient doctrine. During how much of that time those long-suffering believers were asking Mary to intercede for them we do not know, although the *Sub Tuum* tells us the prayers to the Virgin began no later than the third century.

What we also know is that after the hellishness of those early days was at last ended through the instrumentality of Constantine, the first Christian emperor, Mary was impressively and publicly honored. And that almost certainly would not have been the case unless she had been considered a vital part of the Church's heavenly support system.

Indeed, it is interesting to note that the conversion of Constantine himself resulted from the Mary-reminiscent intercession of an earthly woman—Constantine's energetically devout mother, Helena. It was she who had told her iron-willed son about the new religion and opened his thirty-eight-year-old mind to what Christianity could mean for the Empire. And thus, in the year 312, when that remarkable warrior and statesman, on the eve of a battle with his military rivals that would take place inside Rome itself and establish him as emperor—when, on the eve of crossing that new Rubicon, Constantine saw a cross in the sunset and heard a voice say: "In hoc signo vinces" (In this sign you shall conquer), he believed without doubt or scruple. And since, at the battle of the Milvian Bridge the next day, with a bright red cross painted on the shields of his men, he did conquer and did become emperor, it was obvious that mighty changes were in store.

Perhaps they were mightier than the pilgrim Church wanted at that point, but Constantine was not about to be denied. Among other things, he insisted that henceforth he would ride into battle against all enemies of Christ as the "servant of the highest divinity". But first, he rode with Rome's bishop, Miltiades, to the Vatican Hill, where Peter had been crucified 245 years before and where his bones were buried and declared that he would erect a basilica dedicated to the Prince of the Apostles on that very spot. He insisted above all that it have three windows in its façade, one each to honor the Father, the Son, and the Holy Spirit, and that above the windows there be a large mosaic depicting and exalting Jesus, his blessed Mother, and Peter. Needless to say, the inclusion of Mary was highly significant.

Whether Constantine's influence was a good or bad thing has been endlessly debated—especially the question of Christianity's changing from a state-persecuted Church to a state-supported one—but what is clearly beyond argument was the importance of the Virgin to this apparently heaven-sent deliverer. After three centuries of persecution, the Church was coming out of the catacombs, the sun was back in the sky, and at the very center of the Christian family portrait, in the central city of earth, was that serene maternal presence, Mary, Help of Christians. And it spoke, we may be sure, for a Marian reverence that was felt not only by the emperor but by all the sons and daughters of ten generations of blood-witness. How deeply it was felt by Constantine in particular we can judge from the fact that when he decided to move his capital from Rome to what would become Constantinople in the year 330 and build an entirely new city there, it was to the Blessed Virgin that he would dedicate that magnificent eastern Camelot on the Bosporus. The devotion to Mary, we see once again, is far, far older than criticism of the devotion to Mary.

Meanwhile, in the kinder, gentler Roman Empire that developed after the battle of the Milvian Bridge, Constantine undertook any number of dramatic initiatives: slaves could be legally freed within the sanctuary of any Christian place of worship; land grants were made to the Church; Sunday was made a public holiday in honor of the Resurrection; and crucifixion was abolished—on the principle that no malefactor should be allowed to die in the same way as Christ. But while there was peace with the state, there was war in the Church over the vital question of whether Jesus was of the same "substance" as his Father—and Constantine took it upon himself to see that the question was forcefully resolved. He did so in 325 by convening some three hundred bishops at the Council of Nicaea, the first great Church council.

Nicaea was in the northern part of Asia Minor (present-day Turkey), easily accessible to travelers coming from both the Black Sea area and the Mediterranean, and it was there that that great and motley collection of churchmen—some with crippled legs, others missing an eye or a hand from the pre-Constantine persecutions—repudiated the disruptive teachings of the sixty-nine-year-old Libyan-born theologian who was the source of the trouble, a priest named Arius.

Rather like today's Jehovah's Witnesses, Arius contended that Jesus was the first "creature", formed by the Father before the general creation, but as a creature obviously neither eternal nor equal. Since that denaturing view undermined two crucial doctrines, the Incarnation and the Redemption, it had to be decisively refuted. And refuted it *was*—although, like so many other heresies, it would retain its hold on the minds of many and resurface in slightly altered form all down the centuries. The Arians, in any case, were declared to be in error and were banished by "order of the emperor"—an unfortunate, if perhaps unavoidable, intrusion by the state into Church affairs.

Whatever it may have meant in the history of Church-state relations, the Council produced a truly poetic fruit in that beautiful combination of word and thought called the Nicene Creed, still recited today in the Mass of the Roman rite and still insisting on belief in "one holy, catholic, and apostolic church". In his first epistle, Saint Peter had written, "Be ready always to give an answer to every man that asketh you a reason of the hope that is in you", and here was that answer spelled out for every believer in language at once concise and glorious. It reads in part:

Credo in unum Deum, Patrem omnipotentem . . .	I believe in one God, the Father Almighty . . .
Et in unum Dominum Iesum Christum, Filium Dei unigenitum.	And in one Lord Jesus Christ, the only begotten Son of God.
. . . Qui propter nos homines, et propter nostram salutem descendit de caelis.	. . . Who for us men, and for our salvation came down from heaven.
ET INCARNATUS EST DE SPIRITU SANCTO	AND WAS MADE FLESH BY THE HOLY SPIRIT

EX MARIA VIRGINE: OF THE VIRGIN MARY:
ET HOMO FACTUS EST.   AND WAS MADE MAN.

The melodious language reinforces a reality we too often forget: the "INCARNATUS" of the "MARIA VIRGINE" was essential to the "HOMO FACTUS EST", a reality that seems all the more dramatic speaking as it does out of this ancient document setting forth the greatest truths of heaven and earth. And yet only a century later, so tireless is heresy, another dramatic doctrinal statement would be needed. This one would center on Mary and would be proclaimed in Ephesus, that stunningly beautiful site on the western coast of what was then Asia Minor, two hundred miles due east of Athens across the glittering waters of the Aegean Sea.

Ephesus was a Greek city, colonized by Greek soldiers and traders before 1000 B.C. Though it was later captured by the Persians under Cyrus (546 B.C.), two centuries later, Alexander the Great (335 B.C.) easily recaptured it. It was still a thriving Greek metropolis when Saint Paul helped establish Christianity there in the mid-50s A.D. and wrote one of his greatest epistles to its Christian congregation. Later, despite the normally efficient protection of the Roman Empire, the Goths attacked Ephesus (A.D. 262), sacked it, and burned that wonder of the ancient world, Diana's temple, said to be even more beautiful than the Acropolis in Athens. This was the history-rich city, then, with which Mary was to be so unforgettably linked, towering as she does over names as great as Cyrus, Alexander, Saint Paul, and Diana of the Ephesians—towering over them, as we saw in chapter 3, as *Theotokos*, the God-bearer.

Irenaeus, writing in the second century, mentions a tradition holding that the same apostle who "adopted" Mary not only wrote his great Gospel in Ephesus but was put to death there under the emperor Trajan. Since Trajan ruled from 98 to 117, and John was probably born no later than the year 10, it is likely he was well along in his nineties when he won his martyr's crown. And how soul-stirring it is to reflect that in this city touched by triumphant personalities and dramatic historical episodes, the Beloved Disciple, aged but vigorous, perhaps with keepsakes of the Virgin reminding him of that wedding feast in Cana or that gathering under the Cross, set about writing his immortal Fourth Gospel, those great and famous words flowing onto the parchment Greek letter by Greek letter:

> In the beginning was the Word, and the Word was with God, and the Word was God. . . . Except a man be born again, he cannot see the kingdom of God. . . . I am the bread of life. . . . Whoso eateth my flesh and drinketh my blood, hath eternal life and I will raise him up at the last day. . . . He that is without sin among you, let him first cast a stone at her. . . . I am the light of the world. . . . I am the good shepherd. . . . I am the resurrection and the life. . . . In my Father's house are many mansions. . . . I am the way, the truth, and the life. . . . Then saith he to the disciple, Behold thy mother! And from that hour that disciple took her unto his home. . . . This is the disciple which testifieth of these things, and wrote these things: and we know that his testimony is true.

It was in June of 431 that the Council opened—even as footsore Christians were making the long pilgrimage to Palestine that Constantine had begun encouraging a century before, even as the forty-six-year-old Saint Patrick was preaching with spectacular success to the wild Celts of Ireland, and even as China was mourning the recent loss of its great poet Tao Yuan-Ming: "Though wine may melt our sorrows/ Nothing compares with deeds well done." The Council, thanks to the leadership of Saint Cyril, would emphatically produce a deed well done, and produce it before the last rose of summer that year.

As was mentioned earlier, Diana's great temple had been burned 170 years before, and so now a new temple was the all-important one: the basilica in which the Council was held. It was called, significantly, the Mary Church, and excavations have established that it was a decidedly good-sized house of worship, with three naves and twenty-two pillars. And that was only fitting. Behold, a virgin had conceived and brought forth in a Bethlehem cave, not a mystery cult, but God himself, and now, some four hundred years later, in a majestic Ephesus temple that had superseded Diana's, that Incarnation was reaffirmed by the mighty word *Theotokos*. A deed well done indeed.

In Rome the very next year, a delighted Pope Sixtus III built the church of Santa Maria Maggiore (Major) as a memorial of the Council of Ephesus. It was then, and still is, the principal Marian church of the West, and in its huge and spectacular storytelling mosaics, Mary, once the protectress of the Christ-child, is now seen as the protectress of the Church. By no accident at all, the generations were continuing to call her blessed.

To broaden our perspective slightly, let us now move on from fifth-century Ephesus to sixth-century Rome, and to a Marian event in the life of one of the outstanding popes in all history—Saint Gregory the Great. Indeed, he was just what the Eternal City needed. Rome had been through harrowing times with the collapse of the Empire—sacked by Alaric in 410, conquered by the Vandals in 455, and stripped of its last emperor in 476. Among many other accomplishments, Gregory (born in 540) briefly made the city on the Tiber once more sing and be glad: he was its governor at thirty and its bishop at fifty, and he carried out both roles as one born to redeem the time. Though business remained a bit on the slow side and paupers were still occasionally heard to ask, "Brother, can you spare a denarius?" Gregory brought back a sense of energy and purpose that had been missing for almost a hundred years.

By the way, this was the same good-natured man who on seeing blonde and blue-eyed young Anglo-Saxons for the first time made the famous pun, "Non Angli, sed angeli" (Not Angles, but angels). And this was not only the pope who sent a new Saint Augustine to evangelize the pagan English and thus ultimately created Canterbury and its famous cathedral, but also the liturgy-lover who sponsored the supremely beautiful sound called Gregorian chant. And finally, this was the man who showed how strenuously Mary's help was still being sought in the second half of the first millennium.

Not long before this remarkable man became pope, nine months of plague had brought utter misery to Rome and killed seventeen thousand of its inhabitants. Soon after ascending the throne of Peter, Gregory set out to combat the pestilence in the most effective way he could think of: he organized a penitential procession of virtually the entire Roman population and, holding high a portrait of the Virgin, marched at its head through the desolate city, the *Ave Maria* ringing out in a great reverberant chorus. When the procession reached the bridge to Saint Peter's, the Archangel Michael, as a sign that heaven had heard this great cry from Rome's heart, suddenly appeared—and in fact the bridge was thereafter *called* the Bridge of the Angel. Even better, the plague was soon gone. Whether or not that was a direct result of the Virgin's prayerful intercession, what remains is an impression of the overwhelming regard in which she was held—tens of thousands of robed and breast-beating Romans crying "Hail Mary, pray for us" in the same city where once the words had been, "Hail, Caesar, we who are about to die salute you."

Some thirty-five years after Gregory's plague-combatting procession and eight hundred miles to the east, the help of the Virgin was to be dramatically sought by another great and troubled city. This time it was Constantinople, and the enemy was not plague, but siege—the Persian siege of 626. In response, the patriarch Sergius consecrated his city to Mary (as Constantine had done three centuries before) and saw a very happy result: deliverance. During the darkest days, the beautiful Akathist Hymn (already a century old) became a chant both of hoped-for victory and of tentative thanksgiving, and since victory and thanksgiving followed, it is not surprising that that great Marian prayer, all twenty-four stanzas of it, became intensely popular in the Eastern Church. Here is part of one of its deeply reverent verses:

> Rejoice, O star that goes before the Sun.
> Rejoice, O womb of the Incarnate God.
>   Rejoice, for through you all creation is renewed.
>   Rejoice, for through you the Creator became a baby.
> Rejoice, O Virgin and Bride!

So there it was—East Side, West Side, all around the Empire, or what had been the Empire, this remarkable veneration, this treating as a great queen a woman who in her lifetime had probably never worn a piece of jewelry, let alone a crown. The same Holy Spirit who had joined divinity and humanity inside Mary had long since been given by her Son to the pilgrim Church—the Spirit that would "lead you into all truth", and devotion to Mary, it seems, was a considerable part of that truth.

Rome in 590, Constantinople in 626, and in 794, Germany. In that year, only six years before he was crowned Holy Roman Emperor, the great warrior-king Charlemagne built near the warm sulphur springs of Aquis Granum (Aix, or Aachen) what was then the most beautiful structure in Germany, a gold and silver Mary Church. It would give its name to what was soon to become an improbable center of civilization in a world of barbarism: Aix la Chapelle (Aix, the Chapel). Surrounding himself with learned Irish monks and talented artisans, Charlemagne brought learning and beauty—the so-called Carolingian Renaissance—to the dark forests and darker psyche of medieval Germany. Above all, he brought the Blessed Virgin.

Indeed, the death of Charlemagne in 814 was almost like a signal for darkness to resume—especially in the form of Vikings in their longboats stroking down the rivers of France and Germany and burning and looting at a furious rate. Yet even in the two grim, post-Charlemagne centuries leading up to the compelling year 1000, nightingales continued to sing, roses still bloomed in the Mary month of May, and candles burned in ten thousand churches. The sky did not fall, and the end was not yet: vassals still built castles, lords still led armies, monks still illuminated manuscripts, and abbeys and basilicas were still being designed by architects who would never live to see them finished. And all that time, with Thor-worshiping Norsemen ravaging western Europe and Arab horsemen galloping through Italy, prayers to Mary were being set down as fast as goose quill could put ink on parchment. Out of the tumultuous ninth century came the great hymn "Ave Maris Stella" (Hail, Star of the Sea), and out of the no less harrowing tenth century came the beautiful antiphon "Regina Coeli" (Queen of Heaven).

Yet perhaps the most interesting Marian date in those last pre-millennial days was 976, when an abbey was founded halfway up Montserrat, a mountain northwest of Barcelona, rising abruptly four thousand feet from one of those famous plains in Spain. That Benedictine retreat would become a Marian shrine and the repository of a black wooden image of the Virgin, carved, according to a highly uncertain tradition, by Saint Luke. Whether the tradition was true or false, the Abbey almost seemed to speak for that first millennium, symbolizing Mary's vital role in the upward progress of the Church Militant. At that, it was only a sign of things to come, for early in the new millennium, the Virgin's name and fame would soar aloft all over Europe with the spires of the great cathedrals, created for the glory of the universe's unsearchable God and the humble maid of Nazareth.

5

CASTLES OF FAITH:
THE GREAT CATHEDRALS AND
THE MIRACLES OF CHARTRES

The inhabitants of Chartres have combined to aid in the construction of their church by transporting the materials; our
Lord has rewarded their humble zeal by miracles which have
roused the Normans to imitate the piety of their neighbors. . . .
Since then the faithful of our diocese and of other neighboring
regions have formed associations for the same object. They admit no one into their company unless he has been to confession, has renounced enmities and revenges, and has reconciled
himself with his enemies. That done, they elect a chief, under
whose direction they conduct their wagons in silence and with
humility.

—Archbishop Hugo of Rouen
in a letter to Bishop Thierry of Amiens, 1145

Of all the praises ever offered to the Blessed Virgin, perhaps
the ones that most make hearts leap up and pulses sing are
the great cathedrals of France—including, among many others
named specifically "Our Lady", such architectural splendors
as Notre-Dame of Paris, Notre-Dame of Amiens, Notre-Dame
of Rheims, Notre-Dame of Laon, and, above all, Notre-Dame of
Chartres. Here is the faith of the ages expressed in structures as
majestic as any Greek temple and yet as personal as a gargoyle,
structures so interwoven with history—from the traditional
crowning of French kings at Rheims to the trial of Joan of Arc at

Rouen—as to make even the casual visitor aware that he has set foot in a house of spirit and awe: the glory that was Christendom and the grandeur that was Mary.

But how—most people ask, when they first ponder the mystery of why so many of these great buildings came vaulting into existence—how did the cathedrals come to be built in the first place? In fact, there are a number of answers, including not only reverence for the Virgin but also an increasing technical know-how, a growing community spirit, and the simple human desire to create a reality worthy of that emotion so unforgettably expressed by the psalmist: "Lord, I have loved the beauty of thy house and the place where thy glory dwelleth."

Still, an architectural trailblazer was needed, and that role was filled by our old friend Charlemagne when, in the late 700s, he built his strikingly beautiful basilica at Aachen, or Aix-la-Chapelle, "to the Holy Mother of God". Charlemagne, as we saw, died in 814, but his good architectural example lived on, and by 900 or so, the heroic period of cathedral building was under way, with great "sermons in stone" rising all across the continent. Raoul Glaber, a Cluniac monk writing in the early 1000s, summed it up brilliantly: "It was as if the whole earth, having cast off its age by shaking itself, were clothing itself everywhere in a white robe of churches."

In the years between 900 and 1150, those churches were in the so-called Romanesque style—massive, fortress-like structures with round Roman arches exactly like those in the ancient aqueducts. Great as those buildings were, however, they were to be surpassed in beauty and majesty by their architectural offspring, the Gothic cathedrals—they with their pointed arches and soaring spires, their walls interlaced with large and spectacular stained-glass windows and their flying buttresses wedged against them like so many gigantic oars. And these incomparable masterpieces of community effort were not only great buildings, it should be mentioned, they were also an elaborate religious education, presenting the characters and stories of the Old and New Testaments like a Bible in sculpture and glass.

Sir Kenneth Clark, writing in *Civilisation*, his magnificent cultural survey of Western art (and a great BBC series as well), called that Virgin-dominated age of cathedrals and crusades "The Great Thaw" and compared it to the greatest epochs in human history, including Greece in the fifth century B.C., when Socrates taught, Sophocles wrote, and the Parthenon rose in Doric splendor on the Acropolis. "It was like a Russian spring", he wrote. "In every branch of life—action, philosophy, organization, technology—there was an extraordinary outpouring of energy, an intensification of existence. . . . The skill and dramatic invention that had been confined to small portable objects—goldsmith work or ivory carving—suddenly appear on a monumental scale."

Then Lord Clark comes to the heart of the matter: "These changes imply a new social and intellectual background. They imply wealth, stability, technical skill, and above all, the confidence necessary to push through a long-term project. How had all this suddenly appeared in Western Europe? Of course there are many answers, but one is overwhelmingly more important than the others: the triumph of the Church." He points out some of the reasons for that—that "in spite of the number of bishops and abbots from royal or princely families, the Church was basically a democratic institution where ability—administrative, diplomatic, and sheer intellectual ability—made its way. And then the Church was international . . . owing no territorial allegiance." He also points out that the energy the Church seemed to call forth expressed itself in action—"a vigorous, violent sense of movement".

Much of that vigorous and violent sense of movement, he might have added, went directly upward—in arches, pinnacles, finials, and spires. That ferocious energy had found a magnificent focus in the authority of Jesus and the approachability of Mary, and it was largely because of that that a stunning number of those cathedrals were sent soaring above the towns and cities of a dazzled Europe. And there were not merely a few dozen of them, there were hundreds—where there was a bishop in residence, a cathedral was built; where there was not, a church of cathedral size and cathedral majesty was built just the same. And yet while these astonishing structures went up all over Europe in a vast architectural archipelago—who has not heard of Salisbury, Lincoln, and Canterbury in England, Toledo and Santiago de Compostela in Spain, or Cologne and Mainz in Germany?—it was in France, a nation so central to the Virgin in history, that many more of these castles of the faith went up than anywhere else.

It has been said that while a single artist can seem to speak for the soul of a whole nation—as Shakespeare did for England, Beethoven for Germany, and Cervantes for Spain—the soul of France is most truly expressed in its cathedrals. And of the cathedrals, the one that seems to speak most truly for the soul of Mary is Notre-Dame de Chartres.

Even the ground that would one day support the towers and walls of that medieval wonder of the world seemed to have been especially chosen for the Virgin, prophetically honoring her even before Christianity's arrival in that then Celtic corner of northwest France, that land with its waving wheat fields and telescopic horizons. And if the idea of pagan prophecy applying to future Christian reality seems far-fetched, we might look at that famous foreshadowing passage set down by the great Roman poet Virgil, who died a full ten years before the birth of Christ and yet seemed to have foreseen it through a pagan veil. The passage occurs in Virgil's fourth eclogue (a pastoral poem or dialogue) and has long been considered a prophecy of Christ—as if the one great Inspirer had briefly turned Virgil into the prophet Isaiah:

The great cycle of the ages is renewed. Now the Maiden returns, returns the Golden Age; a new generation now descends
from heaven. Yet do thou at that boy's birth, in whom the iron
race shall begin to cease, and the golden to arise over all the
world, holy Lucina, be gracious; now thine own Apollo
reigns. . . . He shall grow in the life of gods, and shall see them,
and shall rule the world. . . . Begin, O little boy, to know and
smile upon thy mother.

And if Mary as mother was prophetically smiled upon in a
pagan poet's Italy, she was all but heralded with the pagan version of the angel choir in Celtic France. In fact, she was prophetically honored not only in words but in one of those
fountains so dear to her heart—and in a wooden statue as well.
(That statue, by the way, would survive from pre-Christian
times until the hate and rage of the French Revolution consigned it to the flames.)

The fact is that a grotto adjoining a well had existed at
Chartres from time immemorial and, long before Christianity
entered the world, the ancient Druids had there set up a
wooden statue of a young woman and dedicated that grotto,
incredible as it may seem, "to the Virgin who shall bear a
son"—*Virgini Pariturae*. In any case, whether it was fantastic coincidence or inspired prophecy, it was over that Virgin-
honoring grotto that all the subsequent churches of Chartres
would be built—including the magnificent cathedral that pre-
sides there today.

And that is only a small part of the story. It is believed that
three fast-stepping missionaries arrived there as early as the first
century, named the Virgin of Nazareth to those who had honored the virgin without a name, and converted most of the
people. Even if the evangelization did not occur then or in that
way, it must have occurred soon after, because it is historically
certain that Celtic Gaul's churches, Chartres included, were the
principal theater of the great persecution, already mentioned,
under Marcus Aurelius (161–180).

In any event, a church was built over the Druid grotto and its sacred well. When the persecutions began, it was into this well "within the Church of the Mother of God" that the bodies of the martyrs were thrown. In their memory it became known as the *Puits des Saintes Forts* (the well of the brave saints), and their sacrifice was said to have imparted miraculous healing properties to the water. Understandably, then, when the persecution ended, the pilgrimages began—the very early forerunners of today's massive pilgrim expeditions to that history-rich site.

But alas, following the Marcus Aurelius persecution, Chartres lived happily ever after only for a very short time. Just about a hundred years later, under Diocletian (284–305), there was yet another persecution, and this time the Christians were all but stamped out. Fortunately, the territory was reevangelized in the tolerant, post-Constantine days of Saint Martin, bishop of Tours (315–397), that gallant Frenchman best known for the episode in his soldiering days when he divided his cloak with a beggar.

It was not a cloak, though, but a tunic that would be the garment most closely associated with faith and reverence in the long history of Chartres. This was the "sacred tunic", or *sancta camisia*, said to have been worn by the Virgin at the birth of Christ. Sacred or spurious as it may have been, it had been presented to Charlemagne by the emperor of Constantinople in the late 700s and had been at Aix-la-Chapelle for a century or so when, in 876, Charlemagne's grandson, the unglamorous Charles the Bald, obligingly transferred it to Chartres. The gesture seemed altogether fitting and proper, for Chartres was even then being called "the preferred residence of the Virgin on earth". As we shall see, what happened with the tunic made even that grand assertion seem a gross understatement.

After the fourth century, fire rather than persecution had been the chief enemy of the Chartres faithful, with, numerous times, a church going up only soon thereafter to go up in flames. Sometimes, of course, it was no accident: when Danish marauders torched it in 858, they did so with both Philistine glee and malice aforethought. In any case, out of the ashes always came a fresh determination to rebuild, and when still another blaze in 1020 destroyed the very large Romanesque cathedral, a certain Bishop Fulbert directed the building of a new one, elements of which—the west towers (including the famous shingle-patterned stone spire) and the stained glass and the façade between them—survive to this day. "These fragments I have shored against my ruins", Eliot wrote in *The Waste Land*, and perhaps no fragments anywhere have shored a ruin as dramatically as did these and two others that survived yet another great fire in 1194.

That blaze initially inspired all-out, hair-tearing grief, for it was thought that both the Virgin's *sancta camisia* and the Druid image of the *Virgo pariturae* had gone up in smoke. Fortunately, two quick-thinking priests had carried those treasures deep into the vaults and closed the protective iron trap doors after them. Falling masonry had buried them under a ton of debris, and it was not until it was cleared away several days later that both the tunic and the wooden statue, not to mention two hungry and claustrophobic priests, were discovered unharmed.

The response to this seemingly miraculous deliverance of those priceless relics was an exuberant resolve to shore up that fire-spared western wall and its towers and add to them a new cathedral greater than any that had ever gone before anywhere. In the popular enthusiasm that followed, all of France dug deep into pocket and purse, and the fervor even reached across the channel: the archbishop of Canterbury donated a magnificent stained-glass window and King Richard Lion-Heart did everything he could to make straight the way of Chartres' fund-raisers in both England and France.

Rebuilding started promptly, and as cathedral construction goes, the new structure was completed in the twinkling of an eye—a little more than sixty years. A boy or girl with the gift of long life who had been ten, let us say, when the great Romanesque cathedral had burned in 1194, would have been seventy-six when its magnificent Gothic successor—the one we know today—was dedicated on October 24, 1260. And that successor was and is, plainly and simply, the greatest of the great: a glorious superstructure with more than ten thousand surviving figures in glass and stone, all of them imbued with a personality and freshness that can still dazzle the imagination and rejoice the heart. Indeed, Chartres is an epic all its own and really needs a book to itself to be adequately appreciated. Still, some idea of its wonder and majesty can be acquired from the comments of the scholars who have so lovingly studied it.

In his *Mont Saint-Michel and Chartres*, for example, Henry Adams, the noted historian, descendant of two American presidents and passionate student of France's greatest cathedral, expressed the common, overawed reaction to its incomparable stained glass, including that magical shade of blue no one has ever been able to duplicate: "One becomes, sometimes, a little incoherent in talking about it; one is ashamed to be as extravagant as one wants to be; one has no business to labour painfully to explain and prove to one's self what is as clear as the sun in the sky; one loses temper in reasoning about what can only be felt, and what ought to be felt instantly."

But Adams goes beyond mere praise to writing with great charm and deep understanding of the Virgin's role in "guiding" the reconstruction of her shrine after the great fire in 1194:

> The architect at Chartres was required by the Virgin to provide more space for her worshippers within the church without destroying the old portal and flèche [spire] which she loved. That this order came directly from the Virgin may be taken for granted. At Chartres, one sees everywhere the Virgin, and nowhere any rival authority; one sees her give orders, and architects obey them. . . . Whether the great rose window was an afterthought or not can never be known, but anyone can see . . . that the vaulting of the main church was not high

enough to admit the great rose, and that the architect has had to slope his two tower-spans upward. . . . The architect has managed to deceive our eyes in order to enlarge the rose; but you can see as plainly as though he were here to tell you, that, like a great general, he has concentrated his whole energy on the rose, because the Virgin has told him that the rose symbolized herself and that the light and splendour of her appearance in the west were to redeem all his awkwardnesses. Of course this idea of the Virgin's interference sounds to you a mere bit of fancy, and that is an account which may be settled between the Virgin and you; but even twentieth-century eyes can see that the rose redeems everything, dominates everything, and gives character to the whole church.

At the same time, Adams took note of another dimension—the colossal scale of sacrifice and spending going on not just in Chartres but throughout all of France—and marveled at the depth of feeling that lay behind it. Herod's great Jerusalem temple (the successor to Solomon's) took forty-six years to build and was the pride of the Jewish nation. In France, temples as great as Herod's were rising east, west, north, and south in staggering numbers. But let John Adams' great-grandson tell it:

In the single century between 1170 and 1270, the French built eighty cathedrals and nearly five hundred churches of the cathedral class. . . . The share of this capital which was—if one may use a commercial figure of speech—invested in the Virgin cannot be fixed . . . but in a spiritual and artistic sense it expressed an intensity of conviction never again reached by any passion, whether of religion, of loyalty, of patriotism, or of wealth. . . . Nearly every great church of the twelfth and thirteenth centuries belonged to Mary, until in France one asks for the church of Notre Dame as though it meant cathedral.

Yet if Chartres was only one ship in a vast Marian armada created by the zeal of a then deeply religious nation, it was unquestionably the flagship. The British historian Christopher Brooke calls the sculpture of the *Portail Royal* (Royal Door) "among the greatest sculpture of all times", adding, "never has

Panoramic view of the city of Chartres, France, showing the Cathedral.

there been a more perfect integration of sculpture and architecture than in these hieratic [priestly] column statues." And in *Civilisation*, Lord Clark similarly exclaims over those so-called "pillar-people"—graceful, elongated figures most notable for "the character of the heads of the so-called kings and queens". In these and countless other gems of craftsmanship, it seems clear the Virgin had inspired not merely a cathedral but a series of individual masterpieces. Indeed, the sculpture alone represented a great revolution in art. As Lord Clark so beautifully expressed it: "Do not the kings and queens of Chartres show a new stage in the ascent of western man? Indeed I believe that the look of refinement, the look of selfless detachment and the spirituality of these heads is something entirely new in art. Beside them the gods and heroes of ancient Greece look arrogant, soulless and even slightly brutal."

Brooke and Lord Clark are also in agreement with those visitors who find a celestial quality in the very air of this great temple. "If anywhere on earth," Brooke writes, "it is at Chartres that one experiences the strange sensation of being transported halfway to heaven. . . . The impact of the jewel-like radiance suffusing the interior is overwhelming." And Lord Clark adds: " 'Men may rise to the contemplation of the divine through the senses.' Well, nowhere else, I think, is this saying . . . so wonderfully illustrated as it is in Chartres Cathedral. As one looks at the painted glass which completely surrounds one, it seems almost to set up a vibration in the air. . . . Chartres is the epitome of the first great awakening in European civilisation."

Yet, far more than an awakening in European civilization, Chartres was also an architectural Nativity, Epiphany, and Resurrection speaking out of the wheat fields of France in the glorious language of the Virgin and her eloquent stone and glass. Perhaps the deeply talented appreciate it most of all. One artist who praised it in all ways and weathers was Auguste Rodin, France's greatest sculptor, who riveted his eye to it again

Jamb Figures, North Portal, Chartres Cathedral, France

and again, studying it inside and outside for days at a time: "To understand, to love this incomparable epic is to increase. It is by a supernatural light that we are enlightened here. . . . This masterpiece, shining over the indifferent city, borrows innovation and perpetual regeneration from the air in which it vibrates. All the hours of the day clothe, adorn, and glorify it. . . . Chartres, our cathedral, splendid among all others. Is it not the Acropolis of France?"

Behind the glory of this transcendent edifice, there is the wonder of how so many nameless artists and artisans could produce statues that rank with Michelangelo's and stained glass that was the envy of Cézanne. Perhaps no one has explained it more concisely than the British writer Cecil Headlam:

> Each part of the Cathedral, like the Cathedral as a whole, is the superb product of the intimate alliance of nameless architects, nameless sculptors, nameless painters of glass, working with the one object of setting forth the Glory of God and His Son and the Virgin to the multitude, of illustrating for all unreading eyes the Word of the Lord. The Cathedral is a Bible in stone, and the porches a gospel in relief, a sculptured catechism, a preface and resume of the book. Each stone, thus understood, is seen to be a page of a great drama. This drama is the history of humanity from the creation of the world to the day of the Last Judgment. . . .
>
> Who conceived, the question arises again and again, this admirable plan, this marvellous whole? . . . What were their names? No one knows. . . . [But] this is in no way surprising when we consider the spirit in which these works were done. The Cathedrals were built and decorated for the glory of God, not for the glorification of the artists. Men dedicated to the Church their money and their labour for the remission of their sins, and not with the object of acquiring fame. . . . A man's labour was his offering: his art very often his best and only alms.

Perhaps the word "miraculous" is used too often in regard to Chartres, and yet no other word seems quite suitable. Even the stone that went into the building was cut from a quarry whose existence was supposedly revealed in a private vision. At the

very least it was a *new* quarry and the stone was decidedly the
"right stuff"—and something more. As Headlam wrote in *The
Story of Chartres*:

> Seven miles distant from Chartres lie the quarries of Berchères
> l'Évêque, whence . . . they brought this miraculous stone. . . .
> Miraculous one may almost call it still, by reason of its quality of
> hardness, its gift of wear, and the exquisite tones which it has
> taken on with the years.

It was the same stone, by the way, that was at the center of the
most remarkable of the many remarkable events in the romance
that is Mary and Chartres—that astonishing spiritual revival that
accompanied the partial rebuilding of the cathedral following
damage from a fire in 1134. The year of that rebuilding was 1144,
and what took place then was a drama even more compelling
than the murder of Thomas à Becket in Canterbury Cathedral
just twenty-six years later. In fact, it was a drama so unprecedented in human experience it was mentioned again and again
in the chronicles and letters of the time. One such account is to
be found in the letter of the Abbot Haimon of Saint-Pierre-sur-
Dives in Normandy writing to the monks of Tutbury Abbey in
England, telling of the great work the Virgin was doing in
France, a work that had begun at the church of Chartres:

> Who has ever seen! Who has ever heard tell, in all the ages of
> the past that kings, princes, and lords, mighty in their genera-
> tion, swollen with riches and honours, that men and women, I
> say, of noble birth have bowed their haughty necks to the yoke
> and harnessed themselves to carts like beasts of burden, and
> drawn them, laden with wine, corn, oil, stone, wood and other
> things needful for the maintenance of life or the construction of
> the church, even to the doors of the abode of Christ? But what
> is even more astonishing is that, although sometimes a thousand
> or more of men and women are attached to one cart—so vast is
> the mass, so heavy the machine, so weighty the load—yet so
> deep a silence reigns that not a voice, not a whisper even can be
> heard.

When they halt on the road, nothing is heard but the confession of sins, and pure and suppliant prayer to God to obtain pardon. At the voice of the priests who exhort their hearts to peace, they forget all hatred, discord is thrown far aside, debts forgiven, and the union of hearts re-established. But if anyone is so hardened that he cannot bring himself to forgive his enemies or if he rejects the counsel of the priest who has piously advised him, his offering is instantly thrown from the waggon as impure, and he himself ignominiously and shamefully excluded from the society of the holy.

Forward they press, unchecked by rivers, unhindered by mountains. You might think they were the children of Israel crossing Jordan, and for them, as for the children of Israel, miracles are wrought. One sees old people, young people, little children, calling on the Lord with a suppliant voice, and uttering to Him, from the depth of the heart, sobs and sighs with words of glory and praise! After the people, warned by the sound of trumpets and the sight of banners, have resumed their road, the march is made with such ease that no obstacle can retard it.

But when they come to the church, they set their waggons in a circle so as to form, as it were, a spiritual camp, and all the following night the watch is kept by the whole army with hymns and songs of praise. Candles and lamps are lit on each waggon; the sick and the feeble are placed thereon, and they bring them the precious relics of the saints for their relief. Afterwards the priests and clerics close the ceremony by processions which the people follow with devout heart, imploring the clemency of the Lord and of his Blessed Mother for the recovery of the sick.

Indeed, who *has* ever seen? Here was an event for the ages, a kind of devotional version of the Day of Pentecost. Or again, it could be looked at as a kind of living fulfillment of the Song of Solomon, the silent marchers beautiful as Tirzah, comely as Jerusalem, and terrible as an army with banners. And can it really have been a coincidence that this softening of hard hearts, this massive reconciling of enemies, this rooting out of pride and egotism in noble and peasant alike, this astounding work of grace—can it really have been a coincidence that such a thing began at Chartres, the very spot on earth where the Virgin was most revered? Or again, is it just by chance that Chartres, this most grace-touched of all cathedrals, with its uncanny Druid prophecy, its well of the saints, its Bethlehem tunic, its incomparable sculpture and stained glass, its ageless stone, its providential history—is it just by chance that this magnificent house of the Lord has in so many ways demonstrated that where God is, there also is Mary?

In the latter part of the nineteenth century, James Russell Lowell, the celebrated American poet, after visiting Chartres and marveling at what he called "imagination's very life in stone", used a striking image to describe the spirit that had created this great work of heavenly glorification. "By suffrage universal it was built", he declared in his poem *The Cathedral*, and then he went on to wonder if the nineteenth century, with its self-absorption, would ever "vote" for such beauty:

> Will what our ballots rear, responsible
> To no grave forethought, stand as long as this?
> Delight like this the eye of after days
> Brightening with pride that here, at least, were men
> Who meant and did the noblest thing they knew?
> Can our religion cope with deeds like this?

Chartres is not only a deed, a city on a hill that cannot be hid, but a kind of perpetual heavenly presence—a presence as brilliant as the gold of the sun shining through its rose windows into a sanctuary built over the waters adjoining a sacred grotto. Indeed, for here as elsewhere, the Virgin speaks in the glorious language of roses, fountains, and gold.

6

FROM ELIJAH TO EDITH PIAF, STAYING IN TOUCH THE OLD-FASHIONED WAY: ROSARY, SCAPULAR, AND ANGELUS

We beseech Thee, that meditating on these mysteries in the most holy rosary of the Blessed Virgin Mary we may both imitate what they contain and obtain what they promise.
—Roman Breviary
Feast of the Holy Rosary

Whosoever dies wearing this scapular shall not suffer eternal fire. —The promise to Saint Simon Stock

The angel of the Lord declared unto Mary. . . .
—Luke 1:28

If Chartres Cathedral shows us the banished children of Eve calling on the Mother of Mercy on the scale of the heavenly city, three contemporaneous developments—the rosary, the scapular, and the Angelus—speak for Marian aid requests on the scale of the earthly prayer closet. And however they may differ, all these instruments of grace were products of a common age and a single mood—ways to get in touch and stay in touch with that gracious advocate whose intercession, it was said, left no one unaided.

Even as Chartres was taking final shape through a century of inspired rebuilding, so were the rosary's brief decades of beads being established through long decades of time. In 1251, meanwhile, just nine years before the great dedication ceremony celebrating the rebuilding of Chartres, Mary, according to a widely accepted Carmelite tradition, was appearing to Saint Simon Stock in the Mount Carmel manor house in Aylesford, England, and initiating the privilege of the brown scapular. And in 1269, the Angelus, already a century old as a morning prayer-greeting to the Virgin, became an evening ceremony as well, thanks to Saint Francis' successors in Assisi.

Part of the appeal of these humble ways of reaching out and up, especially the rosary and the scapular, is that they are so intensely personal—expressions of that part of human nature that in matters of the heart instinctively looks for what it can see and touch. In this respect, they are not so very much different from the great human tradition of keepsakes—the snapshots, pewter mugs, teddy bears, music boxes, and matchbooks.

Ah, but did someone mention the dread word "superstition"? If so, let it be stressed that no one saying a rosary in the spirit of an ancient Chaldean star-ritual or wearing a scapular as if it were a divinely guaranteed rabbit's foot should expect heaven to look down, nod approval, and follow up with an express shipment of manna and quail. That much said, however, rosaries and scapulars can nevertheless move mountains and part oceans—if only because they help the believer to draw concretely closer not only to Mary but to the Author of all things.

Consider a parallel. In his great poem "Fra Lippo Lippi", Robert Browning has that fifteenth-century Florentine painter remark: "We're made so that we love first when we see them painted, things we have passed perhaps a hundred times nor cared to see; and so they are better painted—better to us, which is the same thing. Art was given for that; God uses us to help each other so, lending our minds out." And just as a painting can sometimes speak to us more piercingly than the reality it represents, so can rosary beads or a cloth scapular sometimes move us more than the universe itself. Indeed, the touchable speaking for the incomprehensible is an old story, perhaps best illustrated by that hazelnut God put into the hand of the great fourteenth-century mystic Lady Julian of Norwich, declaring: "It is everything that is made." Archibald MacLeish may have wildly overstated the case, but he was on the right track when he wrote, "For all the history of grief / An empty doorway and a maple leaf."

Obviously, God can answer prayer and perform miracles without the use of any intermediary whatsoever. The fascinating thing, though, is that sometimes he chooses to work explicitly through some particular object or natural element. In the Old Testament, we see him do so, for example, in that first scapular, the high priest's shoulder-supported onyx stones, bearing the names of the twelve tribes (Ex 28); in the mantle of Elijah, when he smote the Jordan waters with it that he and Elisha might cross over on dry land (2 Kings 2:8); and—a wonderful early example of the healing power of the relics of saints—in the story of the dead Moabite who came to life when he was lowered into Elisha's sepulcher and touched the bones of that mighty prophet (2 Kings 13:21).

In the New Testament we see it when the woman with the issue of blood is cured through touching the hem of Jesus' garment (Mt 9:20); when Jesus spits on the ground, makes clay of the spittle, anoints the eyes of the man blind from his birth, and sends him to wash in the pool of Siloam—after all of which he gains his sight (Jn 9); and when God works special miracles by Paul—"so that from his body were brought unto the sick handkerchiefs or aprons and the diseases departed from them, and the evil spirits went out of them" (Acts 19:12). All this granted, then, Mary should be cleared of any suspicion of dealing in "good luck" charms, and the rosary and the scapular should be seen as two more examples of this same idea of spirit working with or through matter, and not as superstitious exceptions to standard divine practice. In any case, let us look at those items both historically and as objects of use. First, the rosary.

The custom of using beads to count repeated prayers is an ancient one in the Eastern world—going back to a time well before the birth of Christ. Its first Christian use, it seems, took place in the third century, when Eastern monks first began bead-counting as an aid to repetitive prayer. Even so, a recognizable form of the rosary did not emerge until at least the ninth century.

Apparently, the original inspiration was the clergy's desire to give the laity a form of supplication modeled on monastic prayer. Because that, in turn, was based on the 150 psalms, the laity, in a very much simplified analogue, were encouraged to recite 150 *Paternosters* (the Lord's Prayer) on a daily basis, and were given beads to facilitate the counting. These were often divided, as were the Psalms, into three sets of "fifties"—and fifty is the key rosary number even today. The practice evidently proved popular: in medieval London, Paternoster Row was a bustling street named after the many craftsmen who produced strings of prayer beads; and in France, Stephan Boyleau's *Livre des Metiers* recorded detailed information about the four guilds of *paternotriers*, as they were called, operating in Paris in the year 1268. Clearly, in that devout age, rosary-making was both a growth industry and a trade that offered genuine job security.

Meanwhile, in addition to the *Paternoster* recitation, there was a parallel practice of using the beads to say the *Ave* (the first part of the Hail Mary) either in "chaplets" of fifty, "groups" of one hundred, or "psalters" of 150. It was inevitable that these two practices would be combined—and in the early 1400s they were: fifty phrases referring to Jesus and Mary were linked to fifty *Aves*. This was called a *rosarium*, or rose garden—and so in the very name of this great bead-counting prayer Mary was once again associated with one of her greatest symbols, the joy-proclaiming rose. The idea of tying these repeated prayers to the joyful, sorrowful, and glorious mysteries soon developed, and by 1483 both the mysteries and the sequence of prayers were all but identical to those of the present day.

In the arrangement of their subject matter, the mysteries might be compared to some momentous piece of music. The joyful mysteries constitute what could be called the "overture": the Annunciation of the angel to Mary, the Visitation of Mary to her cousin Elizabeth, the Nativity, the Presentation of the Child Jesus in the Temple, and the Finding of the Child Jesus in the Temple. The sorrowful mysteries are those representing what could be called the "storm": the Agony in the Garden, the Scourging at the Pillar, the Crowning with Thorns, the Carrying of the Cross, the Crucifixion. And last, the glorious mysteries are those connected with the trumpets and crescendoes of the triumphant "finale": the Resurrection, the Ascension, the Descent of the Holy Spirit on the Apostles, Mary's Assumption, Mary's Coronation.

By no means the preserve of introverted pew-huggers, the rosary has been championed by any number of great-souled extroverts. One such busy beadsman was Saint Philip Neri (1515–1595), the devout and good-humored "apostle of Rome", the priest who used to invite fallen-away young Catholics to his Oratory, where they would soon regularly be going to confession, listening to discourses on the Gospel, laughing at Philip's very good jokes, and saying the fifteen mysteries zealously and en masse.

The rosary received perhaps its greatest *official* encouragement in 1573, when Pope Saint Pius V established the feast of the rosary. He did so in thanksgiving to the Blessed Virgin for her intercessory response to a vast rosary crusade considered vital to the Christendom-preserving naval victory over the Ottoman Turks at Lepanto (see chapter 9).

Yet the most impressive of all the saints who have promoted

the Rosary has been Mary herself. Indeed, in her two most famous apparitions—Lourdes and Fatima—she appeared carrying a rosary. And it was at Fatima, with hell enlarging itself and Lenin slouching toward Russia, that she urged the world's Catholics to pray it daily. No higher recommendation could be given—except, of course, by the Almighty, and since it is he who enables Mary to appear, we must assume it is not a practice he frowns on.

The same can well be said of the scapular, that almost literal application of Jesus' famous invitation in Matthew 11:29–30: "Take my yoke upon you, and learn of me; for I am meek and lowly in heart, and ye shall find rest unto your souls, for my yoke is easy and my burden is light." To be sure, the practice of wearing the yoke and burden of the scapular did not begin with those exalted words in mind. In fact, the original scapular, far from having anything to do with religious devotion, served merely to protect the habits of monks working in the fields. More than anything else, it resembled a poncho—it was a piece of heavy cloth with a head-sized hole in the middle, half of the garment covering the front of the habit, half covering the back. By the way, it got its name from the fact that it hung down over the shoulder (in Latin, *scapula*). Inevitably, it came to symbolize the gentle yoke of Christ and, so that it might be worn in all walks and weathers, was later shortened and made an important part of the full religious habit.

A smaller version was soon to arrive. When lay people began joining the so-called "third orders" of religious communities and were obliged to wear the scapular, they naturally wanted something less hearty for home and office than the jumbo variety worn by monks. As a result, the scapular was miniaturized all the way down to two small (two inches by two inches) double squares of cloth, worn under the clothing and suspended from the shoulders by two slender cords. Today there are close to twenty Church-approved varieties, most owing their existence to a vision granted a particular saint. If nothing else, they bring the force of color and symbol to realities too deep for words, as with the five most popular—the white scapular of the Trinity, the red of the Passion, the brown of Our Lady of Mount Carmel, the black of Our Lady of Sorrows, and the blue of the Immaculate Conception.

Yet of them all, it is the Mount Carmel scapular that seems to attract the most attention both above and below. It is also the most popular, no doubt because of the promise reportedly made by Mary to Saint Simon Stock: "Whosoever dies wearing this scapular shall not suffer eternal fire." However, lest the religious-goods stores be overrun by chartered libertines seeking guaranteed protection against hellfire, it should be pointed out that anyone wearing the scapular must, according to rule, observe a high degree of chastity.

And the chaste and righteous life has been associated not merely with Catholic Carmelites but with Mount Carmel itself for a very long time. Regarded by the ancients as the "holy mountain" and famous for its oracles and its altars, for both the beauty of holiness and the horrors of Baal worship, it was, as we shall see, the scene of a number of unforgettable Old Testament events involving two of Israel's greatest prophets as well as its greatest king.

Carmel, incidentally, is not so much a mountain as a large mountainous spur—a heavily wooded limestone formation suggesting a kind of smaller version of California's Big Sur region: fourteen miles long, eight miles broad, and with an altitude never greater than eighteen hundred feet. It rises from the plain of Esdraelon about sixty miles northwest of Jerusalem, and its picturesque headland juts all the way out into the Mediterranean Sea, near Haifa, Israel's chief port. The Hebrew name, *karmel*, means "orchard", and, fittingly, the mountain was long celebrated for its magnificent forest. Meanwhile, its Arabic name speaks for the drama associated with its most famous ancient inhabitant: *Jabal Mar Elyas*, "the mount of the prophet Elias"—or, as he is called in the Old Testament, Elijah.

It was on Mount Carmel that that great wilderness prophet, so reminiscent of John the Baptist, won his dramatic duel of faith with the 450 priests of Baal by calling down fire from heaven (1 Kings 18). It was also there that Elijah's successor, Elisha, was sought out by the Shunnamite woman whose son he would restore to life in a kind of foreshadowing of the raising of Lazarus. Yet of all the notable Carmel incidents, perhaps the one with the most touching echo was that involving David and Abigail (1 Sam 25). It occurred during the time that King Saul, in his homicidal envy, was hunting down the young hero destined to be his successor, the fearless warrior and inspired psalmist, David.

Between hairbreadth escapes, David and his hungry little band of followers had appealed to a certain Nabal, an affluent Carmel landowner, in the hope of getting a square meal or two, but the man of property had refused in the kind of door-slamming way that was about to win him a quick trip to the afterlife. At that point, his wife Abigail entered the picture, sending bread, wine, corn, and dressed sheep to the future king of Israel, and then dramatically riding down the hill to him, throwing herself at his feet, speaking of herself as "thine handmaid", and otherwise saving both Nabal and the old plantation.

If David is often spoken of as a type of Christ, and he is, then Abigail could well be called a type of Mary—interceding, placating, and even referring to herself by that endearing Marian term, "handmaid". Indeed, the whole episode uncannily prefigures that 1846 episode on another mountain, when the Virgin spoke to the two young cowherds at La Salette about her intercessory burden: "If my son is not to cast you off, I am obliged to entreat him without ceasing."

In spirit as well as letter, then, Mary and Mount Carmel share a long history. Just when the Virgin began to be honored there no one knows, but her name must have been invoked many times in the ancient Mount Carmel monastery, for it was apparently built sometime before 570, and devotion to Mary was by then well established. Here were Carmelites, it seems, in everything but name.

The formal Carmelite Order, in any case, did not come into existence until the Crusades had brought great numbers of Christian warriors to the Holy Land, and many, the fighting over, began seeking a commitment to an eternal cause. It was in 1156 that the order was officially established, the monks taking as their model "the holy and solitary man, the prophet Elijah", and having one essential aim: "To live for the sake of Jesus Christ and to serve him with purity of heart and good conscience." Because of their special consecration to the Virgin, meanwhile, they were known as "Brethren of Saint Mary". Indeed, had it not been for a Saracen resurgence that obliged the Carmelites to leave Carmel behind and resettle in Christian countries, Mary's scapular-inspiring appearance to Simon Stock might have occurred, not in a little English community, but on the holy mountain of Elijah, Elisha, Abigail, and David.

The Carmelites, by the way, are best known, not for the scapular or for Simon Stock or for the fourteen French Revolution nun-martyrs immortalized by François Poulenc in his magnificent opera *Dialogues of the Carmelites*, but for a trio of the greatest saints and mystics ever to climb Mount Carmel in spirit and meet God in person. They were Spain's Saint Teresa of Avila (1515–1582) and Saint John of the Cross (1542–1591) and France's Saint Thérèse of Lisieux (1873–1897), better known as the Little Flower or Thérèse of the Child Jesus. Fortunately, they were not only written about, they were authors in their own right, and while there is no need for a full-scale digression, we might at least briefly look at what they had to say about their encounters with the eternal.

Teresa of Avila, noted as a strict and yet cheerful reformer, wrote powerfully about the interior life of the soul and made the bracing discovery that God not only listens but speaks: "I was wondering what it is the soul does during that time [as it aspires to divine union], when the Lord said these words to me: 'It dies to itself wholly, daughter, in order that it may fix itself more and more upon Me; it is no longer itself that lives, but I.'"

Saint John of the Cross, Teresa's friend and ally in monastic reform, seems to have taken Christ's invitation to deny oneself and take up one's cross with the literal zeal of a pillar saint. Indeed, such was his self-denial and his habit of always choosing the path of *most* resistance that he came to be called the "Doctor of Nothingness" (*doctor de la nada*). As he wrote: "Only when the soul in deepest humiliation has truly been reduced to nothing can it become spiritually united to God. . . . This union consists solely in being crucified alive, in the senses and in the spirit, inwardly and outwardly."

This opponent of laxity in devotion was indignantly imprisoned by his own unreformed order but escaped, according to a remarkable and authenticated tale, with the enthusiastic assistance of the Virgin. (Devotees of miraculous escapes may want to compare John's escape with Peter's angel-aided deliverance from the prison in Jerusalem and Paul's earthquake rescue from the prison in Philippi in the Acts of the Apostles, chapters 12 and 16, respectively.) On August 15, 1578, the feast of the Assumption, Mary appeared to the future saint in the Toledo monastery where he had been shut up and personally guided his getaway—an operation complete with rope ladder and a miraculous opening of heavy locks. It was the kind of experience that might have inspired a lesser man to write detective thrillers, but John was content to produce spiritual masterpieces: *The Ascent of Mount Carmel* and *The Dark Night of the Soul* (to which F. Scott Fitzgerald added the haunting line, "where it's always three o'clock in the morning").

Then there is Thérèse. Few saints exert a greater appeal than the pretty and vivacious mademoiselle who grew up in that late-nineteenth-century world in which Claude Monet was painting with an ice-cream freshness young women strolling about in long green-and-white-striped dresses on dazzling summer lawns. Thérèse had been such a one herself—the unspoiled product of bourgeois comfort and religious austerity. Bright-eyed, merry, and ferociously resolute, she approached heaven, if not as an equal, at least as an heir. One of five devout daughters of a devout and prosperous French couple from the lace-manufacturing town of Alençon, she grew up in nearby Lisieux and there entered the Carmelite cloister her quiet heroism was to make famous.

Though her sufferings from tuberculosis were fearsome (she died in 1897 at the early age of twenty-four), her approachability and relentlessly generous nature remained irresistible—even, it seems, posthumously. She has long been a favorite of those seeking her "little way"—the valiant life on a humble scale—and the conversions inspired by her *Autobiography* have been legion, everyone from athletes and artists to communists and convicts.

One of her more interesting admirers was the celebrated *chanteuse* Edith Piaf, of whom her sister, Simone Berteaut, wrote: "Soon after her birth, Edith developed a cataract. It was not even noticed. She was blind for almost three years. Her grandmother took her to Lisieux. She saw. It was a real miracle for Edith. . . . Since that time she had a real devotion to Saint Thérèse of the Child Jesus. She always had a small picture of the saint on her bedside table." Piaf's haunting rendition of "La Vie en Rose" may not be so far away as all that from the young lace-manufacturer's daughter, who saw her own "life in pink" from the Carmelite perspective: "What happiness that He became man so that we might love Him. If He had not done so, we would not have dared." At least a small part of Thérèse's audacious charm comes through in the invitation she sent out on the occasion of taking her final vows—not quite the usual thing, even for a "bride of Christ":

> Almighty God, Creator of heaven and earth, sovereign ruler of the world, and the most glorious Virgin Mary, queen and princess of the heavenly court, invite you to be present at the marriage of their Son, Jesus, King of kings and Lord of lords, with Mlle Thérèse Martin.

Saints, prophets, monks, and kings—as with Hamlet's "heaven and earth", there are many more things to Mary and Mount Carmel than can be fitted into either Horatio's philosophy or this chapter, but, for a final thought about the scapular, let us look at one great non-Carmelite who wore it, Saint John Bosco (1815–1888). This was the remarkable young priest—acrobat and juggler into the bargain—whose vocation it was to rescue abandoned boys, create hostels for them, and teach them both a useful trade and a living Christianity.

By the time he died, he had under his charge some seven hundred young lads in his Turin hostel and had established numerous other houses throughout Italy. He had also founded his own religious order and experienced some remarkable miracles, including (1) a loaves and fishes episode that dramatically solved the problem when one of his hostels ran short of food and (2) the protection of a mysterious angelic dog, who appeared out of nowhere, ate no food, and sought no comfort but guarded the saint on his travels through the dangerous streets in the slum where he worked. It is no small recommendation, then, that this extraordinary priest, the protector and helper of so many, himself sought the help and protection of Mary's brown scapular.

This section would not be complete without at least a few words about that other great devotion that came out of the

Middle Ages—the Angelus, that simple prayer once recited three times a day by the faithful throughout all of Catholic Europe and a practice still followed here and there even today. "Angelus", of course, is the Latin word for angel, the first word of the opening versicle:

(The) Angel of the Lord declared unto Mary.
And she conceived of the Holy Spirit.

Three additional statements and responses follow, and then comes the concluding prayer:

Let us pray. Pour forth, we beseech Thee, O Lord,
Thy grace into our hearts:
that we, to whom the Incarnation of Christ Thy Son
was made known by the message of an angel,
may by His passion and Cross
be brought to the glory of His Resurrection.
Through the same Christ our Lord. Amen.

Though the entire devotion takes only eighty seconds to recite, it was many years getting fully established. At first—and that was probably in the twelfth century—the Angelus was said only in the morning. Then in 1269, just forty-four years after the death of Saint Francis (second to none, by the way, in his devotion to Mary), the Franciscan Chapter of Assisi exhorted the faithful to greet our Lady just before retiring at the ringing of the evening bells. The evening Angelus soon became widespread, and a midday Angelus was added in 1456.

Under the press of twentieth-century life, the ringing of the bells has long since been discontinued. Even so, art and literature are there to remind us of that beautiful practice. Dante was clearly referring to the Angelus when he wrote in the opening line of Canto 8 of the *Purgatorio*: " 'Twas now the hour that turns back the desire of those who sail the seas and melts their heart, that day when they have said to their sweet friends adieu, and that pierces the new pilgrim with love, if from afar he hears the chimes which seem to mourn for the dying day."

Six centuries later, T. S. Eliot, both a Dante enthusiast and one of Mary's most ardent Anglican admirers, created a beautiful secondary reference in *Four Quartets*: "Also pray for those who were in ships, and/ ended their voyage on the sand, in the sea's lips/ Or in the dark throat which will not reject them/ Or wherever cannot reach them the sound of the sea bell's perpetual angelus." And of course there is J. F. Millet's *Angelus*, the great mid-nineteenth-century painting depicting a farmer and his wife at twilight in the fields just after they have stopped their work at the tolling of that distant bell.

*

Apart from rosary, scapular, and Angelus, perhaps the most fascinating instrument of grace connected with the Virgin is the color "photograph" she left imprinted on the cloak of a New World Mexican in 1531. By then, of course, the Middle Ages had long since passed and the Renaissance was in full flower. But it was a different kind of Renaissance Mary would bring to the Mexico of the 1500s—a rebirth, not of painting and sculpture, but of the human spirit. Indeed, the miraculous souvenir she was to leave behind is still stirring souls and changing hearts the world over—as we shall see in the next two chapters.

7

LUTHER'S CHAPEL AND MARY'S CHURCH: THE WITTENBERG DOOR AND THE HILL OF TEPEYAC

> For where God built a church, there the Devil would also build a chapel. . . . Thus is the Devil ever God's ape.
> —Martin Luther, *Table Talk*, 67

> Know and take heed, thou, the least of my sons, that I am Holy Mary ever Virgin, Mother of the true God for whom we live, the creator of the world, maker of heaven and earth. I urgently desire that a temple be built to me here, to bear witness to my love, my compassion, my aid and protection.
> —Mary to Juan Diego, a converted Aztec, December 1531

On October 31, 1517, the eve of All Saints' Day, Martin Luther, a thirty-four-year-old Augustinian monk and doctor of theology, hammered to the door of the Castle Church in Wittenberg a placard printed in Latin setting forth ninety-five theses challenging not only the legitimacy of purgatorial indulgences but traditional Church authority itself. Thus was the Protestant infant defiantly set down on the Catholic doorstep that Halloween night, and the squalling child would not be easy to quiet. Of all the reactions to it, the most dramatic was the response of a wise and patient mother an ocean away.

On December 12, 1531, just fourteen years after Luther ignited the rebellion called the Reformation, the Virgin Mary appeared to a fifty-seven-year-old Aztec Christian named Juan

Diego. She did so on the hill of Tepeyac, near present-day Mexico City, presented him with a passport of roses, left her full-length image emblazoned on his cape (where it remains to this day), asked that a church be built in her honor, and set into motion the conversion to Christianity of a nation stretching from the Rio Grande to Honduras. Within seven years, some eight million souls would be baptized into the same "idolatrous" Church Luther was even then castigating—a spectacular rebirth that represented the equivalent of as many conversions on each of 2,666 consecutive days as on the day of Pentecost itself, when three thousand hallelujah-shouting sinners joined the fold.

Here, then, only a little more than a decade apart, were two watershed events, both stupendous in their results. Yet while almost everyone everywhere knows enough about Luther either to bristle or to cheer at the sound of his name, only a very small percentage of people are aware of the miracles and triumphs spoken for in the name Our Lady of Guadalupe. There are, of course, at least two good reasons for that. First, Luther's Europe was thought of as civilization itself, singularly powerful and important, while Mary's Mexico, despite its striking architecture and advanced social organization, was naively thought of as "primitive"; and second, war is always bigger news than peace. The religious war Luther inspired in Europe involved famous popes, kings, nations, and cities and inevitably shook the foundations of the established order; the religious peace Mary brought to Mexico involved "little" people and hard-to-pronounce names like Tenochtitlan and Tlaltelolco and was inevitably "overlooked" by historians more interested in the blood of conquest than the water of baptism.

Luther's rebellion, to be sure, was not aimed at Mary—in fact, in the year 1543 that bellicose man peacefully affirmed the Immaculate Conception—but Mary was inevitably a casualty. After all, a belief system tied exclusively to the Bible could

hardly be expected to instruct its adherents in Mary's formidable role following the days of the early Church—the *Sub
Tuum* prayer, the title of *Theotokos*, the Assumption, the miraculous events at Chartres, the devotions, songs, and apparitions.

And so, for countless millions then and since, she became a
figure of fleeting importance, the young woman who gave
birth to Christ, made a number of scriptural appearances, and
passed quietly into a chaste obscurity. Just as nonbelievers pa-
tronizingly declare that Christ was a "great teacher", Luther
created the intellectual climate in which Mary came to be seen
merely as a "good mother". As a result, her dynamic and continuing role in the great matters of heaven and earth is as unknown to numerous people calling themselves Christian as is
the role of Christ in history to numerous people calling themselves enlightened.

One can only wonder how Luther might have reacted if, by
the mercies of grace and a seaworthy German caravel, he had
been present on Tepeyac Hill in December 1531 to stand with
Juan Diego in the Virgin's presence and help gather the winter
roses miraculously blooming there. Would he have thought it
was all either a waking dream, a deception of the devil, or a
sinister conspiracy aimed at undermining scriptural exclu-
sivism? That we do not know. What we do know, first of all, is
that in July 1505, the twenty-one-year-old Luther, knocked to
earth by lightning, desperately cried out not to Mary but to her
mother, Saint Anne (the patroness of miners, Luther's father
having been one): "Saint Anne, help me! I will become a
monk." Thereby he started down the path that led in turn to
compulsive devotion, growing frustration, and finally, furious
rebellion.

We know also that the epistle of Saint James (which Luther
in his wrath called "an epistle of straw") says clearly that "The
wisdom that is from above is first pure, then peaceable, gentle,
and easy to be intreated, full of mercy and good fruits."

Whether Luther would have found that wisdom on Tepeyac Hill we can only conjecture, but it seems his turbulent spirit rarely found it anywhere else. And since, intentionally or unintentionally, it was this fierce and forceful apostate monk who took away the consolations of Mary from so many, we should at least glance at his life and work before we consider the Virgin's mighty answer to it on that hill in Mexico.

Luther was many great things—scholar, speaker, writer, and translator of the Bible into German. But he was also a great oversimplifier. Jesus spoke of the *keys* of the kingdom, a plural image implying a need to deal with complexity and variety; Luther brought everything down to the one and only oracle of the Scriptures. Instead of the set of keys given to Peter wherewith to open the intricate locks of all the many doors leading to truth, Luther asserted the existence of a single passkey and proclaimed that it would work as well for sailors and stonecutters as for the heirs of the apostles. All that was required was to pick up the Bible, put your faith in the Holy Spirit and the translator, activate your God-given intellect, and read. If your God-given intellect reached different conclusions about certain passages than your neighbor's God-given intellect—well, that was what different denominations and splinter groups were for.

In attacking not merely the misuse of Church authority but the *idea* of Church authority, he was attacking the very structure that had preserved the Scriptures through the Dark Ages and defended them again and again against heretical interpretation. As John Henry Newman so brilliantly expressed it a century ago:

> If the revelations and lessons in Scripture are addressed to us personally and practically, the presence among us of a formal judge and standing expositor of its words, is imperative. . . . How are private readers to distinguish what is didactic and what is historical, what is fact and what is vision, what is allegorical and what is literal . . . what is only of temporary and what is of lasting obligation? *The gift of inspiration requires as its complement*

the gift of infallibility. Where, then, is this gift lodged, which is so necessary for the due use of the written word of God? Thus we are introduced to the second dogma in respect to Holy Scripture taught by the Catholic Religion. The first is that Scripture is inspired, the second that the Church is the infallible interpreter of that inspiration.

It must also be remembered that to become the reforming knight on horseback attacking the dragon Church, Luther had to do what no true knight had ever done—break his vows. Here, we must not forget, was a consecrated monk who every morning in the cloister had pulled on his white Augustinian robe and his scapular, sprinkled himself with holy water, and chanted the *Salve Regina* to the Mother of God: "Hail, O Queen, Thou Mother of mercy, our life, our delight, and our hope. . . . Be thou our advocate. Sweet Virgin Mary, pray for us." Indeed, here was someone who, before his final profession of vows, had been told by the prior of his order:

> You have now to choose one of two things, either to depart from us or to renounce the world and wholly consecrate yourself, first to God and then to the Order; for let it be well observed, once you have so offered yourself it is no longer permitted you, on any ground, to shake off your obedience.

These vows, with their solemn promise of obedience and permanence, Luther freely made, freely kept for a time, and then freely broke. We can only wonder what that great champion of the Scriptures made of the many passages in them dealing with vows and the related question of obedience. To take only three examples:

> When thou shalt vow a vow unto the Lord thy God, thou shalt not slack to pay for it; for the Lord thy God will surely require it of thee (Dt 23:21).

> Behold, to obey is better than sacrifice. . . . For rebellion is as the sin of witchcraft, and stubbornness is as iniquity and idolatry (1 Sam 15:22–23).

Obey them that have the rule over you and submit yourselves (Heb 13:17).

The Scriptures obviously take vows and obedience seriously, and how Luther could have overlooked the applicability of these passages to his own case is, to put it charitably, puzzling. After all, he did not overlook the popes and priests in that lax time who violated *their* vows. Granted, Luther had much to complain about in the Rome of his day—the shameless immorality and venality, the simony and cynicism, and all the other embarrassments inevitable when sinful men are put in charge of the bread of angels. Desiderius Erasmus and Thomas More also complained; the difference was that they did not abandon ship and say all truth was now to be found in the lifeboat.

Meanwhile, even as the war between Rome and Luther continued, and Mary stood poised to make her dramatic entrance on the sixteenth-century stage, another tremendously important war was being fought in the Americas. There, too, youth was in the vanguard. At its center was the thirty-four-year-old Hernando Cortez, two years younger than Luther. In February 1519, only fifteen months after Luther had nailed his placard to the Wittenberg door, Cortez assembled his tiny army—six hundred men and sixteen horses—left Cuba, and landed on the coast of Mexico. He was soon making history with every mile traversed and every question asked.

Almost the first thing the adventurous Spaniard discovered was that Mexico's numerous tribal nations were ruled by the far from popular Montezuma, the Aztec whose grandfather had built empire on a systematic tribute of gold and food and at the same time built a grisly mystique on wide-scale human sacrifice. The second thing Cortez discovered was that these subject peoples felt toward their Aztec overlords the traditional smoldering resentment of subject peoples everywhere. Capitalizing on that, and employing shrewd diplomacy, skill in battle, and forthright reliance on heaven and the Virgin,

Cortez did what seemed impossible. He not only conquered
the vast nation of Mexico with an army small enough to fit on
the Carnegie Hall stage, he also paved the way for a stupendous fulfillment of the Great Commission: "Go therefore, and
teach all nations, baptizing them in the name of the Father,
and of the Son, and of the Holy Spirit."

Yet if Cortez made straight the way of the Lord, it would
seem the Lord had earlier made straight the way of Cortez. It
happened in the following manner: In 1509, ten years before
the Spanish forces landed on Mexican soil, the Princess Papantzin, a sister of Montezuma, fell into a coma so deep it met all
the standard requirements of death. She was therefore appropriately mourned over, bundled up, and placed in a royal tomb in
the garden of her palace. There, remarkably, she soon regained
consciousness, cried out, caught the ear of a passerby, and was
thus fortunately delivered from an Aida-like fate.

Breathing clear mountain air again and perhaps sipping at a
welcome glass of fresh papaya juice, she related a remarkable
dream she had had while in the coma: guided by an angel with
a black cross on his forehead, she had stood on the shore of a
great sea and watched several galleons slowly come into sight,
galleons whose sails were emblazoned with black crosses similar
to the angel's. The celestial figure then explained that these ships
were bringing men who would do two stupendous things, the
second no doubt considerably more welcome than the first. The
bad news was that they would conquer her nation. The good
news was that they would bring the knowledge of the one true
God to all Mexico.

Not having a modern psychoanalyst to explain to him that
the dream was only an expression of the princess' repressed
anger toward the Aztec undertaker who had buried her prema-
turely, Montezuma took it quite seriously. And he took it even
more seriously when, a decade later, the galleons arrived, black
crosses and all. He did not strew tuberoses at the feet of Cortez

exactly, but he could not help show the deference of someone witnessing a clear case of manifest destiny. (By the way, speaking of destiny, the angel had told Princess Papantzin she would be the first to receive "the waters that wash away sin", and so it happened. In 1525, four years after Cortez's final triumph, the Princess was baptized, taking the name Doña Maria.)

By then, of course, much of Mexico had at least heard about the Virgin of perpetual help and persistent miracles. In fact, in the earliest days of the conquest, while the Aztec empire's fate wobbled between doom and deliverance, Cortez himself had bravely set up a crucifix and a wood-carved Madonna in the capital's chief sacrificial temple. And he had done so, moreover, after having first destroyed, in the presence of the furious killer-priests, the idol Huitzilapochtli and hurled it down the temple's blood-soaked steps. That dramatic gesture, so vividly recalling Elijah against the priests of Baal on Mount Carmel, was a powerful taste of things to come, when Mexico's version of Baal would be cast out and affection shown the gentle Virgin would replace agony suffered for the Aztec vampire.

But first there were ten years of soldiers, clerks, and missionaries setting up the new order. Gold was no small part of the motive behind the conquest, of course, and, sad to say, the draining away of Mexico's mineral wealth was getting under way even as Franciscan friars were preaching to the Aztecs about a God-man in a far country who had spent his life with the poor.

From a strictly administrative standpoint, incidentally, the new order would have been hard pressed to improve on the old, for Aztec Mexico was at least as well organized as any nation in Europe—even to a complex legal system and a supreme court. The Aztec capital, Tenochtitlan (now Mexico City), was no provincial backwater but a lively metropolis of 350,000 souls living under a highly efficient caste system that could have given cards and spades to social planners the world over. And apart from all else, it had a magnificent natural setting—an island in the center of a gigantic lake (which, alas, like most of Mexico's gold, has long since vanished) and was notable not only for its canals, paved streets, and Venice-like beauty but also for such things as the great palaces of the nobles, the striking pastel colors of the adobe dwellings housing the middle class, the bustling marketplaces, and of course the barbaric splendor of those heart-devouring temples.

Indeed, the Spaniards were so struck by their first view of Tenochtitlan that they compared it to the enchanted city of Amadis, a fictional paradise in a popular romance of the time. And the people who walked its streets, thanks to an elaborate educational system that provided for the mental growth of girls as well as boys, were no grunting savages but a highly intelligent and variously skilled commonwealth of industrious citizens.

Yet the Aztec who mattered most, the devout and patient soul who was to serve as Mary's personal missionary, lived not in the capital but some fourteen miles away in a fair-sized suburb named Cuautitlan. He was a well-educated small landowner and furniture maker named Cuauhtlatohuac, which for the sake of both piety and pronounceability we must be deeply grateful was superseded by "Juan Diego" upon his baptism in the year 1525, when he was fifty years old. From the beginning, he showed himself so zealous for the new faith he thought nothing of walking fourteen miles to church in the capital every Sunday and again every Saturday for the Mass of the Blessed Virgin. And in retrospect, it would almost seem that when Juan Diego's equally devout wife and walking companion died in 1529, the way was being cleared for him to begin a life centered exclusively on the Maid of Nazareth and the great work she needed him for. Indeed, in that friendship lies one of the most beautiful of all stories in the Marian anthology.

The feast of the Immaculate Conception was then celebrated on December 9, and it was on the cold morning of that day in

1531—the same year in which the never bashful Henry VIII declared himself supreme head of the Church in England, and on the very same day when the now forty-eight-year-old Martin Luther saw his fourth child, Martin Jr., turn one month old—it was on that 1531 December morning that the fifty-seven-year-old Aztec met the eternally young woman on the hill called Tepeyac and set the stage for a New World outpouring of grace that would open a door far larger than the ones being closed in England and Germany. Indeed, such marvels and miracles came of that meeting it is not too much to say that to the company of such great and famous hills as Sinai, Carmel, the Mount of Olives, Montserrat, and Saint Francis' Mount Laverna can be added the hill of Tepeyac.

The first sign to Juan Diego that that day was to be different from all others was the glorious birdlike singing he heard in the winter dawn as he approached the hill, a sound so beautiful he quite correctly assumed it was not of this world. But Juan Diego's was a soul imbued with the Aztec equivalent of British reserve and understatement, and the singing neither stopped him in his tracks nor inspired even a mild "Good grief!"

When it ceased, a new wonder followed: he heard a young woman's voice affectionately calling him not merely by his name but by its diminutive form, as a mother would call a very young child: "Juanito. Juan Dieguito!" This too he took in stride, with his Dr.-Livingston-I-presume attitude, and calmly proceeded up the hill. Nor did he pinch himself or look around for peyote smoke when he reached the summit and beheld the Virgin herself, resplendent and radiant, her light so dazzling it brightened the nearby mezquite bushes, prickly pears, and nopal cactus. He simply knelt, and as he did, she asked him in his native language, "Juanito, the smallest of my children, where are you going?" To which the unflappable Aztec responded as calmly as if he were passing the time of day with the Mother Superior at the local cloister: "My lady and my child, I must go to the church at Tlatelolco to study the divine mysteries which are taught us by our priests, the emissaries of our Lord and Savior."

By the way, this extravagantly courteous and formal idiom, which to us may sound like the embroidered diction of diplomats in swallowtail coats in some forgotten Franz Lehar operetta, we owe to the faithful translation from the original Nahuatl language as taken down from Juan Diego by Don Antonio Valeriano. To understand that this is not that Spanish priest's spruced-up version of commonplace speech, but the way Mary and Juan Diego actually spoke with each other, is to feel even more the great charm of that delightful partnership.

For all the balanced phrasing, though, the Lady got right to the point: "Be it known and understood by you, the smallest of my children, that I am the ever Virgin Holy Mary, Mother of the true God, from whom all life has come, of the Creator, close to whom is everything, the Lord of heaven and earth. I ardently desire that a temple be built for me here, where I can show and offer all my love, compassion, help and protection, for I am your merciful mother." She then asked Juan Diego to go to the bishop's palace and make known her request, to which that supremely unexcitable Aztec replied in that same high-diplomatic Nahuatl style: "My Lady, I am going now to carry out your command; for the present your humble servant takes leave of you."

And so to the palace of the bishop, a man just recently arrived from Spain, went Juan Diego, getting past the bishop's major domo and household staff only after they had checked everything but the label in his serape. The bishop was Juan de Zumárraga, a kindly but far from credulous Franciscan, and his initial reaction to Juan Diego's account of his Tepeyac Hill experience was understandably one of prudent doubt. Still, he was careful and polite and ushered his visitor out with the comforting words, "You shall come again, my son, and I will hear what you have to say at greater leisure." Juan Diego did not believe that for a minute, of course, and returned to Tepeyac Hill to confess his failure. The Virgin listened patiently both to his tale of sincerity rebuffed and to his closing argument, one of the most moving declarations of inadequacy ever uttered in Nahuatl or any other tongue of earth:

> So I earnestly entreat you, my Lady and Daughter, to entrust one of the more important people with the message, someone well-known, respected and held in esteem, so that it will be believed; for I am a little man, a thin rope, a little wooden step-ladder, a tail, a leaf, one of the little unimportant people, and you, my Child, smallest of my daughters, my Lady, send me where I am out of place and have no standing. Forgive me if I cause you much grief and make you angry with me, my Lady and Mistress.

Though no doubt touched to the depths of her maternal heart, the Virgin was not about to let him off the hook: "Listen to me, smallest of all my beloved Children, and understand that my servants and messengers are many, and any of them could be ordered to take my message and do my bidding; but it is in every way necessary that you solicit my cause and help me and that it be through your intercession that my wish be carried out." So saying, she ordered her "little wooden stepladder" to call on the bishop the next day, repeat her request that he start work on the temple she wanted, and tell him again "that I in person, the ever Virgin Holy Mary, the Mother of God, send you."

The next day a resolute Juan Diego, again having to talk his way past the bishop's household staff, again delivered his mighty message. And again the bishop heard him out. The difference was that this time he asked for a sign. That was progress, at least, and when the faithful Aztec returned to the Lady's hill and made his report, the Virgin not only showed herself agreeable to the bishop's suggestion, she told her messenger that when he returned the next day, she would give him a sign not to be argued with.

But even heavenly commissions must accommodate dying relatives, and when the Lady's messenger returned home that night and found his venerable uncle, Juan Bernardino, not only hearing the thunderous wingbeats of the angel of death but anxious that his nephew leave before daybreak to fetch a priest, Juan Diego agreed, even though it meant the Virgin would have to be bypassed. The next morning, then, though the way to the priest lay over Tepeyac Hill, Juan Diego made an elaborate detour around it—only to find the Virgin waiting for him on the path.

Fortunately, she was as friendly as ever, did not seem to mind his trying to outmaneuver her, and wasted no time assuring him that his uncle was at that very moment being healed. She then sent him to the top of the hill, the place of the previous encounters, instructing him to gather the flowers he would find there and report back, which he promptly did, an overflowing bouquet wrapped up in his tilma. The "flowers", miraculously enough, turned out to be Castilian roses, flora that had no business blooming on a cold Mexican hill in December—and therefore a rather impressive sign for the good bishop. And so, after the Virgin had done one of the most endearing things in all Marian history—rearranged the flowers in the tilma with her own hands—Juan Diego was off on his third mission to the episcopal palace.

This time, he was again put through his paces by the household staff, who, not content to keep him waiting, attempted to snatch away at least one of those impressive-looking roses he seemed to be hiding inside the folds of his tilma. They failed, in any case, and eventually the relieved Juan Diego, roses intact, again found himself in the bishop's presence. Then, with that worthy cleric looking on and as baffled as ever by this strange visitor with the astonishing tale, Juan Diego—rather in the earnest manner of the Little Prince in the Saint-Exupéry story explaining life on his asteroid to the downed French aviator—made a remarkable three-hundred-word speech, summing up his encounters with the Lady and setting the stage for the fantastic drama that would follow.

Especially did he speak of the sign the bishop had asked for—stressing the miracle of finding magnificent roses growing where "only thistles, thorny bushes, nopal cactus, and mezquite grow among stones". Finally, without flourish or fanfare, he declared: "Behold them here. Receive them." With that, he released his grip, the roses cascading dramatically to the floor. But that, as it turned out, was mere momentary prologue. Almost simultaneously there appeared on his tilma the dazzling full-length image of the Lady of Tepeyac Hill.

Seeing was believing. The bishop and his staff immediately fell to their knees, thunderstruck at beholding this glorious emblem of Paradise. Then, after a few moments, deeply contrite, the bishop asked forgiveness of this heaven-chosen Aztec ambassador for not at once having set to work on what the Virgin clearly wanted and had clearly ordered: her "temple". At last he got to his feet, untied the now-sacred tilma from Juan Diego's neck, and placed it in his oratory. After a day spent in prayer and meditation, he summoned Juan Diego and his own chastened assistants and set off for Tepeyac Hill. They found it just as it had traditionally been, quite bereft of any Castilian roses, but in any case an excellent site for the Lady's temple.

The bishop's staff also went the second mile and accompanied Juan Diego on his visit home. Here they received a kind of aftershock to the earthquake experience of the tilma. Not only did they find the grievously ill uncle up and about and without ache, pain, or sniffle, they found him eager to testify that he had been cured at the exact moment the Lady told Juan Diego he would be. Indeed, in the meantime, he said, the Lady had also appeared to *him*, Juan Bernardino, revealing that she had again sent Juan Diego off to see Bishop Zumárraga. Moreover, during this health-restoring apparition, she had instructed him (the uncle) that for the sake of confirming all these matters, he must relate the story of his cure to the bishop. At the same time, she said, he should make it clear she should henceforth be referred to as the ever Virgin Holy Mary of Guadalupe.

As we will see in the next chapter, there was much more to come—including a question involving some possible confusion of the name "Guadalupe" as translated from the Nahuatl. But already a great answer had been given not only to Luther's placard on the Wittenberg door but to the demon gods of Mexico. The woman clothed with the sun had spoken in the vocabulary of two of her greatest emblems—the roses of Tepeyac Hill and the bright gold of her superimposed image on Juan Diego's tilma. Soon, she would speak in the vocabulary of her third great emblem, the fountain—for in the image of her costume, she had left behind a catechism of meaning that was about to lead a nation from the darkness of human sacrifice to the shining waters of baptism.

8

THE TEPEYAC TILMA AND
THE MEXICAN PENTECOST

I will create enmity between thee and the woman, between thy seed and her seed. She shall crush thy head, but thou shalt lie in wait for her heel.   —Genesis 3:15

And there appeared a great wonder in heaven, a woman clothed with the sun, and the moon under her feet, and upon her head a crown of twelve stars.   —Revelation 12:1

The famous revolutions, as Don Ramon said, began with *Viva!* but ended always with *Muera!* Death to this, death to the other, it was all death! death! death! as insistent as the Aztec sacrifices. Something for ever gruesome and macabre. . . . It ought to have been all gay, allegro, allegretto in that sparkle of bright air and old roof surfaces. But no! There was the dark undertone, the black, serpent-like fatality all the time.
                         —D.H. Lawrence, *The Plumed Serpent* (1926)

If Sherlock Holmes had been called in to investigate the mysterious events on Tepeyac Hill, probably the first thing that would have prompted him to lift his deerstalker cap and scratch his information-packed head would have been the title the Virgin had chosen for herself. It was, after all, a title seemingly unrelated to the great work she was about to undertake in crushing the serpent's head and replacing that counterfeit god with faith in the beautiful and true.

According to the Don Valeriano translation of the original Nahuatl, the name she specified to Juan Diego's uncle, Juan Bernardino, was the "ever Virgin Holy Mary of Guadalupe"— and such it has traditionally remained. Yet the Spanish place name has long been a puzzlement. After all, why "Guadalupe"? Guadalupe was a Marian shrine and village in western Spain having no traceable connection with the events, meaning, or geography of Tepeyac Hill.

Nevertheless, for more than four centuries now, that has been the standard term of reference both for Mary's apparitions in Mexico and for her image on Juan Diego's tilma. It was not until the 1970s, in fact, that "Guadalupe" began to set off the first serious bat-whines of doubt. It was then that the late Helen Behrens, an American living in Mexico who had already become the chief promoter of the Tepeyac apparitions, got a Sherlock Holmes–style "hunch" that led to a highly interesting discovery. Convinced there was a snag somewhere in the translation, she prevailed on Professor Byron MacAfee, a Nahuatl-language authority, to reexamine the original text with frank suspicion and gimlet eye. What the professor uncovered led, in turn, to a dramatic new theory, one whose logic seems compelling. As Helen Behrens summed it up:

> Neither Bishop Zumárraga nor any other Spanish prelate has been able to explain why she wished her image to be called "de Guadalupe." The reason must be that she did not say the phrase at all. She spoke in the Indian language and the combination of words she used must have sounded like "de Guadalupe" to the Spaniards. The Aztec "te coatlaxopeuh" has a similar sound (it is pronounced TE QUATLASUPE).
>
> "Te" means "stone"; "coa" means "serpent"; "tla" is the noun ending, which can be interpreted as "the," while "xopeuh" means "crush" or "stamp out." The last part of the message has to be rearranged in the following manner in order to reveal its true meaning: "Her precious image will thus be known (by the name of) the Entirely Perfect Virgin, Holy

Our Lady of Guadalupe, Tepeyac, Mexico

Mary, and it will crush, stamp out, abolish or eradicate the stone serpent."

If this interpretation is in fact the true one, Mary's role and mission in Mexico are suddenly as unmistakable in declaration as they were in result. The "stone serpent" referred to could only have been Quetzalcoatl, the serpent-god of the Aztecs, to whom had long been offered, like so many grisly valentines, great clusters of still blood-wet human hearts. Now, that glowering Satan-surrogate, whose spiritual ancestry went all the way back to the serpent in Eden, was about to be defanged—and Mary was announcing the fact in the language understood by the people most directly affected. But momentous as that announcement was, she was also saying something even greater— that she was the woman prophesied in Genesis who would crush, or whose seed would crush, her elemental adversary.

As always, the fulfillment of prophecy, the notion that words can fly across the centuries like so many arrows and unerringly find their targets, teaches as nothing else can that there is a Being deeper than time and greater than history. Seven hundred years before the great event in the stable, the prophet Micah wrote: "But thou, Bethlehem Ephratah, though thou be little among the thousands of Judah, yet out of thee shall he come forth unto me that is to be ruler in Israel." A thousand years before the Cross, the shepherd-king David set down in the Twenty-second Psalm a picture of Calvary not only describing those "who part my garments among them and cast lots upon my vesture", but quoting, centuries before they were uttered, the Savior's anguished words: "My God, my God, why hast thou forsaken me?" The fulfillment of the great prediction concerning Mary is no less startling.

While the prophecy is by no means restricted to the events in Mexico, it is nonetheless breathtaking to realize that words uttered in the dawn of human existence would suddenly blossom like those Castilian roses into fresh new meaning in A.D. 1531.

But so it was: the woman and the serpent met in the very center of the New World, and a great prophecy received lasting confirmation not only through the conversion of Mexico but in the divinely imprinted tilma of Juan Diego.

No imprinting could have been more to the point. Here, emblazoned on cloth made from maguey cactus, was a hieroglyphic Book of Revelation written especially for the natives. Theirs, it seems, was a language of symbols, and those on the tilma answered the many questions that had to be answered, for the serpent's poison had long since penetrated to the deep places.

Indeed, to digress just long enough to provide the necessary background to the tilma's dramatic symbolism, the religion that held sway in Mexico was considerably older than Christianity. If the ruins of the ancient monuments are to be believed, the worship of Quetzalcoatl dated back to about 500 B.C.—or roughly to the days when, two oceans away, the Jewish remnant was shambling home from the seventy-year Babylonian Captivity. Quetzalcoatl had thus enjoyed two thousand years of being center stage in the rituals and rhythms of an entire people—and a reign so long, deep, and uninterrupted could hardly have been expected to end just because a few missionaries landed and the Spanish fired off their gleaming cannon.

Something stupendous was needed—something not of land or sea but of the heavens, for Quetzalcoatl, like so many other gods and idols, had himself come slithering down out of the sky, identified with the planet Venus. Theories abound as to how the blameless evening star got itself mixed up with a god who had an almost lascivious taste for human sacrifice, but so it was. One of the more intriguing theories is that as recently as 800 B.C., Venus was not a planet but a comet, and thus in the sight of the more imaginative, a fierce serpent of fire racing through the night sky. In any case, the ancient Mexicans worshiped *some* comet or other, called it Quetzalcoatl, and identified it with the evening star. Carved imposingly in stone, as much dragon as serpent, its fearsome likeness can still be seen today on numerous pyramids throughout Mexico, perhaps most menacingly at the temple of Quetzalcoatl in Teotihuacan.

All these things considered, then, it must have seemed as if a new heaven and a new earth had arrived when the defeat of this venerable comet-serpent-god was announced—and heaven and earth were never more eloquent in announcing it than in that miraculous image on that humble cloak. The tilma represents the conquered god as the black, burned-out crescent on which Mary is standing—an all but literal fulfillment of the prophecy, "She is to crush thy head." (Again, as we saw in chapter 3, while the enmity between the woman and the serpent as described in Genesis 3:15 is indisputable, the question of whether it is Mary as the Second Eve or her "seed" who crushes the serpent's head is in doubt. Obviously, no matter who is the apparent instrument, the power of God is the essential element. That being understood, there is nevertheless a striking poetry in Mary's being front and center during this defeat of the serpent who had beguiled an entire people in Mexico as thoroughly as he had beguiled Eve in Eden.)

To be sure, it is not a feathered serpent on which she stands, but it *is* a heavenly crescent not to be confused with the moon—that, in Aztec hieroglyphics, was always represented as a crescent of light, never black—and its slightly mottled and very dark surface could certainly pass for snakeskin. And if Venus was no comet but rather stood for one, so could this dramatically dead crescent stand for the natives' vanquished sky-god. That, in any case, is what all those millions of new converts understood it to mean.

The tilma also answered another local idolatry—the worship of the sun. The Lady was standing directly in front of the sun, blotting out its center and making it clearly subordinate. And at the same time she was obviously "draping" herself with its rays and thus all but literally asserting her scriptural title: "a woman clothed with the sun". Altogether, the message was unmistakable: If a mere human being was greater than the mighty daystar, obviously it was no god.

Nor did this picto-writing merely cast down: it also built up. There was a brooch enclosing a black cross at the neck of the Lady's tunic. The meaning of that was also not to be missed: The cross was the sign of the Spaniards' religion, for the same black emblem had been on the sails of their ships as well as on the banner of Cortez. Then there was the floral decoration on the Virgin's robe, which celebrated the beauty of earth, her former home, just as the celestial blue on her mantle spoke for the beauty of heaven, her present one. Again, the small gold crown she wore signified regality, and what regality could that be but the regality attributed to her by Juan Diego and the missionaries—that in fact she was the Queen of Paradise? After all, had she not evidently come from there, supported and transported by her cherubic escort on the base of the tilma, whose small arms held her aloft?

Apart from its hieroglyphic particulars, moreover, there was the simple, overwhelming fact of the image itself. No earthly artist had painted it; no earthly weaver had woven it. It was plainly and simply a miraculous portrait, a heaven-sent vision shining out of the tilma's coarse cactus fiber, a divine present the like of which no other religion anywhere had been able to claim since the days when Moses came down from Sinai with the tables of the Law and Aaron's rod burst forth with buds and almonds.

Buddha had sat under the bodhi tree in northeastern India and received a purely abstract "enlightenment"; Mohammed in the desert had experienced the dazzling "visions" that had inspired the Koran; Joseph Smith had beheld through magic spectacles the written revelation of the Mormon angel Moroni; but no tangible relics from these supposedly miraculous events survive. The tilma not only survives, it does so though made of a cloth so feeble it should have disintegrated centuries ago.

At Chartres the question was asked: "Who has ever heard tell, in all the ages of the past that . . . men and women of noble birth have bowed their haughty necks to the yoke and harnessed themselves to carts like beasts of burden?" In Mexico, it might likewise have been asked, "Who has ever heard tell that an entire nation has been converted by a garment?" And indeed, even if the garment had disintegrated (as it normally would have) after twenty or thirty years, would we not still be inclined to believe it had existed—for what else could have changed so many Mexican hearts and minds?

Alas, Juan Diego did not live on to explain it to the other nations of earth as once he explained it to Mexico. For explain it he did, day in and day out—with patience, tact, and astounding success. On December 26, 1531, only two weeks after the tilma miracle, an enthusiastic work force consisting of both Mexicans and Spaniards completed an adobe chapel at the foot of Tepeyac in which to house the sacred image, providing also a small attached room for its Aztec custodian. Juan Diego would live to be seventy-three, and for the last seventeen years of his life it would be his job to interpret the tilma and its symbols to all those tragic-eyed pilgrims who came to his door. He became, in effect, the oracle of Mexico, and though he offered no prophecies, he helped confirm, with every new convert, the great prediction of Genesis 3:15.

Juan Diego died in 1548. But his tilma has survived for almost five centuries, and even as it lives on, it continues to make known amazing new things about itself—especially with the help of modern technology. In 1929, for example, photographic negatives of Mary's tilma-imprinted eyes seemed to show the reflection of a man's face—an image within an image, so to speak. But it was not until 1956 that Dr. Javier Torroello Bueno, an oculist, made it official. After a meticulous examination, he testified that he had found reflected images on the Virgin's cornea—and (a further sign of authenticity) images with the slight distortion normally produced by cornea curvature.

The first eye-enclosed figure to be identified—and for a long time it had been thought he was the only one—was that of Juan Diego. Fortunately, portraits of him existed, and the comparison of the dark and bearded face reflected in the Virgin's eye corresponded convincingly with the earliest known portrait of this striking-looking Aztec. But it seems that Juan Diego was only part of the Virgin's field of vision on that December day in 1531.

In 1962, Dr. Charles Wahlig of Woodside, New York, while examining a portrait enlarged twenty-five times, noticed reflections of two other men—presumably Bishop Zumárraga and an interpreter. What this clearly seems to indicate is (1) that the Virgin, though invisible, was hovering near even as her image appeared on the tilma, and (2) that she was looking down on Juan Diego, the bishop, and the interpreter at the very moment when the Almighty reproduced a physically exact picture of her—including even the tiny human images in her eyes.

We may be sure that also looking on at this remarkable tableau, although with considerably less delight, was the serpent of Eden. In fact, his troubles were just beginning: the stupendous seven-year Marian Pentecost was about to get under way, and to have to hear numberless former idol-worshipers declare, "I reject Satan and all his works and pomps", must have been disagreeable in the highest. Yet to look at the post-1540 history of Mexico is to see that the serpent, head crushed but tail thrashing, made a very considerable comeback. Still, that was to be expected, because the conditions conducive to both spiritual and social revolution were clearly present.

Even apart from human nature's universal tendency to wander off the upward path, there was the friction that inevitably developed among the three main populations—Mexicans,

Spanish, and those of mixed blood, the *mestizos*. There was also an inevitable resentment on the part of the natives toward the Spanish mercantilist system, which, with one glittering eye on gold and the other on silver, was eventually to drain Mexico of most of its underground wealth. There was also the problem of equitable land distribution—or the lack of it. Thus, with enmity, rivalry, and social injustice heating up like so many Mexican volcanoes, it was no wonder the nation seemed to be holding perpetual open house for revolution, counterrevolution, foreign intervention, and general lawlessness. One eventual by-product of all that cyclical chaos was the vicious and diabolical persecution of the Church by secular "reformers".

The most harrowing of those persecutions took place under President Plutarco Elías Calles, who ruled Mexico from 1924 to 1928 and who might more accurately have called himself President Quetzal-Calles. Graham Greene, the wide-ranging Catholic journalist/novelist who described the still-terrible Mexico of the 1930s in his book *The Lawless Roads*, called Calles' rule "the fiercest persecution of religion anywhere since the reign of Elizabeth".

The outrages were as crude as they were predictable: the churches were closed (Mass had to be said secretly in private houses), believers were locked up in prison, priests were shot, and churches were declared private property: hundreds of them were degraded into cinemas, newspaper offices, and garages. At the same time, even as the Church was forbidden to open schools, the government imposed educational programs based on standard satanic utopian principles: rationalism, materialism, and anticlericalism.

Clearly, the serpent was back—not in stone and not with human sacrifice, but with the serene arrogance of all-powerful official authority. Hearts were not being ripped out of human chests, but blood was flowing just as regularly as it had in the old

Aztec days. Indeed, not even the sacred image was safe. Even before Calles became president, his party and political dominance had created an atmosphere of persecution so pervasive and a contempt for religion so complete that the unthinkable happened—an attempt to obliterate the portrait that had spiritually transformed a nation. The attack occurred on November 14, 1921, and only because the government, brazen as it was in its efforts to atomize all signs of faith, was nevertheless afraid to close the Basilica of Our Lady of Guadalupe, the tremendously popular site housing the miraculous image. Instead, whether by a bribe or a nod, the authorities decided to go after the image itself.

And it must have seemed a temptingly simple matter to destroy anything so apparently fragile as the tilma. All the would-be spiritual assassin had to do was enter the church and, as so many others did, leave a bouquet of roses in front of the image—the difference being that, concealed by the flowers and ferns, a high-powered time bomb would be ticking away.

That was arranged, and at 10:30 that November morning, to the lisping of prayers, the rustle of serapes, and the squeaking of huaraches up the long aisles was suddenly added the sound of detonated dynamite. Amid the shouts and screams, stained-glass windows crashed to the floor and an explosion-twisted iron crucifix bounced like a tenpin and came to rest on the main altar. But miraculously, both the Virgin's image and the glass protecting it remained intact. Even with the help of modern explosives, the serpent's head had failed to bruise the woman's heel.

Some idea of the thirsty evil that lay behind this fiendish business can be gathered from the report of an interview conducted many years ago by Earnest Larsen, C.SS.R., with one of the bomb-plot conspirators. By then repentant, this admitted satanist confessed to having machine-gunned numerous believers and to having bribed children with candy simply to get his hands on the consecrated Host. The capture of the living Bread would invariably be followed by a black Mass in which it was horribly desecrated and after which the participants would go out with inflamed vigor to mutilate priests and ravish nuns—a Quetzalcoatl festival if ever there was one.

The turning point for *him*, this evil-doer flatly asserted, was the sight of the tilma standing fast against the dynamite: he had been there in person and had thus witnessed that incomprehensible deliverance with his own eyes. Though he tried earnestly to revive his faith in the power of darkness by visiting one of his organization's largest American shrines and the stone serpent it worshiped—Quetzalcoatl recognizes no boundaries—in the end, by the power of grace, this modern version of an Aztec blood-priest would embrace both the tilma and what it stood for.

All of this, of course, will sound like rabid fantasy to anyone unwilling to believe in the invisible world undergirding and largely shaping this visible one. Yet for those who trust not only the evidence of their senses but the evidence of things not seen, the sacred image of Tepeyac Hill and the implacable malice of Quetzalcoatl speak for that deeper dimension with all the drama of Genesis 3:15 electrifyingly fulfilled.

9

A RAMPART AT SEA (LEPANTO),
A ROCK ON LAND (SILUVA)

O Virgin Mother of God, thou art an unassailable rampart, a fortress of salvation; we beseech thee, destroy the schemes of our enemies, turn the grief of thy people into joy.
—Byzantine Horologion
(ninth century)

Soon after the remarkable events in Mexico, two new and great Marian moments made it clear that the Blessed Virgin was not only an unassailable rampart but also a highly mobile support force. In 1571, forty years after the miracle of Tepeyac Hill and eight thousand miles away, the nation of Ulysses witnessed a new Homeric epic: the Virgin-aided naval victory at Lepanto; and a bit less than forty years after that, in 1608, Lithuania played host to the Virgin's memorable and faith-restoring appearance in the village of Siluva. The battle of Lepanto took place on water; the Siluva apparition on land, a fact that helps explain why Mary's titles include not only Earth Untouchable and Virginal, but also Star of the Sea. The two interventions also demonstrated twice more her proclivity for being at the center of historical dramas with far-reaching consequences.

Especially was that true of Lepanto, that vitally important victory by Christian forces over the Ottoman Turks. Had the battle gone the other way, much of today's Europe would be in all likelihood as Moslem as Mecca. Indeed, some of Europe was already under the crescent—the Ottomans had few rivals in all history at the art of conquering. To appreciate fully the significance of Lepanto, then, it is important to see what those fearsome followers of Islam had previously done in the way of replacing the cross with that symbol curved like a scimitar.

The Osmanlis, or Ottoman Turks, were named for their founder, Osman I (1259–1326; emir, 1299–1326), who at the age of forty, in 1299, called this new empire into being—an empire consisting of people who represented a fusion between Greek natives and Turkish invaders. By the 1350s, having proved themselves formidable on both land and water, they possessed all of Asia Minor and most of the Black Sea nations. A century later, they besieged and captured Constantinople, that ancient Christian citadel which, as we saw earlier, the emperor Constantine had dedicated to the Virgin eleven centuries before.

Had it been Rome itself that had fallen, the shock would have been only slightly greater. Nothing could have made clearer what this new force in the world represented than what happened with the magnificent Greek church called Hagia Sophia (Greek for "Holy Wisdom"). With its spectacular dome, polychrome marbles, and gold mosaic, it was not only the supreme masterpiece of Byzantine architecture, it had been a beacon to believers and a temple of Christianity for nine hundred years. Following the Ottoman victory in 1453, it was converted into a mosque (and a mosque it remained until 1934, when Kemal Ataturk, the founder of modern Turkey, had it turned into a museum).

Western eyes could see the handwriting on the wall, and the script was looking suspiciously Arabic. Obviously, what had happened with Constantinople could happen with Italy and its European neighbors. And in fact what *could* happen *was* happening. By the time of his death in 1566, Suleiman the Magnificent, a kind of Islamic version of Alexander the Great, had brought the Ottoman Empire to the height of its glory—and there it would glitter until Lepanto five years later. In 1521, he conquered Belgrade; in 1522, Rhodes. In 1526, he crushed Hungary at the battle of Mohacs and then calmly went on to new campaigns against Persia and Arabia, acquiring new territory at a furious clip. And in 1529, just two years before Juan Diego saw his vision on Tepeyac Hill, Suleiman was besieging Vienna. Though he failed there, he left no doubt about Ottoman ambitions.

After Suleiman's death, far from relaxing the pace, the Ottomans conducted numerous piratical raids, ravaging areas of Sicily, southern Italy, and even Majorca—the first nibbles at the inviting feast represented by western Europe. Then, in 1571, with their powerful navy already dominant in the Mediterranean, the Ottomans captured the well-defended and strategically vital island of Cyprus and went on to besiege Venice. Who or what would be next? The handwriting on the wall was beginning to look every bit as solid as cuneiform.

Pius V, the white-bearded, ascetic Dominican who, even as pope, continued to wear his friar's habit under his pontifical robes and to walk barefoot in penitential processions, knew the time had come for decisive action. Whatever we in the twentieth century may think of popes wielding temporal power, Pius V wielded it like a man with blood in his veins. Among other things, he had moved vigorously to stamp out prostitution in Rome, had removed all traces of simony from the corrupt Roman curia, had bluntly excommunicated Queen Elizabeth, and had dealt forcefully with heretics (even while rescuing the archbishop of Toledo, condemned by the Spanish Inquisition, and bringing him to Rome for retrial despite the protests of King Philip II of Spain).

Stern but kindly, at once a warm patron of the arts and an unapologetic puritan who had the nudities in Michelangelo's *Last Judgment* discreetly overpainted; above all, a man of principle whom people respected and listened to—this was the spiritual leader and eventual saint who would form the great naval counterforce to Moslem power. It would be called the Holy League, and in creating it, Pius V would enlist the two greatest Italian sea powers, Venice and Genoa (whose vessels formed the bulk of the fleet), and would also prevail on Spain's King Philip for the necessary additional ships, the two men's differences on heresy notwithstanding.

But the forty-four-year-old Philip would contribute something even more important than ships and soldiers; he would supply the commander of the fleet, his illegitimate half-brother, the twenty-four-year-old wonder of the world, Don John of Austria. This strikingly handsome young man, with all the battle talent of a Napoleon and none of the arrogance, had been born in a small Bavarian city, the natural son of the Spanish Emperor Charles V and a beautiful young woman named Barbara Blomberg. In the interests of preventing royal scandal, Don John had been brought up in concealment in Spain under the interesting name of Geronimo—and in fact he would later show himself every bit as much a warrior as his future Apache namesake.

As Wyndham Lewis admiringly wrote of him, he was "a soldier with a fearlessness matching his looks and brains". After the emperor's death, Philip officially recognized him as his half-brother and, noting his princely talent for leading in the field, appointed him commander in chief against the rebellious Moriscos of Granada. Don John at twenty-two was so successful in his campaign against *that* Moslem force that Philip decided he was ready, at twenty-four, to deal with a far larger one. And Philip was proved right: here was the precocious leader and diplomat who would not only inspire but keep together his often antagonistic forces and smooth the feathers of admirals more than twice his age—a kind of latter-day version of Israel's King David.

Enter Mary. With the expeditionary force in place, the Pope brought an even greater force to bear—a vast rosary campaign in which he sought requests for the Virgin's intercession from every Catholic with a set of beads. All that prayer would be in support of a new kind of crusade, one that would be both brief and decisive—not an army setting off for months of war in and near Jerusalem, but a navy setting out to win back the Mediterranean in a winner-take-all battle that would require less than a day to fight. So the prayers were offered and the beads counted off in church, home, and monastery all across Catholic Europe, and in mid-September the 208 vessels of the allies assembled under Don John in the Strait of Messina, that narrow band of water separating Italy from Sicily.

Organization and discipline were no small problem for the young commander. Many of the thirty thousand troops were mercenaries, restless and troublesome when confined on a crowded ship—and deadly fights among them were common. Several of the wilder sort even attempted to assassinate Don John, for which they were promptly hanged. But finally, peace established a beachhead, and, as Wyndham Lewis so gracefully expressed it, "As befitted men sworn to save Christendom or perish, the entire army and fleet from Don John down to the smallest cabin boy went to confession and received the Blessed Sacrament at Messina before sailing." Somewhere to the east lay the Moslem fleet, and the Christian fleet, trusting to God and the four winds, sailed in search of it.

Every level of European society was represented on those oar-powered galleys and on those picturesque sailing ships, and so was virtually every noble Christian family in Spain and Italy, or as G. K. Chesterton put it in his famous Lepanto poem:

> The Pope has cast his arms abroad for agony and loss
> And called the kings of Christendom for swords
> about the Cross.

One of those swords about the Cross belonged to perhaps the second most remarkable of the men who fought in the battle, a young man the very same age as Don John, the bearded, hawk-nosed twenty-four-year-old Miguel de Cervantes, the literary genius who was to enrich the world with his tales of the incomparable Don Quixote and Sancho Panza. Yet it was Lepanto, where he fought courageously until severely wounded (as we will see a bit later) that remained his proudest moment in life or literature.

Meanwhile, even as the Christians were turning themselves into the proverbial irresistible force, assembling a navy that would occupy ten miles of ocean in sailing formation, so were the Moslems lining up as the classic immovable object. When the Christian fleet was spotted, the Ottoman Sultan ordered his number one commander, Admiral Ali Pasha, to seek it out and destroy it. As it turned out, all the commander had to do was proceed to home port and wait. Since he was besieging Venice when word reached him, Ali Pasha at once sailed straight down the Adriatic (to the great relief of the Venetians, whose navy had long since joined Don John) and returned to Lepanto, the fortified Ottoman naval base on the northern shore of the gulf of Corinth. There, sending out fishing boats with false messages designed to mislead his enemy, Ali Pasha made ready, assembling some three hundred ships and packing them with both standard warriors and janissaries (the elite guard).

Even before one of the world's great battles began, one of history's great spectacles would be on view—under a flawless blue sky, more than five hundred ships swarming with close to one hundred thousand men, bright banners flying on every vessel, great banks of oars rhythmically stabbing the turquoise sea, cannon being primed, scimitars flashing, archers dipping their arrows in poison. Had a filmmaker been there, the senior camera crew would no doubt have been assigned to Don John, who commanded the main Christian squadron of sixty-two vessels, and took the center position in the attack. His richly decorated man-of-war, the *Reale*, the largest in the battle, flew the bright blue Venetian pennant—a large square flag emblazoned with the traditional gold Venetian winged lion holding aloft a cross. To his left, flying yellow banners, were the thirty ships of the reserve squadron, and just in front, like a kind of nautical battering ram, were six massive cannon-packed Venetian galleasses, the so-called "floating fortresses".

An hour after sunrise on October 7, lookouts on the advance galleys began to cry out that enemy ships had been sighted inside the inlet to the gulf. And an hour or two later, one can imagine the rush of adrenaline as the Christian vessels swung around the headland and the whole Ottoman navy came into view directly facing them, hundreds of long, curving sails silhouetted ominously against the rising sun. But there was still plenty of time for final preparations: sand was spread about on the ships' decks for better footing; the surgeons got ready their operating tables; all the galley slaves (unless they were Moslem prisoners of war) were unchained, given weapons, and promised their freedom if the Moslems were defeated; and triple portions of wine were issued to one and all, it being thought the juice of the grape increased men's fighting ability. But even after drinking their courage-supplement, some of Don John's lieutenants, eyeing the size of the Moslem fleet, asked him to reconsider. His reply was as brief as it was memorable: "Gentlemen, the time for counsel is past, and the time for battle has come."

Following classic sea-battle etiquette, the Moslems fired off one cannon blast and the Christians answered with two as a signal to fight. With that, Ali Pasha's flagship, the *Sultana*, hoisted a large green silk banner decorated with the Moslem crescent and Arabic inscriptions, even as his men blew horns, clashed cymbals, and fired muskets. By contrast, following a single trumpet blast from Don John's flagship, the Christians knelt in prayer as a crucifix was raised aloft on each vessel.

The symbolism was as powerful as it was elemental: cross versus crescent. David versus Goliath in the valley of Elah could have been no more dramatic than this duel to the death in that narrow inlet off the Ionian Sea. And now, with the fleets only two miles apart, yet one more astonishing thing took place: as if on signal, the westerly breeze died away, leaving the Gulf of Lepanto ominously still. And just as remarkably, the sea retained an uncanny glasslike surface for the rest of the day—with, as we shall see, one providential exception. The stillness only added to the drama of a spectacle beyond the wildest dreams of Cecil B. de Mille—hundreds of warships with brilliantly colored sails and banners coasting slowly toward each other across the entire width of the gulf, a kind of *High Noon* on the high seas.

The battle commenced at midday and continued through four long hours of cannon blasts and clanking swords. Of all the thousands of close-encounter clashes, the most dramatic occurred when Ali Pasha's *Sultana* rammed Don John's *Reale*. Even as muskets boomed and poisoned arrows flew, Don John led his men forward onto the *Sultana*, broadsword in one hand and battle-ax in the other. Seeing him, Ali Pasha rushed ahead over the wet sand and fallen bodies, hoping to meet his great young rival in hand-to-hand combat. No such luck. He was stopped by a musket ball and toppled off the deck onto the uppermost rowing benches. Thereupon a Christian galley slave, savoring his moment in the sun, grabbed a scimitar and severed the Ottoman admiral's head, which a Spanish soldier at once hoisted triumphantly aloft on a pikestaff. Don John then ordered Ali Pasha's green, crescent-emblazoned silk banner cut down from the mainmast and a large Holy League banner raised in its place for all to see—the fifteenth-century equivalent of the Marines raising the Stars and Stripes on Iwo Jima. In both cases, it was the prelude to victory.

And Lepanto was a victory to make even the fish take notice. Of the three-hundred-plus Ottoman ships, fewer than fifty managed to escape, and 117 were captured intact. While the casualties were heavy on both sides, the Christians had much the best of it. Though they lost some eight thousand men to sword and sea, the Ottomans lost at least twice that many. At the same time, Don John's forces rejoiced the hearts of untold rosary-saying wives and mothers by liberating some ten thousand Christian galley slaves.

In addition to the Don John-Ali Pasha free-for-all, another battle within the battle not to be overlooked was the one starring the young Spaniard destined to become one of the world's great writers. Like Don John, Cervantes was a soldier with a Don Quixote gallantry already burning in his adventurous soul. When the signal to open fire was given, he was lying prostrate with fever below decks, but, vowing that he would rather die in action for God and King than skulk below, he begged for a dangerous assignment and got one—the command of twelve men in a longboat. Fever-ridden though he was, he led a spirited series of attacks on Moslem vessels until he was finally knocked out of action by three gunshot wounds—two in the chest and one that permanently disabled his left hand. As he later wrote of himself: "He lost in the naval battle of Lepanto his left hand, which was struck by a shot from an arquebus—a wound that, although it appears ugly, he regards as lovely, because he received it on the most memorable and lofty occasion that past centuries have beheld, nor can those to come hope to see the like."

And there was yet one more battle within the battle that should be underscored in red pencil—a battle decided by a sudden wind out of nowhere. As we noted earlier, the sea was eerily wind-free all day—except, it seems, when a wind was needed. It was needed because Admiral Andrea Doria, commanding the fifty-ship squadron to the right of Don John, was maneuvered by his Moslem opposite number into separating from the center force. As a result, he and his squadron were suddenly on the verge of being cut off, surrounded, and obliterated. But somehow a wind arose, blew the attacking Moslem

squadron off course, and allowed Andrea Doria not only to recover but to gain the upper hand. What makes his deliverance
especially fascinating is that his ship was the only one in the fleet
under the special protection of Our Lady of Guadalupe.

It seems that Bishop Zumárraga's successor, Bishop Fray
Alonso de Montufor, had sent a small reproduction of the miraculous tilma image to King Philip of Spain, suggesting that
when the time came, it would serve the Christian cause very
well indeed. The time came soon after Philip presented it to
Admiral Doria. The admiral promptly had it installed in his
cabin, hoping, no doubt, that if a miracle were needed, a
miracle there would be. And, though a sea-breeze off Greece
may not have been as dramatic as Castilian roses on a Mexican
hill, no one was quibbling. There is, of course, no way to know
whether prayers to the Virgin of Tepeyac brought the rescuing
wind, but the fact remains that Admiral Doria's crew un-
hesitatingly attributed their deliverance to her intervention.

Pope Pius V, in any case, even though he was probably un-
aware of the presence of the Guadalupe image on the famous
admiral's vessel, credited the victory to Mary's intercession following the countless rosary petitions she received and to the
divine wisdom in choosing the right man for the job: the won-
der-working Don John. As the Pope so beautifully summed it
up simply by quoting the first chapter of the Fourth Gospel:
"There was a man sent from God, whose name was John." With
the Spanish king's young brother playing the Duke of Welling-
ton out of John the Baptist, the victory had been every bit as
decisive as Waterloo. It broke the back of Moslem sea power in
the Mediterranean, reassured Christendom that prayer and reso-
lution could turn back a force many had thought irresistible,
and delivered all of Europe, Protestant as well as Catholic, from
the ominously lengthening Ottoman shadow.

As with the events at Chartres and Tepeyac Hill, the events at
Lepanto justify those great rhetorical questions of the Abbot

Haimon: "Who has ever seen! Who has ever heard tell?" In the waters off Greece, as earlier in the plains of France and in the mountains of Mexico, Mary had once again lived out the words of the Magnificat: "My soul doth magnify the Lord", and "All generations shall call me blessed."

✦

There could hardly be a sharper contrast than that between the bright coastal waters of Greece and the sandy, barren soil of central Lithuania around the small town of Siluva—yet the Virgin's influence was soon to be felt every bit as much there as in the smoke and blood of Lepanto. In 1608, only thirty-seven years after Don John's great naval victory, she appeared in the very center of that Baltic nation, and the result was equally profound. And, as at Lepanto, a religious war was the occasion of her being called on. Yet this new war was Christian all the way: Catholics versus Calvinists.

Siluva gets its name from "silas", the local term for a pine tree forest, the pine being the one tree able to thrive in that sandy soil. Yet despite the land's hostility to vegetation, a two-thousand-member community, made up for the most part of small farmers, was somehow able both to scratch out a living and maintain a rich faith. A zealous noble named Pietras Giedgaudas had built Siluva's Catholic church in 1457—significantly, in honor of the Blessed Virgin—and every September 8, pious pilgrims came pouring in to commemorate her birthday. That happy custom lasted for seventy-five years. But then in 1532, following that boisterous dispute in nearby Germany, the Reformation's influence began making itself felt, and beginning in 1550, the Calvinists swept all before them, either taking over or burning virtually every one of Lithuania's Catholic churches.

Siluva's church, leveled to the ground, was one of the more eloquent casualties. Fortunately in 1570 or so, or just about the time of Lepanto, the last Catholic pastor was prudent enough to remove the treasured image of the Madonna and Child, some ecclesiastical vestments, and some official church documents, place them in an oaken chest, and bury them secretly near a huge rock about a half-mile from the church.

Some twenty years later, as Lithuanian politics moved in the direction of greater tolerance, Catholics were given the right to repossess their churches and other property unjustly seized. For Siluva, however, there would be a long wait, since it seemed no one knew where to find the documents establishing that Pietras Giedgaudas had in fact given the land and the long-since-obliterated church to the Catholic authorities. Then, in 1608, the necessary miracle took place.

By way of background, it should be noted that traditionally in Siluva the older children tended the flocks while the younger ones played around that same large rock near which the forgotten oak chest lay buried. In any case, one hot summer day exactly a dozen years before the Pilgrims landed at that far more famous landmark, Plymouth Rock, Siluva's tykes and toddlers looked up to see, not one of their own, but a striking-looking young woman sitting just above them on that favorite rock of theirs. They described her as having beautiful long hair and attractive, loose-fitting garments and holding a child in her arms. But they also reported that this lovely image of motherhood was weeping. Whatever it signified, one of the children ran to tell the local Calvinist responsible for catechetical instruction that something highly *un*-Calvinist had been going on. The next day, curious if not convinced, both the catechist and the Calvinist seminary's rector were on hand along with many of the townsfolk when the woman once again appeared on the rock.

"Why are you crying?" asked the catechist.

"Formerly in this place", the woman replied, "my Son was adored and honored, but now all that the people do is seed and cultivate the land."

With that she disappeared, and the catechist and the rector, understandably annoyed at this arrant violation of their doctrine, could only insist it was all the work of the devil. And there the matter might have rested except for one thing: there was a blind man present in possession of a crucial secret, and though he alone of all those gathered there could not see the vision, he was moved by what he heard the woman say. He then revealed that he knew by touch exactly where the oaken chest was buried—and proceeded to prove it. (Why he had withheld the information until then remains a mystery.) The chest was promptly dug up, at any rate, and the indispensable documents were recovered.

Eventually, the tribunal in the capital city of Vilnius decided in favor of the Catholics, and in 1624, the Catholic pastor, Jonas Kazekevicius, built a small wooden church to replace the one destroyed fifty-odd years before. By then word of the apparitions had spread far and wide and so had news of the recovery of the Madonna-and-Child image, now resting above the main altar of the church. As a result, pilgrims soon began arriving in thunderous numbers. To accommodate the crowds, a much larger edifice was put up in 1641. Finally, on September 7, 1789, the Virgin's own birth was heralded with the solemn consecration of a new stone church in Renaissance style, and a chapel was built over the rock of the apparition.

But though the pilgrims flooded in and the devotion grew— Pope Pius VI in 1775 had officially approved the cult of Our Lady of Siluva—persecution followed as the night the day. In 1795, at the time of the great Polish partitions, Lithuania (Poland's northern neighbor) was annexed by Russia. After the takeover, not only was the teaching of the Lithuanian language forbidden, but no religious book could so much as be printed, let alone read. It would be a total eclipse of the nation lasting over a hundred years—until a revolution in 1904 made it possible to reclaim some privileges, and a declaration of independence at war's end in 1918 created twenty-two years of freedom, during which devotion to Our Lady of Siluva spread rapidly. On September 8 of that Armistice year, almost one hundred thousand pilgrims were at the shrine to participate in the services commemorating the 1608 appearances.

Alas, in 1940, the Soviet version of the Russian bear—red in tooth, claw, and flag—made itself a present of the little Baltic nation, just as the Czarists had done 145 years before, and happily set about ripping it to pieces. Whatever their arrogance, the Czarists had at least left the religious symbols in place, whereas the Communists wanted everything spiritual torn out, root and branch, cross and crucifix. Bishop Fulton J. Sheen, one of many appalled observers, called the persecution following the Communist takeover unlike anything the world had seen since the time of Nero—a third of Lithuania's population either massacred or exiled to Siberia. Today, fortunately, for however long, that nation again breathes free—even as the rock of Siluva continues to speak for a people who have done indescribably more than "seed and cultivate the land".

Pius XI, pope from 1922 to 1939 and onetime nuncio to Poland (Lithuania's long-suffering neighbor), knew Lithuania's story to the last teardrop—bedeviled by its enemies, consoled by the Virgin. He called it "Terra Mariana"—the land of Mary. The land covers a mere twenty-five thousand square miles, or about 1/160th of the continent of Europe. Yet because of the significance of Siluva alone, Lithuania must be reckoned a great rose in the crown of the woman all generations call blessed.

10

IN PRAISE OF MARY: GREAT WORKS OF
PEN, BRUSH, CHISEL, AND SONG

Frequently images badly painted distract and cause devotion to
be lost, at least in those who possess little; and, on the contrary,
those that are divinely painted provoke and lead even those
who are little devout and but little inclined to worship to contemplation and tears.

—Michelangelo Buonarotti

"Praised be the fathomless universe", wrote Walt Whitman, "for
life and joy, for objects and knowledge curious, and for love,
sweet love—but praise! praise! praise!" The poet wasn't telling
us anything our instinct for admiration has not told us a thousand times just as insistently—for it would seem that a far
greater Poet than Whitman long ago put the praise-impulse
deep inside the human soul. As the author of the true, the good,
and the beautiful, the Creator understandably wants true, good,
and beautiful things praised, and as the architect of voice, eye,
hand, and all else that makes praise possible, he not unreasonably
insists that he be honored first and last, even above Picasso and
Andy Warhol. Or as Psalm 113 so beautifully expresses it: "From
the rising of the sun unto the going down of the same, the
Lord's name is to be praised."

The Hebrews, those exemplary praisers on the trumpet, harp,
timbrel, and cymbals, followed that advice so thumpingly in

both letter and spirit they even referred to the human tongue as "my glory"—that is, as the chief instrument for giving glory to their Maker. And they gave him that glory not only in tongue-praise but also in music, costume, sacrifice, and ceremony. It was for Christianity to bring in something entirely new: the image.

The reason for that was as simple as it was obvious: the New Testament faithful had been given for eye to see and hand to carve and paint what the Old Testament worshipers had not: God the Son and his immaculate human Mother. Infinity had walked the earth for thirty-three years with human feet and spoken in a human voice; humanity had been given perfection in a handmaid whose soul magnified the Lord. Human artistry could only marvel and exclaim at these wonders in every way it knew how, even to the unprecedented act of depicting the image of the Almighty.

Jesus is of course the greatest sight human eyes have ever beheld, and it is small wonder that his name, praise, and image fill the world. But Mary is the second greatest sight ever witnessed by human eyes, and the wonder is that, great as her praise has been, it has been begrudged by so many in the Christian world—including, all too often these days, the Catholic world. Fortunately, it has not been neglected by those who can best make praise live, shine, and soar—the deeply talented in the realm of art.

Even as the cathedrals, those psalms written in stone and stained glass, continued to rise all over Europe, other forms of hosanna were finding gigantic new talents to set them forth. In 1265, only five years after Chartres Cathedral's final dedication, the city of Florence saw the birth of Dante Alighieri, who was to become not only one of the world's supreme poets but also one of its greatest Mary-praisers. In the *Paradiso*, his soaring vision of the celestial afterlife, he set down an image for all time: the Queen of Heaven seated on her glorious throne even as "that Love which first descended to her, singing: *Hail Mary, full of grace* now spread his wings before her and the divine canticle answered from every side"—all of this taking place in that "realm of divine light" where the angels have faces of living flame and where the redeemed are seen, rank upon rank, as the petals of a gigantic rose. (As always, it seems, the rose and the Virgin are never far apart.)

Dante is told to "look now upon the face which is most likened unto Christ; for its brightness, and no other, has power to fit thee to see Christ." Dante not only looks upon the Virgin's face, he prays to her, and she, pleased with his devout request that she "vanquish human ferments", answers by showing him the perfect way to do so: she calmly looks into the eternal light of the Trinity. Dante follows suit, and, before long, his sight becoming "purged", he is able to "unite my glance with the Worth infinite" and see at last the glorious "book" of ultimate meaning: "ingathered, bound by love in one volume, the scattered leaves of all the universe". No more poetic treatment of Mary's assertion that "My soul doth magnify the Lord" has ever been penned.

Then there was the great John Donne (1572–1631), poet, Anglican divine, and dean of Saint Paul's Cathedral. In his powerful series of poems entitled *The Litany*, he places Mary immediately after the Trinity and in praise of her achieves a truly stunning eloquence:

> For that fair, blessed mother-maid
> Whose flesh redeem'd us, that she-cherubim
> Which unlock'd paradise . . .
> Whose womb was a strange heav'n, for there
> God clothed himself and grew.

Few images, if any, have ever outshone that last one—the idea of God slowly adorning himself with Mary's flesh, for nine amazing months adding glory to glory—the tiny sacred heart slowly growing larger and all the while beating a foot away from its Mother's immaculate one.

Apart from Dante and Donne, perhaps Mary's greatest praiser in the world of poets is a distinctly modern one, Gerard Manley Hopkins (1844–1889). In "The Blessed Virgin Compared to the Air We Breathe", he gives us eloquence and celebration in a key all his own. Employing an image fresh in every sense, Hopkins speaks of the "world-mothering air" that gives us life, telling us how it reminds him of that spiritual oxygen Mary has given us through Christ and continues to give us through grace. Finally he goes on to declare, in a chain of phrases that magnificently link heaven to earth:

> I say that we are wound
> With mercy round and round
> As if with air: the same
> Is Mary, more by name.
> She, wild web, wondrous robe,
> Mantles the guilty globe,
> Since God has let dispense
> Her prayers his providence:
> Nay, more than almoner,
> The sweet alms' self is her
> And men are meant to share
> Her life as life does air.

These, of course, are only a few of the countless stairway-to-Paradise lines offered in praise of the Virgin over the past two thousand years, and though many more might be quoted here, there is only one too haunting to be bypassed before we move on to the praise offered Mary in other forms of art. It is by the wonderful G. K. Chesterton (1874–1936), and is part of "The Arena", the poem he wrote about the University of Notre Dame when he gave a series of lectures there in 1930 and, incidentally, saw his first game of American football. The statue of Mary on the Golden Dome captured his imagination and *he* captured *it*:

> I have seen, where a strange country
> Opened its secret plains about me,
> One great golden dome stand lonely with its golden
>   image, one
> Seen afar, in strange fulfillment,
> Through the sunlit Indian summer
> That Apocalyptic portent that has clothed her with
>   the Sun.

If poets have found the Marian phrases that bring heaven down to earth, at least one composer has found the Marian notes that go all the way up. Indeed, of all the "Stabat Maters", "Salve Reginas", and "Ave Marias" that have attempted to capture the special quality that is Mary's alone, there is none with quite the magic of Franz Schubert's "Ave". Somehow the young Austrian composer found that Jacob's ladder of perfect chords on which the angels of music are forever ascending and descending and listened well enough to set down a masterpiece.

So exquisite is that melody, so perfectly does it capture the tone of an earthly soul reverently beseeching the help of the Mother of Mercy that few can hear it without feeling that music so poignant must speak for something greater than itself. The world first heard it in 1825—just thirty-three years, or the length of her Son's life, before Mary appeared to Bernadette at Lourdes—and Saint Cecilia herself conducting the seraphic choir could not have provided a more beautiful fanfare. Heaven's reaction to this literally transporting new piece of music we can only guess at; earth's was immediate and profound. As the twenty-eight-year-old Schubert wrote to his father:

Especially have my new songs from *The Lady of the Lake* earned
me success. Much have I surprised people by the religious feeling I have expressed in a hymn to the Blessed Virgin and
which, it appears, grips every soul and turns it to devotion. The
reason, I think, is that I never force myself to think religiously
and never write sacred music unless something stronger than
myself urges me to it; but then, that, surely, is more likely to be
genuine religious feeling.

The "something stronger" that urged him to write his "Ave
Maria" he did not specify, but supernatural grace would seem to
be the prime suspect, having earlier apparently made all the
necessary connections of text, translation, and circumstance. If
Henry Adams was right in asserting that the Virgin gave orders
to her architects at Chartres until she got just what she was after,
then here, surely, was the melody she wanted as her own. To
bring it about, Mary, or other heavenly power or powers, first
had to inspire Catholic sympathies in the Protestant heart of Sir
Walter Scott, *The Lady of the Lake*'s author. Done. Next, there
had to be in Scott's writing the fresh, human note that would
get his work read and admired far beyond the borders of Scot-
land. There was. Next, that work had to find a German translator who would do justice to the original. It did. Finally, the
right composer with the right melodic gifts and quality of soul
had to read that work, like the songs, and feel the right sort of
inspiration. Enter Schubert.

Inspired by P. A. Storck's translation of Scott's epic narrative
poem, Schubert promptly set to music the three songs sung by
the tale's young Catholic heroine, Ellen Douglas. The first two
have not been heard in public since the second Grover Cleve-
land administration, but the third, the "Ave Maria", sung by
Ellen sitting at her harp on the tiny midlake island where she
lives with her father, is still drawing iron tears down the faces of
hardened sinners. Indeed, it would almost seem that a *celestial*
lady of the lake was breathing through the melody that Scott's
word's referred to:

It is the harp of Allan-bane
That makes its measure slow and high,
Attuned to sacred minstrelsy.
What melting voice attends the strings?
'Tis Ellen, or an angel, sings.

Somehow, in spirit or dream, Schubert had sat at that lake-island harp and, "attuned to sacred minstrelsy", found his sacred muse. He would die at thirty-one, but in his short life he had written, among a hundred superb compositions, one supreme one. Never was it truer that the song is ended, but the melody lingers on.

☙

If names as great as Dante and Schubert have praised the Virgin in poetry and music, names as great as Michelangelo and Leonardo have praised her in sculpture and painting. Indeed, of all the Mary-honoring works ever to proceed from the hand of genius, the most famous is undoubtedly Michelangelo's *Pietà* (an Italian word that can mean devotion, piety, or pity, but here seems to mean something far more), that supremely eloquent white-marble statue of the bereaved Mother holding her lifeless Son.

As with Schubert's great melody, the *Pietà* leaves the beholder wondering what argument or theological fine point could ever stand against a work of art so overwhelming—not just a sermon in stone, but theology in marble. When Saint Paul wrote (2 Cor 3:2), "You are our epistle written in our hearts, known and read of all men", he went on to say, "written not in tables of stone, but fleshy tables of the heart". Michelangelo's triumph was to produce an epistle written in *both* stone and heart—and an epistle every serious believer should rejoice at having. When Walt Whitman wrote in *Leaves of Grass* "Camerado, this is no book; who touches this touches a man", he struck the note all great art aims at. But Michelangelo's triumph was to express not only his human presence but the deepest sorrow this world has ever known.

The great Florentine sculptor was only twenty-five years old and, in his own words, following not the conventional sculptural wisdom but "the heart's image" when he created it, and it made his reputation immediately. (Schubert at twenty-eight, Michelangelo at twenty-five—were there ever such masterpieces of youth inspired by a common subject as these two?) And it seems not only a touching reality but a fitting one that, after a very long life in which he established himself as perhaps the greatest artist of all time, Michelangelo finished his magnificent career where he had begun it—working on a new *Pietà*. As the British writer Michael Ayrton so concisely expressed it:

> On the 12th of February (1564) he worked, standing all day, at this last *Pietà*, drastically recutting the stone so that it remains now in a state of transition between two quite different conceptions of the same subject. . . . It is unfinished, and it is finished. Six days later, on February 18th, it was all finished. Michelangelo was dead. He was not quite 89 years old.

Perhaps better than anyone else, this cloud-borne genius from the Tuscan hills appreciated the majesty befitting sacred art and the responsibility assumed in undertaking it:

> It is not sufficient merely to be a great master in painting and very wise, but I think it is necessary for the painter to be very good in his mode of life, or even, if such were possible, a saint, so that the Holy Spirit may inspire his intellect. . . . And even in the Old Testament God the Father wished that those who only had to ornament and paint the *arca foederis* should be masters not merely excellent and great, but also touched by His grace and wisdom, God saying to Moses that He would imbue them with the knowledge and intelligence of His spirit so that they might invent and do everything that He could invent and do.

It would seem that it was for the greatest artist to say the wisest thing, and generally speaking, Michelangelo followed that prudent counsel. It is no secret he kept beside him and constantly studied copies of the flame-tipped sermons preached by another great Florentine and contemporary—the Dominican prophet Fra Savonarola.

Another Savonarola admirer and Madonna artist of the first rank was Sandro Botticelli (1444–1510), too much praised for his paintings of Venus and the three graces of spring and too little praised for his magnificent religious compositions. Indeed, if Michelangelo's *Pietà* is the greatest work of one man's hands ever to honor the Virgin, Botticelli's merry and magical *Nativity* (cover), with its ring of angels dancing in the air, its newborn Babe reaching up in joy, and a spirit of happy innocence overflowing in every detail, is right behind.

Three centuries later, Keats would look at figures on a Grecian urn and exclaim: "What pipes and timbrels? What wild ecstasy?" But no pipes and timbrels were needed for the wild ecstasy Botticelli created in his great celestial dance on canvas. Savonarola's preaching had briefly purified the polluted moral air of Florence in the 1490s, and Botticelli, like Michelangelo, had breathed deeply of that new and Gospel-brightened atmosphere.

In both the life of the people and the art of genius, the effect was profound. For all the wild stories of how the giant 1498 "bonfire of the vanities" devoured great works of art, the fact was it devoured mostly false hair, mirrors, veils, perfumes, and pornographic books and pictures. If any masterpiece perished in the flames, its name is unknown to art historians. Indeed, one of the most beautiful of all the results of Savonarola's Christ-first example was that in 1500, only two years after the bonfire, the world was gloriously enriched by those two towering works of genius, one depicting the birth and the other the death of Christ in the company of his Mother.

The most fitting praise of the *Pietà* was Michelangelo's own, for in undertaking that great subject he had agreed to carve "the finest work in marble which Rome today can show". He clearly succeeded. Botticelli's great work, on the other hand, would have to wait almost four hundred years for the praise that came closest to doing it justice. Once again, it came from that giant of wit and thought, G. K. Chesterton:

The Nativity of Botticelli

Do you blame me that I sit hours before this picture?
But if I walked all over the world in this time
I should hardly see anything worth seeing
    that is not in this picture.

If Florence produced two titans of sacred art in whose work Mary lives forever, so did the supremely civilized hillside town of Urbino when it gave us Raphael and Barocci. Raphael's is the greater name, of course, and the range and depth of his work are astounding, considering that when he died, in 1520, he was just thirty-seven years old. But in the matter of sacred art alone, Federico Barocci created masterpieces that compare very favorably with the best work of Raphael, the man he forever regarded as his master, though he was born thirty-two years too late to meet him.

Raphael's *Sistine Madonna* (no connection with the Sistine Chapel: he painted it for the monks of San Sisto in Piacenza, and it now hangs in the Royal Gallery in Dresden) is probably his greatest sacred work—a Christ-Child with an uncanny serenity of expression and a Mother serious, simple, barefoot, and so free from either human or artistic affectation as to recall the words of Saint Paul: "Let love be without dissimulation." But as great as it is, it has nothing on the best works of Raphael's Urbino heir, Barocci, an artist who vigorously followed Michelangelo's prescription for being not merely "a great master in painting and very wise", but also "very good in his mode of life".

Barocci's early biographers spoke of his "strict morality and piety", and, fittingly, he was not only closely associated with the Capuchin branch of the Franciscans, he became a member of its Third Order at the age of thirty-one. Here, then, was a devout spirit wedded to deep talent, a life-giving combination if ever there was one. The result was an innocence, a freshness, and a lyricism free of any of that saccharine piety that spoils so much religious art. Indeed, if Schubert's "Ave Maria" has a canvas counterpart, it would be Barocci's two greatest works, his *Nativity* and *The Rest on the Flight to Egypt*—masterpieces that all but sing.

A Marian artist not to be overlooked, of course, is perhaps the only Renaissance master whose talent ran head-to-head with Michelangelo's—the great Leonardo da Vinci, that universal genius for whom painting was just one more undertaking in a world of perpetual intellectual challenge. Fortunately for posterity, he found enough time in his crowded schedule to create two of the greatest of all Madonna paintings: *Virgin and Child with St. Anne and John the Baptist* and *The Virgin of the Rocks*. Not far behind was Titian, yet another great Italian master, who was to capture the first of the joyful Marian mysteries in his luminous *Annunciation*.

The list of great artists who have depicted Mary is lengthy, but in the hope that the reader will not merely glance at but linger over the masterpieces in this miniature gallery, the selections made here are deliberately few. In addition to the familiar Italian names, the offerings of two great Spanish masters—Zurbarán and Murillo—are included. Astonishments all, they are of course only the barest sample of the reverent outpouring of Parnassian talent Mary has inspired all down the centuries.

Michelangelo once said of Ghiberti's magnificent gold low-relief sculptures on the baptistery at Florence that they were worthy to be placed on the gates of Paradise. If there is an art gallery within, surely all these brilliant works of pen, brush, chisel, and stone will someday be placed on permanent exhibition.

Michelangelo Buonarotti, *Pietà*, St. Peter's Basilica, Vatican

Titian, *Annunciation* (1556–58)

Zurbaran, *The Nativity*

Murillo, *Adoration of the Shepherds*

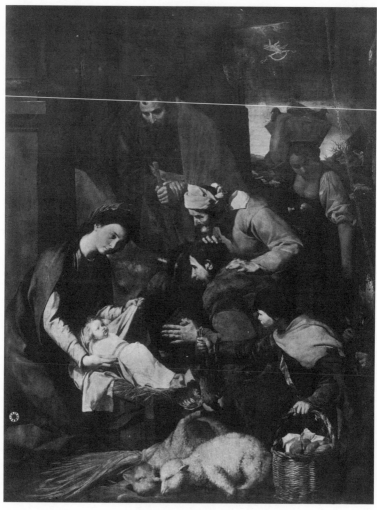

Barocci, *The Nativity*

Barocci, *Rest on the Flight into Egypt*

Leonardo da Vinci, *The Virgin and Child with St. Anne
and John the Baptist*

Leonardo da Vinci, *Madonna of the Rocks*

Raphael, *Sistine Madonna with Saints Barbara and Pope Sixtus IV*

MARY AND THE ELDEST DAUGHTER
OF THE CHURCH

England is an empire; Germany is a nation, a race; France is a
person.

—Jules Michelet, *Histoire de France*

"France is a person." As strange and paradoxical as the statement
is, somehow it carries the ring of truth.

After all, here is a society as touchy about its breeding as any
dowager, a land where every cook and cobbler thinks of himself
as an artist, where a national academy guards the pristine French
language from foreign invasions, and where a party politician in
an off-the-rack suit will talk as solemnly about Gallic grandeur
as Charles de Gaulle lecturing on national purpose at the palace
of Versailles. The person that is France may look like Joan of
Arc or sound like Maurice Chevalier, yet beneath the surface it
possesses not only a sense of grandeur and majesty but also bed-
rock faith, a deep feeling of community, a warrior spirit, and a
pointed wit, and something at once as close to the earth as the
red wine and rich food of its farmers and as determined to be
above it as those Parisian entrepreneurs who build drugstores as
elegant as opera houses.

And then there are those personality aspects that speak for an
entirely different side to the national character—the worship of
the reason, the vogue for intellectual novelty, the passion for

dragging everything into the light, the polar extremes of the puritanical Jansenists on the one hand and the Parisian flesh markets on the other. Perhaps all these elements help to explain why France has played so large a part in the Virgin's apparitions in recent centuries, for if France is indeed the Church's eldest daughter, the one to be treated as first among equals, she has also played the willful child and spoiled brat.

In fact, France has been something of an *enfant terrible* ever since the sceptics and freethinkers in the so-called Enlightenment first began complaining about the crown-and-miter alliance of the royalist state with the propertied Church. To be sure, there was much to complain about. Royalty had taken the words "self-indulgent" and "fiscal irresponsibility" to a level that would be exceeded only by the wild spending of the mad King Ludwig of Bavaria a century later, and Versailles, the monarchy's most resplendent symbol, had become a kind of monetary black hole, swallowing the nation's taxes without regret or apology. More and more the state was employed as a supple tool for preserving the wealth and privileges of a corrupt aristocracy not only against the oppressed poor but against the industrious new capitalists of the rising bourgeoisie. And the Church, with her vast property holdings (10 percent of the nation), seemed altogether too comfortable and too accommodating to the status quo to be considered the blameless bride of Christ.

Inevitably, the winds of change began to blow, and before long they reached hurricane force, uprooting an entire way of life and shaking a nation loose from its foundations. The French Revolution, beginning in 1789 and never really ending, was at once a revolt, an inquisition, and a Pandora's box releasing two shadows of tyranny for every sunbeam of freedom. That momentous event not only changed the earth's religious climate forever, it left France a social war zone, with Church-state skirmishes both inevitable and frequent.

No doubt the Revolution was one of those events to which the Gospel words apply with an extra helping of truth and fury: "It is impossible but that offenses will come: but woe unto him through whom they come!" (Lk 17:1). Whether or not he had that passage in mind, Joseph de Maistre in his *Considerations sur la France* (1796) described the Revolution not only as a death struggle between Christianity and a diabolical philosophy but also as a trial permitted by Providence to revivify Catholicism. He might also have described it as a death struggle between traditional authority and intellectual megalomania. In any case, its early residue was a sullen mutual hostility and a dilution of faith, an atmosphere in which the Virgin's utterances would seem more than ever light speaking out of darkness.

When the Revolution began, the state was considered Catholic and the king a kind of "bishop of the exterior"— God's magistrate on earth. When it ended, the state would be as separate from the Church as if the flaming sword of Genesis had been placed at the entrance to the door of government—a sword that just then looked suspiciously like a guillotine. But so it was, and in the end the new France, left-of-center, republican, and proudly irreligious, would be hopelessly at odds with the old France, rightist, monarchist, and Catholic—the legacy of a religious persecution never to be forgotten.

Like so many things with dark consequences, the Revolution had begun with bright promises. In those first heady days of 1789, the freedom-intoxicated members of the Constituent Assembly, all but dancing about with vine leaves in their hair, enthusiastically set forth the Declaration of the Rights of Man. It asserted that all men are free and equal, with freedom to think and write as they might wish, and it promised that no one would be harassed for his opinions, not even on religion. (Somehow this comforting pronouncement would be forgotten altogether when it came time to fasten the ideological shackles on Catholicism.)

The step from benevolently declaring freedom to tyranni-
cally imposing it was a short one—and the heel of the boot
came down with maximum force on religious congregations.
They were simply "freed" out of existence. In the spring of
1790, in an act of breathtaking absurdity and towering arrogance, the Assembly forbade religious vows in the name of the
inalienable liberty of the individual. Here was George Orwell's
"doublethink" 160 years before George Orwell: "I declare you
absolutely free, but I absolutely insist that you are not free to
take a vow."

But these tyrants of liberty were just warming up the bath
water for the baby they would soon be throwing out with it.
Next, without so much as consulting the Holy See, the Constituent Assembly enacted on its own authority a new statute
defining the status of the Catholic clergy. It then demanded that
priests, as salaried civil servants, take a civil oath to uphold the
Civil Constitution. Suddenly, the "separation of Church and
state" meant that the state would separate the Church not only
from the state but also from her bishops—and at the same time
turn consecrated priests into state employees.

The collapse of the throne in 1792 only accelerated the attempts of the state to have either a servile Church or none at all
and led to an unrelenting attack against Catholicism and Christianity in general. Between May 1792 and October 1794, the
state carried out the policy called "de-Christianization", a
shameless attempt to eradicate not only Catholicism but also the
Huguenots and whatever other groups dared to call themselves
Christian.

This root-and-branch persecution by the Legislative Assembly, so reminiscent of the old Roman Empire's persecutions, set
into motion such outrages as the deportation and execution of
ecclesiastics, the closing of churches, the decapitation of religious statues and the desecration of religious monuments, and
the sponsoring of a general prohibition against worship and re-

ligious teaching. Serious Catholics suddenly found themselves aliens in their own nation—a nation that had been as Catholic as Rome for fourteen centuries.

On October 1, 1793, going one step farther, the Assembly passed a law that made all suspected priests and all persons who harbored them liable to death on sight—a law, incidentally, that proved easier to enforce in the more "liberal" parts of France than in the more "traditional" ones. Indeed, in 1793, the devoutly Catholic peasants of the Vendée region teamed up with the local nobility to launch a formidable insurrection, for a time controlling most of northwest France. Elsewhere the victories were scarce and the losses severe, whether in the field or on the scaffold. At Lyons in November 1793, 135 priests were shot to death; in Compiègne, sixteen Carmelites were executed; in Orange, thirty-two Ursulines met their death. In a little more than the twinkling of an eye, the French Revolution had become the French Inquisition.

Meanwhile, the "Goddess Reason", the Revolution's novel idea of a replacement deity, had been outraging faith, stealing its altars, and dressing up in priestly robes. Civic celebrations honoring the "goddess" were soon the order of the day, and in that same grim November of 1793, her "feast" was spectacularly commemorated in Paris' great Notre-Dame Cathedral: "Hail Goddess, full of reason."

After that choice bit of logical lunacy had set the tone, churches were routinely converted into auditoriums for popular meetings or even turned into boutiques. Not even the Gregorian calendar (which of course bore the un-Revolutionary name of Pope Gregory) was safe. In October 1793, the Convention abolished it and replaced it with a revolutionary calendar purged of those annoying Sundays and saints' feast days. Indeed, the Convention insisted that the Year One henceforth begin not with anything as trifling as the birth of Christ but instead with that curious event combining rationalism, rage,

arrogance, and lunacy—the foundation of the Republic on
September 22, 1792. Before long, the Reign of Terror and the
Reign of Error were one.

While this failed to destroy religious life, it did drive it underground. When the Revolution began, there were 135 bishops in
France, and while 110 of them were either exiled or simply
considered it prudent to flee the wrath to come, twenty-five
courageously stayed put. Indeed, some of them spent the entire
Reign of Terror watching over their imperiled flocks while living incognito in Paris. To be sure, there were long-term spiritual
benefits, for persecution invariably deepens faith. One such
benefit was the example of Jean Marie Vianney, later to become
the great saint popularly known as the Curé of Ars. He had
imbibed the spirit of heroism he associated with the priesthood
when, as a young boy living in the early days of the Terror, he
attended Masses said in haylofts by hunted priests.

Nor was this reason-crazed revolution willing to confine itself to France. In the eyes of the ruling rationalists, the problem
with their staunchly Catholic subjects was that they paid too
much attention to Rome. The solution, then, seemed as obvious as it did logical: Destroy the papacy. And, incredible as it
may seem, that is exactly what they attempted to do. In February 1798, General Louis Bertheu's army entered the Eternal
City, dispersed the papal court, and proclaimed the Roman Republic. For good measure, Pope Pius VI, though eighty-one
years old and in tottering health, was spirited off to France as a
prisoner of the new freedom. When, on August 29, 1799, the
"eldest daughter of the Church" watched him die forsaken on
the eldest daughter's own soil, it must have struck the aged Pon-
tiff, playing King Lear to France's Regan and Goneril, as a fate
both cruel and ironic.

But the rationalists were not grieving. To them it seemed that
their irresistible juggernaut of pure reason had crushed its most
serious rival forever and that the world could now march in step

with the Goddess of Reason in a festive new spirit of logic un-limited, with thrilling premises and postulates for all.

To faithful Catholics, by contrast, when the Pope died that warm August day, it must have seemed like the beginning of the great persecution reserved for history's end times: all that was missing was the Antichrist. And when the thirty-year-old Napoleon returned in triumph from Egypt that autumn and launched his successful coup d'état (November 9–10, 1799), many must have felt that the last piece of the ghastly puzzle was in place.

Fortunately, the conquering hero was content to be emperor and leave the role of Antichrist to posterity, and in fact, to the relief of almost everyone, he soon made it clear he was as deft a politician as he was a soldier. Desiring the support of all of France and not merely that of its rationalists, Masons, and priest-haters, he set about accomplishing his purpose with *sang-froid*, *savoir-faire*, and good sense. While he declared the Revolution ended, he promised to guarantee its "conquests", such as liberty of belief, equality among religions, and sale of religious property. At the same time, however, he permitted the return of the refugee priests and bishops, asking only a simple promise of fidelity to the constitution. With that, public worship resumed, and in 1801 the emperor went farther yet—agreeing to a concordat reestablishing the French hierarchy in communion with the Holy See.

Irreparable damage, of course, had already been done by the time Bonaparte seized the reins, and to a lesser degree it would continue to be done thereafter. In particular, the popes saw in the Revolution the source of all those modern ideas injurious to serious faith—doctrinal indifferentism, ultrasecular rationalism, and all-tolerant liberalism. More than that, they saw a door opening on endless innovations dangerous to the family and destructive to society—including civil marriage, secular education, and the quack formula of the Reason, the Whole Reason, and Nothing but the Reason.

For generations to come, including our own, reason un-
tempered by charity would continue to be a monster eating its
own children—even to the eldest daughter. And that, in large
part, was responsible for the strange and sullen France the Virgin
would so dramatically enter in 1830 at Paris, in 1846 at La
Salette, and in 1858 at Lourdes. There she would remind this
freedom-obsessed and humanity-worshipping nation that the
children of light were created for the purposes of a Being far
greater than the Goddess of Reason.

12

THE APPARITIONS BEGIN:
A CHAPEL IN PARIS

O Marie conçue sans péché priez pour nous qui avons recours à vous. [O Mary, conceived without sin, pray for us who have recourse to thee.]

> —Inscribed on a frame round the Virgin
> in Catherine Labouré's first vision

While no one can say precisely when the modern world first came, saw, and conquered, 1830 has as much claim to that dubious honor as any other year. Six years after the death of Lord Byron though it was, the romantic movement was going stronger than ever; machines were making towns and factories seem more important than farms and fields; democracy was supplanting aristocracy in government; and that very year the juggernaut of the Industrial Revolution gave birth to the speeding machinery that best symbolized it—when the first railroad line, the Liverpool and Manchester Railway, formally opened to goods and passengers. Finally, it was in 1830 that Eugène Delacroix, as a kind of cherry topping on the cake of modernity, produced his revolution-celebrating masterpiece, *Liberty Leading the People*—in which Notre-Dame Cathedral, as if to speak for the diminished state of religion, appeared in the distant background, forgotten and forlorn.

Yet there is always one thing more modern than the modern—the eternal. And thus the most truly modern reality of

1830 was not steam, speed, romantic music, or political liberty, it was the appearing of the Virgin Mary to Catherine Labouré, a twenty-four-year-old nun, in the chapel of the motherhouse of the Daughters of Charity, located in Paris at 140 Rue du Bac. Mary's great series of modern apparitions had begun. While passionate political and artistic arguments raged in the cafés, and quill pens and paintbrushes set down glum visions of life in steamy garrets, the Virgin of Nazareth one midsummer night gave a humble young woman a series of sublime revelations deeper than reason and greater than art.

Yet even had the event been reported in the newspapers, it is doubtful anyone would have paid serious attention. The apparition took place in July, and Paris' Revolution of July 1830, which deposed the wildly unpopular monarch Charles X, was even then monopolizing the headlines. (Lest the reader wonder how the monarchy had returned so soon after the Revolution, it was simply that after the allies defeated Napoleon in 1814—they would have to defeat him again a year later at Waterloo—they understandably insisted on a conservative, stable, and non-threatening France. That meant a king, and while their first appointee, Louis XVIII, worked out reasonably well, his successor and brother, the waspish and arrogant Charles X, managed to inspire a whole new revolt after a mere six years on the throne.)

And France had another great source of excitement just then: Victor Hugo's anti-royalist play *Hernani* was provoking riots and demonstrations left and right—a kind of reliving of the 1789 revolution without gunpowder. At the same time, Paris was becoming ever more the city of the muses, far less interested in saints than in artists—and in 1830, already overflowing with famous painters, it could also claim such glittering young writers as the twenty-eight-year-old Hugo, the thirty-one-year-old Balzac, and the twenty-eight-year-old Dumas as well as such notable composers as the twenty-seven-year-old Berlioz and the thirty-eight-year-old Rossini (with the twenty-one-year-old Chopin due to arrive the following year). Few shrines were honored as much as Apollo's—although, to be sure, religion in France was far from dead in 1830. As just one example, in the village of Ars, the forty-four-year-old Jean Marie Vianney, the Curé, was living out a life of stupendous sanctity, frequently spending seventeen hours a day in the confessional.

Meanwhile, all eyes were on Paris—that city which for better or worse seemed to be changing the world even as it captured its heart. Artists, bookstalls, little bridges over the Seine, cabmen and cabhorses, open-air markets, men in stovepipe hats and women in hats almost as large ornamented with flowers and ribbons, poets drinking absinthe in the waning yellow gaslight, horse-chestnut trees along the boulevards, and statues of Roman emperors in the fountain-sprinkled parks—it was a Paris even more picturesque than the one we know today. Then as now it was called the City of Light, but, in the spiritual realm at least, it was woefully lacking in that staple when Mary suddenly arrived in town and produced an illumination for the ages.

The Daughters of Charity had been founded some two centuries before by that great helper of the poor, Saint Vincent de Paul, and, by what would seem no coincidence at all, it was in the last hour of the eve of his feast day itself (July 19) that the Virgin appeared to Catherine Labouré. It was a drama to inspire awe—then and now. But to see it in perspective, we need to look at the events that led up to this great dawning of a whole new Age of Mary, this moment that above all others anointed 1830 as the beginning of the modern world.

Those events were centered in the life of an attractive young woman who sought both first and last the Kingdom of God. Devout from an early age and so determined upon a religious life that she rejected three proposals of marriage, Catherine Labouré found her earthly mission through the influence of two remarkable dreams. In the first, she assisted at the Mass of an old priest, a stranger to her. In the second, she visited a sick friend and again encountered the priest. In both dreams she fled. But in the second, the old priest called after her: "You do well to visit the sick, my child. You flee from me now, but one day you will be glad to come to me. God has plans for you; don't forget it." It would be four years later, in the visitors' parlor of the Hôpital de Saint Sauveur in Châtillon, that Catherine would recognize the old priest in a portrait of Saint Vincent de Paul and know that God meant her to be a Daughter of Charity.

Meanwhile, Catherine's earthly father had been putting every possible obstacle in her path, even sending her to work in her brother's café in Paris for a full year. The incongruity of this future cloister saint waiting tables in a public restaurant was exceeded only by the folly of her brothers and sisters "rescuing" her by enrolling her in a fashionable finishing school in Châtillon. Never a student of anything but the celestial, she now had to deal with the snobbery of classmates who ridiculed her for knowing little about academics and less about fashion. Still, all things work together, and it would be in Châtillon that the portrait of the old priest of her dreams would look at her and into her.

Finally, her father gave his reluctant consent, and Catherine was soon a twenty-four-year-old postulant at the Daughters of Charity in that same little town on the Seine River. After three months there, where, by the way, she was spoken of ever after for her remarkable goodness, she entered the novitiate on the Rue du Bac in Paris on April 21, 1830—not quite ninety days before the night the Blessed Virgin first appeared to her.

Even before the great events of July, Catherine was a living example of the beatitude "Blessed are the pure in heart, for they shall see God." Soon after arriving at the Rue du Bac, she received a vision of Jesus truly present in the Holy Eucharist. Indeed, it was given her every time she entered the chapel during the nine months of her novitiate. Nor was that all. On Trin-

ity Sunday, June 6, 1830, our Lord appeared to Catherine during
Mass, robed as a king. At the reading of the Gospel, the symbols
of his kingship fell from him, and Catherine immediately experienced the heart-knowledge that the King of France, the same
Charles X mentioned earlier, would be overthrown—as he was
the very next month in the July Revolution.

In truth, the *real* July revolution of 1830 was what took place
in the chapel on the Rue du Bac on July 18 and 19. Providen-
tially, we possess Catherine's own handwritten accounts, and
her precisely chosen words, as charming as any tale by Scheher-
azade, capture that night of miracle as no paraphrase could:

> On the eve of the feast of St. Vincent, good Mother Martha
> spoke to us of devotion to the saints, and to the Blessed Virgin
> in particular. It gave me so great a desire to see her that I went
> to bed with the thought that I would see my good Mother that
> very night—it was a desire I had long cherished.
>
> We had been given a piece of a surplice of St. Vincent's. I
> tore my piece in half, swallowed it, and fell asleep, confident
> that St. Vincent would obtain for me the grace of seeing the
> Blessed Virgin.
>
> At eleven-thirty, I heard someone calling my name:
> "Sister, Sister, Sister!"
>
> Wide awake, I looked in the direction of the voice. Drawing
> the bed-curtains, I saw a child clothed in white, some four or
> five years old, who said to me:
>
> "Come to the chapel; get up quickly and come to the chapel:
> the Blessed Virgin is waiting for you there." . . .
>
> He followed me, or rather I followed him; he kept to my
> left, and was surrounded with rays of light. Wherever we went,
> the lights were lit, a fact which astonished me very much. But
> my surprise was greatest at the threshold of the chapel: the door
> opened of itself, the child scarcely having touched it with the
> tip of his finger. . . . To see that all the torches and tapers were
> burning—it reminded me of midnight Mass. I did not see the
> Blessed Virgin. The child led me into the sanctuary, to the side
> of *M. le Directeur*'s chair. There he remained the whole
> time. . . .

Finally the hour came; the child announced it to me, saying: "Here is the Blessed Virgin; here she is."

I heard a noise like the rustling of a silk dress, which came from the direction of the tribune [a raised platform or dais] near the picture of St. Joseph; a lady was seating herself in a chair on the altar steps at the Gospel side. . . .

I doubted whether it was the Blessed Virgin. Again the child, who stood by the whole time, said to me:

"This is the Blessed Virgin."

It would be impossible for me to describe what I felt at that moment, or what passed within me, for it seemed to me that I did not look upon the Blessed Virgin.

It was then that the child spoke, no longer as a child, but as a grown man, and in the strongest terms.

Looking upon the Blessed Virgin, I flung myself toward her, and falling upon my knees on the altar steps, I rested my hands in her lap.

There a moment passed, the sweetest of my life. I could not say what I felt. The Blessed Virgin told me how I must conduct myself with my director, and added several things that I must not tell. As to what I should do in time of trouble, she pointed with her left hand to the foot of the altar, and told me to come there and to open up my heart, assuring me that I would receive all the consolation I needed. . . .

I could not say how long I stayed with her. When she left, it was as if she faded away, becoming a shadow that moved toward the tribune, the way she had come. I got up from the steps of the altar and saw that the child was where I had left him. He said:

"She is gone . . ."

We went back the same way, always surrounded with light, the child still keeping to the left.

I believe that this child was my guardian angel, who showed himself that he might take me to see the Blessed Virgin, for I had often prayed to him to obtain this favor for me. . . .

Having returned to my bed, I heard two o'clock strike. I slept no more that night.

Catherine added to this general account a far more detailed record of the words spoken by Mary during that astonishing night. With her characteristic precision, she called it: *July conversation with the Most Blessed Virgin, from 11:30 in the evening of the 18th until 1:30 in the morning of the 19th, St. Vincent's Day.* It tells us the Virgin began by saying, "My child, the good God wishes to charge you with a mission. You will have much to suffer but you will rise above these sufferings by reflecting that what you do is for the glory of God. . . . You will see certain things; give an account of what you see and hear."

"The times are very evil", the Virgin continued. "Sorrows will befall France. . . . The whole world will be plunged into every kind of misery." (And here is first sounded that apocalyptic note that was to be heard once again at La Salette in 1846 and, most dramatically, at Fatima in 1917—and whose echo has been heard ever since in our increasingly catastrophic age.)

Mary also spoke of practical matters; the most interesting of them involved a prophecy in the last of a brief series of requests. (It would be fulfilled nineteen years later.) Referring to the congregation's director, the Virgin said, "Tell him for me to guard against useless reading, loss of time, and visits. When the rule is restored in vigor, a community will ask to be united to your community. . . . God will bless those who take them in. (This, it would turn out, was a reference to Mother Elizabeth Seton's group of sisters from Emmitsburg, Maryland. They would one day petition to be united with the Saint Vincent community and would be admitted in 1849.)

Another prophetic vision, a truly dark one, dealt with events a full forty years in the future:

> There will be victims (the Blessed Virgin had tears in her eyes when she said it)—among the clergy of Paris there will be victims—Monseigneur the Archbishop—(at this name the tears came afresh).
> My child, the cross will be treated with contempt; they will hurl it to the ground. Blood will flow; they will open up again the side of Our Lord. The streets will run with blood.

Monseigneur the Archbishop will be stripped of his garments.
(Here the Blessed Virgin could no longer speak; her anguish
was depicted in her face.) My child, the whole world will be in
sadness. (At these words I wondered to myself when this would
be, and I understood clearly, *forty years*.)

Forty years later meant July 19, 1870, and incredibly enough,
that was precisely the day and the year when the Franco-Prussian War began—the war that would bring the siege of Paris,
the horrors of the inevitable famine, the creation of the Paris
Commune, and the murder of Archbishop Darboy. One can
only conclude that even as Catherine was beholding the vision
of Mary, Mary was herself beholding, and emotionally experi-
encing, bloody events taking place forty years in the future. And
yet as truly staggering in every way as was this first night of
revelation given to Catherine, a greater one would follow just
four months afterward. And, pleasant to relate, it would be one
that would have far more to do with remedy than with calamity.

It occurred in late November of that same larger-than-life
1830, and, almost like a new Annunciation, it poured forth a
whole new world of light and truth about the stupendous symbolic reality of the Virgin's Immaculate Heart and the unfath-
omable mystery of her grace-dispensing office. In fact, so
dazzling was the vision one has to wonder if perhaps the Almighty reserved it for the City of Light simply to underscore
the gulf between man-made light and the true Light that en-
lightens every man who comes into the world. One imagines
the half-believing Balzac in the Dominican robe he put on
when he wrote, scribbling furiously away in his Paris garret,
drinking numerous cups of the coffee he was so fond of, resolutely lecturing the world all about "real life", while a stone's
throw away in a quiet chapel, the Blessed Virgin was calmly telling a twenty-four-year-old innocent about a far deeper "real
life"—what the poet William Blake called "portions of eternity
too deep for the eye of man".

Again, since no paraphrase can do justice to the brilliantly precise account of the saint and witness, let us once more have the original:

On November 27, 1830, which fell upon the Saturday before the first Sunday of Advent, at five-thirty in the evening, in the deep silence after the point of the meditation had been read— that is, several minutes after the point of the meditation—I heard a sound like the rustling of a silk dress, from the tribune near the picture of St. Joseph. Turning in that direction, I saw the Blessed Virgin, at the level of St. Joseph's picture. The Virgin was standing. She was of medium height, and clothed all in white. Her dress was of the whiteness of the dawn, made in the style called "*à la Vierge*," that is, high neck and plain sleeves. A white veil covered her head and fell on either side to her feet. Under the veil her hair, in coils, was bound with a fillet ornamented with lace, about three centimeters in height or of two fingers' breadth, without pleats, and resting lightly on her hair. Her face was sufficiently exposed, indeed exposed very well, and so beautiful that it seems to me impossible to express her ravishing beauty.

Her feet rested on a white globe, that is to say half a globe, or at least I saw only half. There was also a serpent, green in color with yellow spots. [Compare Genesis 3:15 and Quetzalcoatl.]

The hands were raised to the height of the stomach and held, in a very relaxed manner and as if offering it to God, a golden ball surmounted with a little golden cross, which represented the world. Her eyes were now raised to heaven, now lowered. Her face was of such beauty that I could not describe it.

All at once I saw rings on her fingers, three rings to each finger, the largest one near the base of the finger, one of medium size in the middle, the smallest one at the tip. Each ring was set with gems, some more beautiful than others; the larger gems emitted greater rays and the smaller gems, smaller rays; the rays bursting from all sides flooded the base, so that I could no longer see the feet of the Blessed Virgin.

At this moment, while I was contemplating her, the Blessed Virgin lowered her eyes and looked at me. I heard a voice speaking these words:

"This ball that you see represents the whole world, especially France, and each person in particular."

I could not express what I felt at this, what I saw, the beauty and the brilliance of the dazzling rays.

"They are the symbols of the graces I shed upon those who ask for them."

This made me realize how right it was to pray to the Blessed Virgin and how generous she was to those who did pray to her, what graces she gave to those who asked for them, what joy she had in giving them.

"The gems from which rays do not fall are the graces for which souls forget to ask."

At this moment, I was so overjoyed that I no longer knew where I was. A frame, slightly oval in shape, formed round the Blessed Virgin. Within it was written in letters of gold:

"O Mary, conceived without sin, pray for us who have recourse to thee."

The inscription, in a semi-circle, began at the height of the right hand, passed over the head, and finished at the height of the left hand.

The golden ball disappeared in the brilliance of the sheaves of light bursting from all sides; the hands turned out and the arms were bent down under the weight of the treasures of grace obtained.

Then the voice said:

"Have a Medal struck after this model. All who wear it will receive great graces; they should wear it around the neck. Graces will abound for those who wear it with confidence."

At this instant the tableau seemed to me to turn, and I beheld the reverse of the Medal: a large M surmounted by a bar and a cross; beneath the M were the Hearts of Jesus and Mary, the one crowned with thorns, the other pierced with a sword.

This astounding three-part vision—(1) an epiphany showing Mary as granter of grace to this golden ball of earth, (2) a confirmation of the Immaculate Conception written in letters of gold, and (3) a revelation that Mary's heart is so important in the plan of heaven as to be paired with the heart of her divine Son—this astounding vision then disappeared from Catherine's sight "like a candle blown out". With that, the former Paris waitress was left to carry out a task that must have seemed difficult indeed: to remain absolutely obscure while seeing that the medal became abundantly popular. In fact, she was to say nothing of it to anyone except her confessor. Among other problems, that meant saying nothing to the archbishop of Paris, who wanted her to testify in person at the first official inquiry into the origin of the medal (1836). Fortunately, in the fullness of time the archbishop was persuaded even without direct testimony by the star witness.

Thus was born the Medal of the Immaculate Conception, worn since by countless numbers of Catholics and popularly known as the Miraculous Medal. And so it was that out of that cross-grained and cross-hating France—oppressively liberal and depressingly anticlerical—a supposedly dead faith began not only to revive but to flourish. It was almost as if Notre-Dame Cathedral had suddenly begun to vault upward in the background of Delacroix's great painting—eventually to overshadow all those earnest and embattled human figures in the foreground. But of course—because, for a time at least, it was no longer bare-bosomed Liberty leading the people with the French tricolor held high, it was the chaste and modest Catherine Labouré, holding up a small gray medal inscribed with two tiny hearts and a simple cross.

Presumably in keeping with Mary's wish that she remain obscure, Catherine said goodbye to the Rue du Bac in 1831 and lived out the remaining forty-five years of her saintly life at a convent on the outskirts of Paris. There, she looked after the poultry, acted as doorkeeper, and helped care for elderly, poverty-stricken men. She was canonized in 1947 by Pope Pius XII. Her incorrupt body, returned after Catherine's death to the place most precious to her, lies beneath an altar built on the very spot where the Virgin appeared to her with rings on her fingers and the world on her toes.

13

HOW BEAUTIFUL UPON THE MOUNTAINS:
THE APPARITION IN THE ALPS

There is a glorious Lady in heaven who has taken so great compassion on this soul distressed that the hard law she has chosen to restrain.

—Dante, *The Inferno*, canto 2

How beautiful upon the mountains are the feet of him that bringeth good tidings, that publisheth peace; that bringeth good tidings of good, that publisheth salvation; that saith unto Zion, Thy God reigneth!

—Isaiah 52:7

To think of great religious moments associated with mountains is to think of Noah and his ark anchoring amid the peaks of Ararat, Moses meeting the Lord on Sinai, or Elijah triumphing in blood and fire over the 450 priests of Baal in that great duel of faith on Mount Carmel. To those great high-altitude dramas we might well add the visit of Mary to the French Alps, for it was there, only sixteen years after the apparitions at the Rue du Bac, that the Blessed Virgin once again sought to inspire by presence and precept an irreligious France and an unbelieving world.

The apparition occurred on the mountain named for La Salette, a parish some fifty miles from Grenoble, comprising a half-dozen hamlets nestled in a nature-lover's paradise: snow-capped peaks, bright green plateaus, and wandering mountain streams—one of which was to play a dynamic part in the drama. As always, the date was significant. The apparitions at the Daughters of Charity had come on the eve of the feast day of the congregation's founder, Vincent de Paul; the apparition at La Salette came on the eve of the feast of Our Lady of Sorrows (for it was a sorrowful Lady indeed who greeted two young cowherds on an alpine meadow and made known to them the disappointment of heaven in the behavior of earth).

It was September 1846, and while the French Revolution had been over for half a century, its effects lingered even in the far-off provinces. And La Salette was provincial indeed—three hundred miles southeast of Paris in both distance and demeanor. If that part of the world had learned anything from the Revolution, it was not a greater understanding of the rights of man, it was a grosser indifference to the rights of God. Hearts were hard; Mass was ignored except by the few; Sunday was one more work day; the Angelus was only a bell; blasphemy was part of the local idiom; the cabarets were full; and to all appearances, the Pentecostal flame was down to its last flicker. In brief, La Salette and France were desperately in need of bracing counsel. The Virgin was called on to provide it, and like her Son many centuries before, she chose to preach her sermon on a mount.

The audience consisted of Mélanie Mathieu, a careworn fourteen-year-old cattle herder and occasional baby sitter, and Maximin Giraud, the eleven-year-old son of the local wheelwright. They were there, along with Maximin's frisky little dog, Loulou, simply because they had been the only children available at the time to hire out as guides and guards for a local farmer's one goat and eight cows. Here were perhaps the two strangest children of earth ever to find themselves in the company of the Blessed Virgin: Mélanie, a rail-thin introvert whose pale melancholy was accentuated by her peasant garb—bootlength skirt, apron, and white cap tied under the chin; and

Maximin, a chronically restless, forgetful, and notoriously undependable runner of errands and doer of odd jobs.

This was the unpromising pair who on the sunny afternoon of September 19, 1846, after locating the cows they had carelessly let wander off, would suddenly behold, near a stream bed in a mountain ravine named La Sézia, a dazzling circle of light moving swiftly to a position a dozen feet away from them. The frightened Mélanie dropped her staff; the audacious Maximin girded his loins. "Hold onto that staff of yours," he told her, "and I'll hold onto mine, and if *that* attempts to hurt us, I'll give it a hard whack."

But no such rude response was called for. To the children's astonishment, the dazzling globe of light opened up, and within it they could see the figure of a radiant woman. But here was a Virgin far different in mood and aspect from the one who had cheerfully greeted Juan Diego on Tepeyac Hill or the one who had serenely addressed Catherine Labouré in a Paris convent—here was a Virgin, elbows on knees, face in hands, and *weeping*.

Weeping or not, she was resplendent almost beyond description. She wore a golden crown incorporating roses of many colors, a long white dress sprinkled with pearl-shaped gleams of light, a shawl trimmed with roses and golden lace, a large golden apron, and rose-bordered white slippers decorated with pearls and gold buckles. But the most interesting item of all had nothing to do with splendor. On her breast she wore a crucifix hanging from a chain and flanked by a hammer and a pair of half-open pliers—the hammer that drove in Calvary's nails and the pliers that pulled them out, instruments that asked the everlasting question: Which will *you* choose?

The Virgin's first words were reassuringly down to earth: "Come to me, my children. Don't be afraid. I'm here to tell you something of the greatest importance." But the opening part of her sermon was anything but comforting.

"If my people will not obey," she said, "I shall be compelled to loose my Son's arm. It is so heavy, so pressing that I can no longer restrain it. How long have I suffered for you! If my Son is not to cast you off, I am obliged to entreat him without ceasing. But you take no heed of that. No matter how well you pray in future, no matter how well you act, you will never be able to make up to me what I have endured in your behalf."

As the Virgin continued this straightforward rebuke to La Salette and France, she began employing phrases that seemed to indicate she was essentially speaking the words of God the Father himself:

> I have appointed you six days for working. The seventh I have reserved for myself. And no one will give it to me. This it is which causes the weight of my Son's arm to be so crushing. The cart drivers cannot swear without bringing in my Son's name. These are the two things that make my Son's arm so burdensome.
>
> If the harvest is spoiled, it is your own fault. I warned you last year by means of the potatoes. You paid no attention. Quite the reverse, when you discovered that the potatoes had decayed, you swore, you abused my Son's name. They will continue to be spoiled, and by Christmas time this year there will be none left. If you have grain, it will do no good to sow it, for what you sow the beasts will eat, and whatever part of it springs up will crumble into dust when you thresh it. A great famine is coming.

After this plain-spoken expression of divine displeasure, the Virgin broke off to confide a secret to Maximin and another to Mélanie (and this, it seems, involved Mary's first warning ever concerning the Antichrist—for later, in an interview, confiding her secret to Church authorities, Mélanie would ask how to spell that grimmest of names). When she resumed, it was with a highly welcome note of cheer, for in the tradition of the Lord speaking to the Israelites, she followed the threat of calamity repaying sin with the promise of prosperity rewarding virtue:

"If people are converted, the rocks will become piles of wheat, and it will be found that the potatoes have sown themselves."

She then struck a personal note, asking the children how much they prayed—very little was the answer—and then urging them to do so no matter what the circumstances: "At least say an Our Father and a Hail Mary." She also demonstrated her powers of clairvoyance after Maximin had replied "No" on being asked if he had ever seen spoiled wheat:

> But you, my child, must have seen it once, near Coin, with your papa. The owner of a field said to him, "Come and see my spoiled wheat." The two of you went. You took two or three ears of wheat in your hands. You rubbed them, and they crumbled to dust. Then you came back from Coin. When you were only a half-hour away from Corps [where Maximin lived], your papa gave you a bit of bread and said, "Well, my son, eat some bread this year, anyhow. I don't know who'll be eating any next year if the wheat continues to spoil like that."

And that settled that. On having it recalled to him, the young herder at once conceded: "It's very true, Madame. Now I remember it. Until now I didn't." Mary had now convinced her future messengers; could they now convince others? The Virgin seemed to think so, for her next words were also her last: "Well, my children, you will make this known to all my people." As she turned to go, stepping across the narrow stream bed, she repeated those precise words. She then walked the length of the ravine, the excited children tagging along. As Maximin described it, far from crushing the roses with which the soles of her slippers were framed, she glided effortlessly above ground level. When she reached the top of the ravine, she paused, gracefully rose into the air, looked up to heaven, looked out over the world—even as both she and the circle of light surrounding her shone ever more brilliantly—then gradually faded into the vastness of the sky.

Amazingly, even after this astonishing vision-*cum*-revelation, the ragamuffin pair still had no idea who the Lady was. "Perhaps", said Mélanie, "she was a great saint." It wasn't until the odd little couple had proven themselves convincing witnesses by giving virtually identical descriptions and details without the other being present and, later that day, had settled down at their employer's dinner table that the words "Blessed Virgin" were first spoken. Word quickly passed from the farmer and the farmer's wife to friends and neighbors, and while some believed and others scoffed, all agreed the priest should be told the next morning, which happened to be Sunday.

Remarkably, in a response totally out of keeping with the normally sceptical stance of a churchman hearing the uncomfortable word "apparition", the priest, a Father Perrin, not only accepted the story, he believed with a credulity that would have rejoiced the heart of a three-card monte operator. Indeed, he believed so unblinkingly that in an abrupt departure from the Church's tradition of prudent doubt and patient investigation, he proceeded to tell the tale from the pulpit that very morning, tears streaming down his bliss-transfigured face.

The congregation was not merely baffled at hearing this sudden announcement of a personal visit by the Queen of Heaven to a bumbling pair of junior cowherds, it was embarrassed. And Mayor Peytard, present at Mass that day and no doubt wondering if perhaps a new strain of Alpine fever was going around, was not merely embarrassed, he was incensed. Afterward he tracked down Mélanie and successively tried to reason, threaten, and bribe her out of this strange delusion of hers—all to no avail. The next day he cornered Mélanie's eleven-year-old sidekick and had no better luck. Undaunted, he and the local sergeant of police the following Sunday marched the children all the way up to La Sézia. There, on the very stage, so to speak, where the drama had taken place, the cowherds relived the story so enthusiastically and persuasively that even the mayor had to wonder. So did the officer of the law.

"Tell me where this woman went", said the sergeant of police to Maximin.

"She disappeared into the light, and the light prevented us from seeing where she went."

"Well, she's been found. Some soldiers have seized her and put her in prison."

"Clever indeed, the person who could seize *her!*"

The next figure of consequence to enter the story was Father Melin, the parish priest at nearby Corps (population thirteen hundred and the largest village in the La Salette area), cool, correct, and formerly an assistant at the cathedral in Grenoble, whose bishop he knew well. This clear-minded cleric, not quite knowing what to make of a tale that seemed to combine majesty and farce, summoned the young visionaries, heard them out, said little, and then with five other adults of sound mind and sober manner repeated the mayor's experiment, marching the children once again all the way up to the site of the apparition. And once again the children, far from getting the fidgets or exchanging nervous glances, acted out their singular experience with zest in every gesture and delight in every detail. Here they had eaten their lunch, there they had napped, here they had found the cows grazing, there they had seen the light, here was the place where the Lady had become visible, here was the rock she had sat on. Hallucination or hysteria it may have been, but one thing was clear: the witnesses were in no way fabricating.

And when it was time to leave, a remarkable thing happened: the little spring in the ravine, which normally gave water only after heavy rains or when the snow high on the mountains was energetically melting, began gushing water in a steady stream. Coincidence? Father Melin, prudent to the end, took a wine bottle that had been emptied during the party's lunch and collected a fair-sized stream sample.

Later, a second remarkable thing happened. It took place after

the priest gave some of the spring water to a very sick parish-
ioner, a certain Madame Anglot, whose condition was such that
she could retain no food and was slowly wasting away. Madame
Anglot at once began a novena to our Lady, each day drinking a
swallow or two of the water—the one thing she seemed able to
keep down. On the ninth day, she got out of bed, went to the
dining table, and ate heartily.

And now it was time for the bishop to take over—and fortunately, a remarkable bishop he was. Philibert de Bruillard was
then eighty-one years old, but his vigor was legendary. He had
been ordained at the age of twenty-four way back in 1789, the
year the Revolution had begun—and nothing he had seen or
done since had been able to slow him down. Young Father
Bruillard's first priestly assignment had been to teach philosophy and theology at Saint-Sulpice, the famous seminary in
Paris. He remained in that Revolution-convulsed city, minister-
ing to all the serious Catholics he could find even as the Terror
raged. After the worst of that frenzy had passed, he had served
successively as pastor of two Paris churches, been spiritual director of a future saint (Madeleine Sophie Barat), and demonstrated a gift for both scholarship and administration. At the age
of fifty-six, he had been named bishop of Grenoble.

Soon after hearing from Father Melin, Bishop de Bruillard
sent a letter to each priest of his diocese, beginning, "Doubtless
you know of the extraordinary events that are said to have taken
place in the parish of La Salette, near Corps." He then went on
to forbid them to speak or write of any miraculous occurrences
until an "exact and rigid" examination had been completed.
That done, he dispatched to the apparition site the superior of
the minor seminary and three members of the seminary faculty.
With characteristic thoroughness, he then appointed two separate commissions to evaluate the complete file gathered by the
investigators.

Meanwhile, interesting things were continuing to happen in

those little hamlets high in the Alps, starting with impromptu pilgrimages and increasing references to "the Mountain of Our Lady". Maximin's wheelwright father—a hard-drinking asthmatic and a scoffer of the first magnitude—was touched, in spite of himself, when his son, mentioning that the Lady had recalled to him the day they had visited the farmer with the spoiled wheat, said the magic words, "The Lady spoke of you, too."

Intrigued, the senior Giraud made his own pilgrimage to the high-altitude ravine and returned a changed man. He ceased to drink, declared his asthma was gone, and began assisting at daily Mass. Likewise, a parish that had consisted of the lukewarm, the indifferent, and the invisible underwent a kind of Pentecostal revival. Sunday was once again the work-free Lord's day, Mass drew large numbers, confession lines were samba-length, and communicants increased from the dozens to the hundreds.

Yet all of this, bracing as it was, was a mere preamble to the electrifying events of November 17, the day of the first official pilgrimage—a scant two months after the apparition. The procession started from Corps, and six hundred of the town's thirteen hundred residents took part, an astonishing number under any circumstances, let alone for an uphill journey of four hours. In any event, the highlight of that day would be the stupendous drama involving forty-eight-year-old Marie Laurent, the wife of the town baker.

Madame Laurent had for the past eight years been so crippled by rheumatism she could move only with the aid of crutches, and even that was so painful she did little more than sit in a chair all day. Each morning she had to be lifted out of bed, and each night she had to be carried back to it. Still, despite her Job-like misery and an immobility suggesting a character trapped in one of the bleaker plays of Samuel Beckett, this patient soul had continued to hope for deliverance through her eight long years of suffering. And so, although she obviously could not go on the climb herself, she asked her neighbors to remember her when they reached their goal. They promised they would.

Singing hymns all the way up to the top-of-the-world meadow where that dry stream was still pouring forth its living water, the pilgrims could not know they would that day see a miraculous fulfillment of Psalm 46: "There is a river, the streams whereof shall make glad the city of God." Long before they were made glad, in any case, the city of God's Corps representatives fell to their knees and offered a mighty mountaintop prayer on behalf of Marie Laurent. Soon after, they again fell to their knees to drink of that same little stream before commencing their return journey.

The supreme moment of an exhilarating day came as they were marching reverently through Corps on their way to gather in the church for a final moment of thanksgiving. When they reached the Laurent home, Madame Laurent, without crutches or other support, suddenly walked out like a new Lazarus to greet them. Jesus himself had wept at that miracle in Bethany, and now, no doubt, there was not a dry eye in all of Corps—especially when, in a crowning touch, Marie Laurent took her place in the procession.

The moment became even sweeter in retrospect when the pilgrims heard the full story. That afternoon, the invalid, just after drinking some water taken from the celebrated stream (as she had every day during the novena she was embarked upon), had felt a great desire to get up and walk. She at once tried and found she could not only move about crutch-free, she could run—and run she had, first to tell her husband and next to give thanks in the church. And when had that occurred? At the very hour, it seemed, when the six hundred on the mountain had been making the very sky echo on her behalf. The response of the returning pilgrims to this faith-confirming news was a resounding rendition of the Magnificat right there in the cobblestone square facing the church: "My soul doth magnify the Lord, and my spirit has rejoiced in God my Saviour."

Astonishing as it had been, that resurrecting day would be rivaled by many others in the months and years that followed, for the healing miracles continued, the word spread, the faith grew, and "La Salette" began to tower as a name every bit as much as it towered as a mountain. In Grenoble, meanwhile, without fanfare or flourish, Bishop de Bruillard began his exhaustive juridical inquiry (it would last four years). Whether by grace or coincidence, he launched it on July 19, 1847—seventeen years to the day after the Virgin's appearance to Catherine Labouré in the Rue du Bac.

By the way, the contrast in public attention paid to the two apparitions could not have been greater. Almost literally, news of the Rue du Bac had been whispered in a corner, whereas news of La Salette had been shouted from the mountaintop. As a result, La Salette was soon the talk of France—including France's government, which was in no mood to break out the champagne. *Au contraire.*

Even as the state's sycophantic press twisted what few facts it knew about La Salette, a government that prided itself on its liberty, equality, and fraternity was showing itself not only illiberal and unfraternal in its dealings with a fourteen-year-old girl and an eleven-year-old boy but unequal to refuting them. With a great display of fuss and feathers, prosecutors and investigators, it insisted that the "concocters" of this "pretended apparition" must be found and punished. But the authorities in Paris soon realized that La Salette had become a reality beyond the power of even a national government to resist. On September 19, 1847, the first anniversary of the apparition, with a dozen Masses being celebrated on open-air altars set up on that mountain meadow, fifty thousand people stood in line for as long as five hours simply to drink, touch, or bottle a bit of that high holy fountain with the water of life.

Physical healing there had certainly been—twenty-five authenticated cures. But there had also been spiritual healing of vast numbers of people, whose return to devout Christian living was beyond the power of the Revolution to undermine or explain. And thus it continued year after year—remarkable things happening, Bishop de Bruillard's investigators checking them out. Finally, after countless interviews and a marathon of truth-sifting, it was time for a conclusion.

The doctrinal pronouncement was issued by Bishop de Bruillard in collaboration with his close friend Bishop Ville-court of La Rochelle, who had conducted his own inquiry. It was signed on September 19, 1851, the fifth anniversary of the apparition. Here are a few of its opening paragraphs:

> Five years ago we were told of an event most extraordinary and, at first hearing, unbelievable, as having occurred on one of the mountains in our diocese. It was a matter of nothing less than an apparition of the Blessed Virgin, who was said to have been seen by two herders on September 19, 1846. She told them of evils threatening her people, especially because of blasphemy and the profanation of Sunday, and she confided to each a particular secret, forbidding that these be communicated to anyone.
>
> In spite of the natural candor of the two herders; in spite of the impossibility of collusion by two ignorant children who hardly knew each other; in spite of the constancy and firmness of their witness which has never varied either when confronted by the agents of the law or by thousands of persons who have exhausted every trick to involve them in contradiction or wrest their secrets from them, it has been our duty to refrain for a long time from accepting an event which seemed to us so marvelous. . . .
>
> While our episcopal duty imposed on us the necessity of waiting, pondering, fervently begging the light of the Holy Spirit, the number of wonders noised about on all sides was constantly growing. . . . Sick people in desperate straits, either given up by their doctors as certain to die soon or condemned to long drawn out suffering, have been reported restored to

perfect health after invocation of Our Lady of La Salette and the use, with faith, of the water from a spring at which the Queen of Heaven appeared to the two herders.

From the very first days, people have spoken to us of this spring. We have been assured that it had never before flowed steadily, but gave water only after snows or heavy rains. It was dry that September 19; thereafter it began to flow and has flowed constantly ever since: marvelous water, if not in its origin, at least in its effects.

The bishop then went on to outline the process of inquiry followed, the reports commissioned, the investigative accounts studied, the discussions insisted on, the voices both assenting and dissenting (oh, yes, a few doubting Thomases there were), and finally, what he called "the impossibility of explaining the fact of La Salette in any other way than by divine intervention". He concluded with three gracefully phrased declarations:

1. We give judgment that the apparition of the Blessed Virgin to the two herders on September 19, 1846, on the mountain of the Alpine chain situated in the parish of La Salette, in the territory of the archpriest of Corps, bears in itself all the marks of truth, and the faithful have grounds to believe it indubitable and certain.

2. We believe that this event acquires a further degree of certitude . . . from the abundance of marvels which have come in the wake of this event and a very great number of which cannot be called in doubt without violating the rules of human testimony.

3. Therefore, to demonstrate our lively thanks to God and to the glorious Virgin Mary, we authorize the cult of Our Lady of La Salette.

Given at Grenoble September 19, 1851, the fifth anniversary of the famous apparition.

Philibert, Bishop of Grenoble.

Eight months later, the bishop would give added life to this proclamation by announcing that a basilica would be built on the site of the apparition and that he would be founding a community of priests who would be assigned to the church—the

Missionaries of La Salette. Remarkably, the bishop himself, though eighty-seven years old at the time and in far less than euphoric health, somehow made the climb and laid the cornerstone in May 1852.

La Salette was again "in the news", so to speak, some twenty years later—when the Virgin's warnings at both La Salette and the Rue du Bac about trouble ahead for the nation of France were grimly fulfilled in the events surrounding the Franco-Prussian War of 1870–1871. That disaster not only involved a scorching military defeat that would cost the nation Alsace-Lorraine, it also brought two separate sieges of Paris with all the horrors of famine and slow death.

In protest against the humiliating peace terms agreed to by the royalist majority in the National Assembly, the republicans and radicals formed a governmental unit called the Commune to govern Paris. Besieged and starving though they were, the Communards led a forceful revolt against the National Assembly. But the siege went on for two full months, and as the horrors multiplied, the Communards slew their hostages—including, as Mary had foretold in her 1830 conversation with Catherine Labouré, the archbishop of Paris.

The eldest daughter of the Church or not, France was in a bad way, spectacularly unhappy and bitterly divided. That was never more apparent than when a national pilgrimage was proposed—a pilgrimage of reparation to that same Alpine mountain where the Virgin had brought her message of plain rebuke and conditional deliverance. Adolphe Thiers, the president of that devastated nation, remarked with icy contempt: "Pilgrimages are no longer among our customs." But events proved him wrong, for in 1872 pilgrims from every corner of France converged on La Salette in unprecedented numbers to ask heaven to deliver their troubled land from evil. Seven years later, in 1879, that hope seemed to take on a new concreteness when the great basilica was at last consecrated. And though it did not of

course bring lasting peace, the La Salette pilgrimage was to enjoy a forty-two-year afterglow: it would be 1914 before war
again assailed the nation Mary had done so much to exalt and
defend.

Meanwhile, the story of La Salette would not be complete
without a brief discussion of the controversy surrounding the
secret confided by the Virgin to Mélanie, a secret that was to
remain largely unknown though published under episcopal im-
primatur and that was to be as resolutely defended by its cham-
pions as relentlessly attacked by its foes. Since it was no simple
one-sentence revelation, but rather a largely uneducated young
woman's detailed account containing not only a grim warning
of apostasy among the clergy and the religious communities but
also the soul-freezing statement that "Rome will lose the faith
and become the seat of the Antichrist", it is easy to see why it
would be challenged. Apart from the sensational nature of a
prophecy that would seem to cast into doubt the idea of a
Church against which the gates of hell would never prevail,
there was the question of personal credibility: though unshake-
able in her La Salette testimony and undeniably devout, Mélanie
would later write an autobiography mentioning supernatural
experiences in early childhood that from all accounts owed
more to a creative memory than to hard fact.

In any case, the young seer first put her secret into writing on
July 3, 1851—almost five full years after the apparition. She did
so at the request of Pope Pius IX and in the presence of witnesses who included the canon of Grenoble Cathedral. Reportedly, she filled three large pages, breaking her silence only to ask
the meaning of the words "infallibly" and "Antichrist" and how
to spell the latter. Twenty-eight years later, in 1879, Mélanie
herself published (with the help of a pious patron) a somewhat
longer version of the secret—a version that bore the imprima-
tur of her spiritual director, Bishop Salvatore-Luigi Zola of
Leone, Italy.

Just as there were two versions of the secret—the second fuller but by no means contradicting the first—so there have been two versions of Mélanie, highly contradictory. Her critics, including many who thoroughly believe in the authenticity of the La Salette apparition, have painted her as vain, unstable, and attention-seeking, an individual whose head had been turned by celebrity and who therefore moved restlessly from one order to another without ever becoming a professed religious—four years with the Sisters of Providence at Corenc, a brief stay with the Daughters of Charity at Vienne; other brief stays with the Carmelites in the English town of Darlington and the Sisters of the Compassion in France.

Her admirers, on the contrary, describe a very different Mélanie—not a restless neurotic but a holy young woman plagued by the curious and opposed at every turn by sceptical clerics, especially in France, sceptics presumably influenced by the kind of Modernist thinking that was to provoke an all-out condemnation and counterattack by Pope Saint Pius X in the early 1900s. Her greatest champion was the aforementioned Bishop Zola, who was to defend her every bit as staunchly as another Zola—Émile—was to defend Captain Dreyfus. The bishop was to write of her:

> This pious girl, this virtuous and privileged soul whom wicked people have tried to vilify by making her the butt of their detestably gross calumnies and proud disdain, I can attest before God is in no way deceitful, crazy, deluded, prideful, or motivated by self-interest. On the contrary, I had occasion to admire the virtues of her soul, as well as the qualities of her mind throughout the period of time I had her under my spiritual direction, that is to say from 1868 to 1873. . . . I can affirm that to this day her edifying life, her virtues, her writings have deeply impressed on my heart the sentiments of respect and admiration.
>
> In 1879, our Holy Father Leo XIII deigned to honor Mélanie with a private audience and also charged her to com-

pile the rules for the new order recommended and requested by Our Lady of La Salette under the title of the Apostles of the Latter Days. In order to complete a draft of this kind, the ex-shepherdess stayed in Rome for five months at the convent of the Salesian Sisters. During this time she became better known and more highly esteemed, especially by these good nuns, who furnished a very favorable report.

Indeed, Pope Leo XIII was to honor Mélanie with not one, but two audiences. Further, he not only accepted her account of the apparition, he asked a noted attorney to "draft a brochure explaining the whole secret so that the general public could understand it properly". (Incidentally, that same pope was himself to receive a chilling forecast of things to come. Saying Mass one day, he suddenly collapsed and for some minutes was to all appearances dead. When he recovered, he described a terrifying vision of dark spiritual forces in control of the Vatican. In response, he wrote the famous end-of-Mass prayer beginning "Saint Michael the Archangel, be our defender in the day of battle.")

But while there may have been papal favor, there was also serious Vatican opposition, and in 1915, the Holy Office issued a decree forbidding all discussion of the secret and in 1923, another "proscribing and condemning" the entire brochure. It was not until 1966, when Pope Paul VI abolished the Index of Forbidden Books, that the secret was free to be read by one and all—assuming they could find a copy. After all, few had heard it so much as mentioned for more than forty years. And by then, of course, there was little point in warning the faithful about a "frightful crisis" involving the clergy and the religious communities when the crisis was already visibly under way. It would seem Mélanie Mathieu was destined to be a modern Cassandra, her warnings largely ignored until the Trojan horse was inside the walls and the city in flames.

Whether true prophet or well-meaning dreamer, the peasant girl who had gone from obscurity in the Alps to center stage in

Rome was ultimately to retire to a spot far from the madding crowd, finally settling in the small Italian town of Altamura and spending her last years there in a rented room. She died peacefully in that room in 1904, wearing an outmoded black dress and black bonnet that showed an admirable indifference to the fashion of this world, a seventy-two-year-old woman familiar to the townspeople, not because of her celebrity, of which they knew nothing, but because she faithfully attended the same daily Mass.

Maximin Giraud, meanwhile, he who had been nicknamed "Perpetual Motion" for his inability to sit still (and who frankly admitted to fidgeting with a stone even while the Blessed Virgin was speaking with him), would remain on the move all his short life. At fifteen, he entered the Grenoble minor seminary but proved an erratic student. He then tried monastic life, a job as a mechanic, another seminary, a college, six months in Rome as a papal zuave, and the French army. Finally, he returned in ill health to the little house in Corps where he had grown up. There, in 1875, after making the touching request that his heart be buried in the new basilica (it later would be), he died at the early age of forty.

Only one decision in his impetuous life did he truly regret. In Grenoble, some young Madison Avenue–style entrepreneurs had decided to market a liqueur called "Salettine" and promote it for its associations with the miraculous stream at La Salette. Desperate for cash, Maximin endorsed it in haste and repented at leisure. No matter. La Salette lives on; Salettine has gone the way of all those expensive alternatives the world has always preferred to the free, clear water of faith.

14

LIGHT AT LOURDES:
THE SONG OF BERNADETTE

"Que soy era Immaculado Conceptiou."
—the Blessed Virgin to Bernadette Soubirous,
March 25, 1858, the Feast of the Annunciation

Like flashes of lightning, startling but brief, Mary's appearances at the Rue du Bac in Paris (1830) and at La Salette (1846) had brought the Blessed Virgin to the revived attention of Catholic France. Her 1858 appearances at Lourdes, by comparison, were more like an aurora borealis, a long series of illuminations that would both amaze and instruct the entire Catholic world.

France had become more than ever Mary's private stage, and the brilliant drama called "Lourdes" would not only stir hearts from Dunkirk to Marseilles, it would make a small village in the Pyrenees a synonym for miraculous healing—a new Bethesda. And there was one name more that would forever set Lourdes apart—the title by which the Virgin identified herself there. At the moment of the Annunciation, the angel Gabriel had announced to Mary that she was blessed among women and would bear the Son of God. On the *feast* of the Annunciation, March 25, 1858, Mary herself made it clear that from the moment of her own conception she had been the pure and perfect vessel required for that incomparable honor, so much so that she could even be *called* "the Immaculate Conception".

At the same time, there were striking similarities to her own earlier French visits and indeed to all her other visits past and yet to come. As at the Rue du Bac and on the hill of Tepeyac, she appeared to a single witness; as at La Salette, she brought life and hope out of a fountain of water; and as in all her visits everywhere, she appeared as a beautiful young woman appareled in celestial light and eager to speak the heart-piercing words of a concerned and consoling mother. Yet at Lourdes she did that one thing more: she asserted an identity setting her apart from any other mere human being. On Mount Sinai, the God of the Hebrews had declared to Moses in fire and majesty, "I AM WHO AM." In Bethany, Jesus had serenely spoken of his divine identity to Martha, the sister of Lazarus: "I am the Resurrection and the Life." At Lourdes, Mary confirmed to Bernadette Soubirous the glorious truth about her superhuman purity: "I am the Immaculate Conception."

In fact, it was heaven's confirmation of Rome's declaration, coming just three years and three months after the doctrinal pronouncement in December 1854. Why heaven waited so long to settle the issue is of course a mystery. In any case, for many centuries, one of the more vexing questions of Catholic doctrine was the matter of whether or not Mary had been free every moment of her existence not only from personal sin but from original sin, that soul-staining susceptibility to evil that has been part of the human condition ever since Adam and Eve strayed from the narrow path. To be sure, Mary had generally been given the benefit of the doubt: the feast of the Immaculate Conception had been celebrated in the Eastern churches as early as the seventh century and in many Western churches starting in the eleventh and twelfth centuries, when the scholastic theologians were reasoning up a storm and putting pen to vellum with the results. Not surprisingly, great minds did not always agree.

Even that superheavyweight among medieval metaphysicians,

the ultraorthodox Thomas Aquinas (died 1274), had his reservations. The Angelic Doctor felt that if the Blessed Virgin had been sanctified before her conception, she would not have needed redemption and salvation by her Son, and thus Christ would not be, as Scripture insists he is, the savior of all men. But another muscular thinker, Duns Scotus, an Oxford Franciscan (died 1308), argued that a spiritual "immunization" preserving Mary from all sin, personal and original both, would not only not detract from the redemption but would instead be an especially glorious fruit of it.

Over the centuries, the Duns Scotus view—prevenient (or preceding) redemption—gradually prevailed. *Extremely* gradually, one is tempted to say. The great Council of Trent (1562–1563), while sympathetic to the Scotist opinion, felt that the time was not yet ripe for any sort of pronouncement, and nearly three additional centuries would pass before a sudden spiritual ground swell, stimulated by the vision given to Catherine Labouré ("Mary conceived without sin") inspired Pius IX to begin considering the matter doctrinally. The vivacious response of the bishops told him that the view of Duns Scotus had indeed taken hold and that a doctrinal pronouncement would be welcome— provided that Mary's gift of immunity be affirmed as a fruit she received from her Son's sacrifice. And so it was that on December 8, 1854, Pius IX declared that the Virgin "from the first moment of her conception, by a singular grace and privilege of almighty God, in view of the merits of Jesus Christ the Savior of mankind, [was] preserved free from all stain of original sin".

Yet it is one thing for a pope to define a doctrine and another for a heavenly being to set it to music. Mary did so at Lourdes not only by her own winning presence but by choosing as her ambassador an appealing young shepherdess. If the music was Mary's, the song was Bernadette's. Lourdes is generally considered one of the three greatest Marian apparitions (the other two being Guadalupe and Fatima), and apart from its doctrinal importance, it is notable for its unprecedented number of appearances (eighteen) and for the sustained drama centering on the young Bigourdane peasant girl, tiny in her person (four feet seven inches tall) but irresistible in her personality.

She was born January 7, 1844, twenty months before Mélanie Mathieu and Maximin Giraud saw the Virgin at La Salette—or, from another point of view, fourteen years after the Rue du Bac and fourteen years before the apparitions began at Lourdes. Those privileged to behold the things of heaven normally must endure, as did the great Apostle, a thorn in the flesh, and Bernadette was to endure several. At the age of six she began suffering the asthma attacks that would afflict her for the rest of her short life; and at eleven, she survived a case of cholera. (A persistent and eventually fatal tuberculosis would come later.) She also had to survive the hardships brought on by a father whose unbusinesslike ways soon turned prosperity into poverty, cost him the mill he had operated, and obliged the family to live in a single dank room, formerly a jail. Still, from all reports, the family was devoutly and unconquerably cheerful, whether skies were gray or black.

At one point, Bernadette helped out by boarding with an aunt and working in her uncle-in-law's cabaret. She also gained experience in a more conventional occupation for the heaven-chosen: watching over sheep, which she did for a stretch of six months in a nearby farming community. The fresh air agreed with her, and she might have stayed with the sheep till the cows came home if she had not been so eager to get back to Lourdes for the catechism classes she needed to prepare her for her First Communion. She therefore returned home in late January 1858—just two weeks, as it turned out, before the Blessed Virgin would appear to her. Catherine Labouré had encountered Mary on a warm summer night; Mélanie Mathieu and Maximin Giraud on a golden September afternoon; Bernadette Soubirous would meet her in the dead of winter.

The river Gave flows through Lourdes and past the grotto of Massabielle (from *masse vieille*, old rock), a formation as forbidding as anything in a Brontë landscape, and it was there that the visionary-to-be, with a sister and a companion, had gone in search of firewood on the cold Thursday of February 11, 1858. Bernadette was abruptly left behind when the other two removed their boots, sprinted barefoot across the frigid stream blocking their path, and went on their way, ungallantly leaving the asthmatic to shift for herself. But all of this is to get slightly ahead of one of the world's most fascinating stories, which more properly begins with Bernadette's own account of that day:

> We came down by the side that leads near the Gave and, having arrived at Pont Vieux, we wondered if it would be best to go up or down the river. We decided to go down and, taking the forest road, we arrived at Merlasse. There we went into Monsieur de la Fitte's field by the mill of Savy. As soon as we had reached the end of this field, nearly opposite the grotto of Massabielle, we were stopped by the canal of the mill we had just passed. . . .
>
> The water was cold and I for my part was afraid to go in. Jeanne Abadie and my sister, less timid than I, took their sabots in their hands and crossed the stream. However, when they were on the other side, they called out that it was cold and bent down to rub their feet and warm them. All this increased my fear, and I thought that if I went into the water I should get an attack of asthma. So I asked Jeanne Abadie, who was bigger and stronger than I, to take me on her shoulders.
>
> "I should think not," answered Jeanne. "You're a mollycoddle; if you won't come, stay where you are."
>
> After the others had picked up some pieces of wood under the grotto they disappeared along the Gave. When I was alone I threw stones into the bed of the canal to give me a foothold, but it was of no use. So I had to make up my mind to take off my sabots and cross the canal as Jeanne and my sister had done.
>
> I had just begun to take off my first stocking when suddenly I heard a great noise like the sound of a storm. I looked to the

right, to the left, under the trees of the river, but nothing moved; I thought I was mistaken. I went on taking off my shoes and stockings; then I heard a fresh noise like the first. I was frightened and stood straight up. I lost all power of speech and thought when, turning my head toward the grotto, I saw at one of the openings of the rock a rosebush, one only, moving as if it were very windy.

Almost at the same time there came out of the interior of the grotto a golden-colored cloud, and soon after a Lady, young and beautiful, exceedingly beautiful, the like of whom I had never seen, came and placed herself at the entrance of the opening above the rosebush. She looked at me immediately, smiled at me and signed to me to advance, as if she had been my mother. All fear had left me but I seemed to know no longer where I was. I rubbed my eyes, I shut them, I opened them; but the Lady was still there continuing to smile at me and making me understand that I was not mistaken.

Without thinking of what I was doing, I took my rosary in my hands and went on my knees. The Lady made a sign of approval with her head and herself took into her hands a rosary which hung on her right arm. When I attempted to begin the rosary and tried to lift my hand to my forehead, my arm remained paralyzed, and it was only after the Lady had signed herself that I could do the same. The Lady left me to pray all alone; she passed the beads of her rosary between her fingers but she said nothing; only at the end of each decade did she say the "Gloria" with me.

When the recitation of the rosary was finished, the Lady returned to the interior of the rock and the golden cloud disappeared with her.

As soon as the Lady had disappeared Jeanne Abadie and my sister returned to the grotto and found me on my knees in the same place where they had left me. They laughed at me, called me imbecile and bigot, and asked me if I would go back with them or not. I had now no difficulty in going into the stream, and I felt the water as warm as the water for washing plates and dishes. . . .

We bound up in three fagots the branches and fragments of wood which my companions had brought; then we climbed the slope of Massabielle and took the forest road. Whilst we were going toward the town I asked Jeanne and Marie if they had noticed anything at the grotto.

"No," they answered. "Why do you ask us?"

"Oh, nothing," I replied indifferently.

However, before we got to the house, I told my sister Marie of the extraordinary things that had happened to me at the grotto, asking her to keep it secret.

Throughout the whole day the image of the Lady remained in my mind. In the evening at the family prayer I was troubled and began to cry.

"What is the matter?" asked my mother.

Marie hastened to answer for me and I was obliged to give the account of the wonder that had come to me that day.

"These are illusions," answered my mother. "You must drive these ideas out of your head and especially not go back again to Massabielle."

We went to bed but I could not sleep. The face of the Lady, so good and so gracious, returned incessantly to my memory, and it was useless to recall what my mother had said to me; I could not believe that I had been deceived.

Bernadette also went on to describe the beautiful lady in detail:

She has the appearance of a young girl of sixteen or seventeen. She is dressed in a white robe, girdled at the waist with a blue ribbon which flows down all around it. A yoke closes it in graceful pleats at the base of the neck; the sleeves are long and tight-fitting. She wears upon her head a veil which is also white; this veil gives just a glimpse of her hair and then falls down at the back below her waist. Her feet are bare but covered by the last folds of her robe except at the point where a yellow rose shines upon each of them. She holds on her right arm a rosary of white beads with a chain of gold shining like the two roses on her feet.

Here, then, is the eyewitness account of Bernadette Soubirous, teenager, shepherdess, peasant, dutiful daughter, and future saint. To be sure, the witness' credibility would be established only after much cross-examination and numerous marvels and miracles, but still what she said *was* true: for the third time in a mere twenty-eight-year span, the Blessed Virgin had appeared in France. And this time she had scarcely set foot there when she performed the astounding act of joining her young petitioner in the saying of the rosary—perhaps the most dramatic illustration ever of the importance of that particular prayer tool. And an especially convincing detail of Bernadette's account of that dual rosary recitation was that the Virgin said only the Gloria. (That of course made perfect sense: glorifying the Trinity would be as appropriate for Mary as for Bernadette, whereas it would have been absurd for Mary to pray to herself in the Ave Maria or ask to be led not into temptation in the Our Father.)

The rosary also figured in the second apparition, which took place only three days later, when Bernadette, following an inner prompting, returned to the grotto on Sunday, February 14. By now, word had spread, and she was joined in this second grotto visit by a flock of other young bead-carrying girls in their Sunday best, all of whom were soon resolutely praying alongside. Fearing diabolical impersonation, the girls had brought along a vial of holy water, and when the Lady appeared (again, only Bernadette saw her), they urged her to sprinkle away. When Bernadette did so, chorusing "If you come from God, stay, but if not, go away!" the Lady only smiled. Bernadette then went back to her beads, soon passing into an ecstasy so complete her worried companions wondered if she was about to lift off with full rocket thrust.

Meanwhile, the odious Jeanne Abadie, Bernadette's sneering companion of the first visit, arrived on the scene and, resentful at having been left behind, fiendishly proceeded to roll a large stone down the hill on which she was standing, aiming it directly at the rosary-sayers, no doubt expecting them to scream and scatter—which they did. All, that is, except for Bernadette, who remained motionless even as the stone crashed by within a few feet of her. This apparent insensibility to dangerous moving objects so increased the girls' alarm that they summoned

Antoine Nicolau, a nearby millowner, who, helped by his be-
wildered mother, managed to push and pull the tiny mystic all
the way to the mill even as she continued to gaze adoringly in
the direction of the grotto. This whole uproarious drama, combining deep faith with elements of narrow escape and slapstick
comedy in a style anticipating the early silent films of Charlie
Chaplin, neither edified nor amused Bernadette's mother. Summoned to the mill and embarrassed to the bone, she made clear
her displeasure in the language of Poe's raven: Nevermore.
Nevermore the grotto.

And that interdict might have remained in effect perma-
nently had it not been for the efforts of the wealthy widow
Jeanne-Marie Milhet, a social climber whose thirst for status
was by no means confined to the terrestrial. What enabled her
to get in on the heavenly action, so to speak, was that she knew
Bernadette's mother, having occasionally employed her as a
doer of odd jobs. When the widow's dressmaker, the devout
Antoine Peyret, suggested the two women call on Madame
Soubirous with an eye to making straight once more the path of
Bernadette to the grotto, the widow responded enthusiastically.
Massabielle was not Paris exactly, but what did that matter if
going there would enable her to meet someone from the high-
est level of aristocracy anywhere? Together, in any case, the two
visitors managed to persuade the worried mother that with
themselves as escorts, Bernadette could safely return to
Massabielle—and this they did, bearing a candle and rosaries, on
February 18.

The day was to be a tissue of sorrows for Madame Milhet. As
the three approached the rock on which the distinguished visitor normally stood, the Lady made herself visible (as was of
course her custom) only to Bernadette and added another stab
to the widow's heart by making a sign for only Bernadette to
advance. Nor did these soul-destroying snubs end there.
Bernadette soon thereafter informed the dressmaker that the

Lady had looked at her a long time, while presumably ignoring Madame Milhet. Could human flesh bear more? "It was the candle she was looking at!" shrieked the widow. "No," said Bernadette, with more truth than tact, "the Lady looked and smiled." It is not recorded whether the widow then clutched her throat and staggered backward in the manner of Sarah Bernhardt playing Camille, but she did at least manage to invoke the curse of the wounded woman of property: "If you are lying, God will punish you!"

Somehow, Bernadette was spared the divine wrath. Moreover, on the walk home, she revealed that during this third appearance the Lady had reversed the roles of heaven and earth by asking the humble peasant girl: "Will you do me the favor of coming here for a fortnight?" Bernadette, exalted from earthly drudge to heavenly auxiliary, had of course said "Yes." But there was to be a price: "I do not promise you will be happy in this world, only in the next."

Meanwhile the authorities began working overtime to discourage Bernadette's Massabielle visits. After numerous warnings had failed, the local inspector of police subjected her to an inquisition only slightly less aggressive than one of Robespierre's. Despite his threats, Bernadette, with vast crowds looking on, continued to engage in what seemed to be a kind of impromptu fanaticism: kissing the ground, walking on her knees up to the grotto, and weeping like Rachel for her children. Her explanation? The Lady had asked her to do these things in penance for the conversion of sinners.

That there was a method in all this madness became clear on Thursday, February 25. In the middle of her vision that day, before a crowd of muttering sceptics and hushed believers, Bernadette abruptly got up, walked toward the river, and then, looking puzzled, stopped, selected a spot, fell to her knees, and began scratching the hard winter earth—searching, it would turn out, for a stream. At last, the stream appeared—at first little more than a muddy rivulet. Repeatedly, Bernadette tried to swallow a bit of its dark water from her cupped hands—not succeeding till the fourth attempt. She then splashed some on her face and, to complete what must have appeared to the on-lookers like a human imitation of rhesus-monkey behavior, plucked some nearby unsavory herbs and calmly began chewing them.

Later, Bernadette would explain just what she had been up to. First, the Lady had told her to go drink and wash at "the spring". Since no spring was visible, she had started toward the river. The Lady then made it clear she had not meant the river and pointed to a spot some distance away. That was why Bernadette had stopped and looked puzzled and finally begun clawing at the earth, where of course she found what she was supposed to find—with drinking, washing, and penitential herb-chewing to follow.

Plausible as it may have sounded, all of this was fervently dis-believed by almost everyone until a curious fact at last regis-tered: the little muddy trickle had irresistibly become a clear and vigorous body of water, swiftly finding its way to the nearby river. And in time it would be found that there was something still more interesting about it: by the grace of God, it cured. Indeed, it restored sight to the eye of a man who had been so severely injured no organic basis for sight remained. The waters of Lourdes, like the waters of La Salette, were soon being bottled, drunk from, washed in, and, not always and everywhere, but often and astoundingly, performing miracles.

Meanwhile, as the Lady's requested "fortnight" continued, the visions continued, the harassment continued (the imperial prosecutor, picking up where the inspector of police had left off, threatened both Bernadette and her mother with prison), and the crowds continued to grow. Perhaps the most signifi-cant—and least welcome—words of the Lady during all this time were those expressing her wish that her young witness "go to the priests" and tell them she wanted a chapel built at the grotto.

To Bernadette, that meant the not very cheerful prospect of relaying the message to her pastor, the formidable Dean Dominique Peyramale, with his prison-warden face and no-nonsense manner. Here was a courageous soul who had won the hearts of his parishioners three years before by fearlessly tending the sick and the dying during a cholera epidemic, but here was also a man not likely to see in an undersized teenager a second Moses coming down from the mount.

Reluctantly, Bernadette duly went forth to beard the priestly lion in his den. The dean's response was in character—bluster and incredulity followed by two down-to-earth questions: What was the Lady's name, and was she going to come up with the money for the chapel? And by the way, if the Lady had made a request of him, let him also make one of her: cause the rosebush near where she was standing to bloom.

When, at her next visit to the grotto, Bernadette relayed the dean's response, the Lady smiled a no doubt indulgent smile. But since heaven was not in the habit of obeying earth, she was not about to repeat the miracle of Tepeyac Hill and bring forth winter roses. Rather, she simply sent the nervous Bernadette back to the fire-breathing pastor with an amplified request: Not only the chapel but also processions to the grotto. This time, not surprisingly, the dean ushered her out of his rectory even more briskly than he had the time before, telling her not to call again. But she did that very night, having forgotten part of the Lady's request and being determined to carry out her charge in full. One of her neighbors made it easier by accompanying her and acting as a kind of buffer.

And now, whether by the grace of God or a good supper, the dean remained calm and conversational as not only he, but his two curates, quizzed the little courier in detail. The interview ended with the dean insisting on one absolute condition: Unless he was told the Lady's name, there would never be so much as an architect's sketch, let alone a chapel. Relieved, Bernadette was also resolved: She would get the Lady to tell her her name and thus put an end to this maddening tug-of-war in which she seemed to be serving as the rope.

But the name was a long time coming, for as we can see now in hindsight, the Lady was saving it for the feast of the Annunciation, still weeks away. In any case, the "fortnight" of appearances ended on March 4, and no soccer crowd could have been more disappointed in a World Cup cancellation than were the twenty thousand in attendance that day on learning, as they soon did, that while the Lady had appeared, she had declined to identify herself. Dean Peyramale would have to wait and so would Lourdes—and that might be forever.

As it happened, Bernadette felt no urge to return to the grotto until precisely three weeks had passed. It was March 25 when she went back and, considering the long hiatus, she was no doubt greatly relieved when the Lady appeared. Bernadette promptly popped the crucial question, and when the Lady merely smiled, she repeated it: "Madame, O Madame, please be so kind as to tell me who you are." Finally, the moment came: the Lady opened wide her arms, lowered them, joined her hands, brought them prayerfully to her breast, and raised her eyes. Then, as one commentator has beautifully expressed it, she "surrendered her secret in words that this world could not have invented": "*Que soy era Immaculado Conceptiou*" ("I am the Immaculate Conception" spoken in the local Bigourdane dialect). Appropriately, this tremendous announcement was made on the anniversary of the angel's tremendous announcement to Mary: the feast of the Annunciation. Bernadette had her answer.

Comedy and triumph followed. Repeating the words over and over so as not to forget them, Bernadette hurried off to tell the dean the good news. Bursting into his room without preamble or explanation, she exclaimed, "I am the Immaculate

Conception!" A kind of sickly horror must have registered in the dean's features, for quickly she amended her statement: "Aquero ("That"—her name for the Lady)—Aquero said 'I am the Immaculate Conception.' "

The dean was not appeased. On the contrary, he was shocked, angry, and mystified. "A lady cannot bear that name!" he shouted. What set him off was the idea of Mary (if Mary it was) naming herself after a single aspect of her being: while Mary's conception was no doubt immaculate, to say she *was* her own conception sounded like immaculate nonsense. "You're mistaken!" he thundered at the waif. "Do you know what you're saying?" Bernadette shook her head. "Then how can you say such a thing if you don't understand?" "Because", said Bernadette, "I repeated it all the way here from Massabielle."

This ignorance was of course a tremendous point in Bernadette's favor: had she been fabricating her story, it is unthinkable she would have chosen, instead of a proper name, the name of a doctrine she knew nothing about. (Nor is it surprising she was not familiar with the term; for all her piety, it should be remembered, she was yet to make her First Holy Communion.) In any case, Bernadette had kept her part of the bargain in finding out the Lady's name, and now she did not hesitate to add: "She still wants the chapel." Half-convinced, half-confused, the dean sent the child on her way, promising to think it over and get back to her. Later, he was to become her champion.

That afternoon, Bernadette had the term "immaculate conception" explained to her and felt not only enlightened but vindicated. After all, she had consistently reported only what she had seen and heard, never claiming the lady of her vision was anyone in particular, in fact never referring to her as anyone but "Aquero"—"That". Now, to her unspeakable joy, she realized the Lady of her vision was Mary of Nazareth.

So did the inhabitants of Lourdes soon realize it—and their delight was matched only by the exasperation of the civil authorities. All else having failed, the government brought in the medical examiners, hoping to get Bernadette certified as a lunatic. But try as anyone might, whether patient doctor or prodding official, there was no tripping her up, catching her out, or proving her mad. As Dean Peyramale summed it up in a letter to his bishop after witnessing an intensive examination by a former member of the Assembly: "Everything about the girl deeply impressed him [the examiner]. He subjected her to a most detailed line of questioning, but the child answered all his questions with ability far above her age level and, what seemed to me, far above her intelligence."

One of the more telling moments of that interview followed on Bernadette's comment that the Virgin had spoken in patois (the region's Bigourdane dialect). The former legislator objected: "The Blessed Virgin could not have spoken patois. God and the Blessed Virgin don't speak that language." Bernadette's reply stopped him in his spats: "How is it *we* know it if *they* don't?"

On April 7, Bernadette again felt that inner tug that told her it was grotto time. Though it was only 5:30 in the morning when she arrived, a scattering of believers were already there, muttering prayers in the early dawn and never suspecting that another startling event was on the way. It seems a local wine merchant had given Bernadette a long and heavy prayer candle, and this she rested on the ground directly in front of her. To keep it burning, since there was a brisk wind, she cupped her hands around the flame even as she prayed. And she left them cupped and in place even when the Virgin appeared and the visionary went into her customary ecstatic trance. The conscious Bernadette had of course been able to adjust her hands to the wind-shifting of the flame; the entranced Bernadette moved them not at all, and soon it was obvious that the darting candle-fire was repeatedly touching, and presumably burning, those reverent little fingers. Understandably, gasps and murmurs were heard from all sides.

A certain Doctor Dozous, however, sensing that something beyond normal physics was at work, insisted that Bernadette not be interfered with. For fifteen minutes the suspense continued. After the vision, Bernadette uttered not so much as a whimper when the doctor examined her hands. Indeed, he pronounced them burn-free. Previously undecided, the medico now joined the ranks of the believers, and the so-called "miracle of the candle" was added to the list of the numerous miraculous occurrences connected with Massabielle, this new rock of the faith.

All the while, it should be remembered, these singular events were taking place within the borders of a nation whose government still saw through the Cyclopean eye of the Reign of Terror. To be sure, Polyphemus had calmed down considerably, but he was still ready to smite any new Ulysses who might oppose him too strenuously or try his patience too much. Since *l'affaire Bernadette* promised to become an embarrassment on the grand scale, much as La Salette had been, the giant soon stepped in with both boots, protesting that the people were committing the impertinent crime of starting a "cult" without the state's permission. On June 7, the regional ruler, the prefect of the Hautes Pyrenees, ordered the mayor of Lourdes to close the grotto without further ado. Barricades went up on June 15 and, after they were indignantly torn down by the faithful, were rebuilt a week later. For good measure, trespassers were arrested.

Despite the state's mailed-fist approach, the disturbances continued, and adventurous souls persistently slipped inside the barricades to collect water from the Virgin's spring. Some of it, in fact, made its way north to Paris and into the very household of the emperor, Napoleon III. Whether or not it was responsible for healing his deathly sick young daughter is not certain, but it *is* certain that after his daughter recovered, he sent a memorandum dated October 2, 1858, permitting everyone everywhere access to the grotto.

Meanwhile, Bernadette had had one final vision—the vision

of July 16, the feast of Our Lady of Mount Carmel. The barricades were still up then, so Bernadette had waited until sunset, concealed her tiny frame inside an oversized cape, and smuggled herself past a lackadaisical guard all the way to her usual spot. This time the Virgin said nothing, but as if to compensate for the absence of words, she added something in the way of splendor—appearing more beautiful, said Bernadette, than she had ever seen her.

Twelve days after that farewell apparition, the bishop of Tarbes, Bertrand Laurence, set up a commission that would sit for three years and test the validity of all claims. That meant not only clerics and experts on theological matters, it also meant the hydrologists, chemists, and geologists who would examine the claims made on behalf of the water that was later to become so famous. (By the way, to the acute disappointment of the mayor, who assumed that all the reported cures must mean the stream came from a mineral spring and thus would soon make Massabielle the Marienbad of France, a Toulouse professor pronounced it ordinary spring water.)

After exhaustive interviews with Bernadette, with the beneficiaries of miraculous cures, and with numerous other witnesses expert and ordinary, the commission delivered its verdict on January 18, 1862:

> We hold that the Immaculate Mary, Mother of God, actually appeared to Bernadette Soubirous on the eleventh of February, 1858, and on subsequent days to the number of eighteen, in the grotto of Massabielle, near the town of Lourdes; that the apparitions bear all the signs of authenticity and that the faithful are free to consider it true.

The chapel the Virgin had requested—indeed, no mere chapel was it to be, but a great steeple-crowned basilica—was completed in 1871, and the processions she had requested began soon after. Indeed, they have never really stopped: Lourdes now draws some four million pilgrims every year.

And Bernadette? Hers was, as the Virgin had left no doubt it would be, a life short on champagne and truffles. After several years of schooling made onerous by asthma-related suffering and after being wooed by many orders and convents, she joined the Sisters of Nevers, one of the few orders that did *not* try to get her to join. Nevers, on the Loire in central France, was a very long way from Lourdes, but Bernadette's fame pursued her even there. Again and again, she was summoned forth to be "gawked at", as she put it, "like some freak animal" for the edification of drop-in celebrity-seekers—most of them, sad to say, bishops. As Sister Marie-Bernard she lived out a life exactly half as long as the biblical three-score-and-ten, undergoing a prolonged martyrdom caused not only by her worsening asthma but by the tuberculosis of the bone that would first cripple and then kill her. The waters of Lourdes, it seems, were not for its most famous citizen.

In 1877, only two years before her death, the bishop of Nevers, soon to depart for Rome, prevailed on her to write a letter to Pius IX, promising to deliver it personally and to return with a papal blessing. Though bedridden at the time and in great pain, Bernadette wrote a brief and tremendously touching letter to the same Pope who had defined the doctrine that had flowered, so to speak, over the rosebush at Massabielle. She concluded:

> It seems to me that every time I pray for your intentions that from heaven the Blessed Virgin must often cast her eyes on you, most Holy Father, because it was you who proclaimed her Immaculate, and that four years later, I did not know what the word meant. I never heard the word before. Since then, on thinking it over, I told myself that the Blessed Virgin is good— it would appear that she came to confirm the word of our Holy Father.

After sustained and excruciating suffering that reached its peak in Easter week, Bernadette made the sign of the cross in the beautiful, deliberate, dignified way in which she had seen the Virgin sign herself at the grotto twenty-one years earlier, inclined her head, and died. It was April 16, 1879, and this pure-hearted witness who alone had been privileged to see the heavenly visitor in Lourdes presumably saw her soon again. Bernadette was beatified in 1925 and canonized on December 8, 1933, the feast of the Immaculate Conception. Today her incorrupt body rests in the main chapel of the convent of Nevers. So lifelike does she appear she might almost seem to be awaiting yet another visit from above.

A postscript:

In the last frantic days of June 1940, the sudden collapse of France under the Nazi onslaught made it imperative for Franz Werfel, the celebrated Jewish novelist, to exit that nation with all deliberate speed. He and his wife, the equally celebrated Alma Mahler, widow of the great composer/conductor Gustav Mahler, tried desperately, as did countless other refugees, to cross the Spanish border into safety, only to find that the Nazis had sealed it off with hermetic finality. Separated from their luggage, caught in a nightmarish world where arrest seemed imminent and where no end of other fugitives jammed the trains, roads, and hotels, the Werfels heard what seemed almost a whisper from heaven: a family they chanced to meet told them that Lourdes was the one place in France where they might still find a room. There they arrived after a harrowing thirty-kilometer taxi ride, and there they indeed found shelter.

"It was in this manner", Werfel later wrote, "that Providence brought me to Lourdes. We hid for several weeks in the Pyrenean city. It was a time of great dread. The British radio announced that I had been murdered by the National Socialists. . . . But it was also a time of great significance for me, for I became acquainted with the wondrous history of the girl Bernadette Soubirous and also with the wondrous facts concerning the healings of Lourdes. One day in great distress I made a vow. I vowed that if I escaped from this desperate situation and reached the saving shores of America, I would put off all other tasks and sing, as best I could, *the song of Bernadette*."

That graceful writer did reach the saving shores of America, and, in a book bearing that musical title, he not only fulfilled his vow but told that wondrous story in rich and beautiful detail. Franz Schubert had written the incomparable "Ave Maria". Franz Werfel added a new set of words to the new and glorious "Ave" sung by the eternal Bernadette.

15

THE SILENT APPARITIONS:
PONTMAIN AND KNOCK

Hark! on the fragrant air,
Music of France, voices of France, fall piercing fair.
Poor France, where Mary's star shines,
    lest her children drown.
                —Lionel Johnson, "Our Lady of France" (1891)

Mary, Star of the Sea!
Look upon this little place:
Bless the kind fisher race,
Mary, Star of the Sea.
                —Lionel Johnson, "Cadgwith" (1892)

In her appearances at Paris, La Salette, and Lourdes, the Blessed Virgin had not only been visible but audible, speaking words that resound to this day: "The times are very evil; sorrows will befall France" . . . "If my Son is not to cast you off, I am obliged to entreat Him without ceasing" . . . "I am the Immaculate Conception." In her last two nineteenth-century apparitions, however, she was content to let the image speak for the phrase. And indeed, if it is true that a picture is worth a thousand words, those silent apparitions spoke libraries.

Interestingly, the first of those appearances was for children only; the second was for all ages—to the extent of an unprecedented eighteen witnesses ranging in age from thirteen to seventy-plus. Interestingly, too, while the first silent visitation was in France (Mary's fourth consecutive appearance there), the second was also in a nation where Catholics had recently suffered for their faith—Ireland. And finally, each of the two apparitions provided its own special type of consolation at opposite ends of a decade that in France began in bloody war (Mary appeared at Pontmain in 1871, when the Franco-Prussian conflict was raging) and that in Ireland ended in uneasy peace (she appeared at Knock in 1879, when the effects of the potato famine and a Simon Legree–style eviction policy were still being felt).

Pontmain is in the Breton-flavored province of Mayenne, which borders the region of Brittany (that westernmost part of France, jutting out like a great thumb into the Atlantic, an area of transplanted Celts, deep faith, and a Celtic language still spoken today—Breton). In 1871, the province was being overrun by Prussian troops, and though there was anxiety in the small town of Pontmain, fortunately the only occupier the citizens had to contend with on January 17, 1871, was a thick blanket of snow.

Despite the presence of foreign marauders nearby, that day the good people of Pontmain continued their useful toil along the cool sequestered vale of life, entrusting graver matters to Providence. Two of the workers were the very young Barbedette brothers, Eugène and Joseph, who were helping their father prepare feed for the horses in the family barn, little realizing they were about to go from standing in hay to staring at heaven.

Shortly before six o'clock, Eugène walked outside, there to be stopped in his tracks by the sight of a beautiful Lady startlingly near in the winter sky. Heavenly she seemed in every sense, for she wore a golden crown and a dark blue robe sprinkled with stars, and almost immediately smiled and regally spread her hands in a welcoming gesture. She was still smiling when Joseph, hearing his brother's wild cries, rushed out to see what was up. Soon he too was shouting the Breton version of "Come and see!" That brought their father, looking up and around for all he was worth but unable to find anything unusual in the deep purple of early evening. Thus also with Madame Barbedette when she left the pots simmering in her warm kitchen to see what all the racket was about. Vision or no vision, then, the family returned inside for the evening meal, the parents dubious, the boys almost too excited to eat.

The senior Barbedettes may have felt a bit of onion soup and some good French bread would restore their sons to a normal field of vision, free of apparitions, delusions, gold crowns, and star-spangled robes—but far from it. Returning to the wintry outdoors, the lads once again looked up and once again saw the Lady. This time, wanting either clear confirmation or flat refutation, the parents summoned a couple of the nuns at Pontmain's Catholic school. These good sisters, it seems, were so eager to see the Lady they had been praying to for so long (if she it was) they rushed over to the Barbedette barn with two of their lower-grade schoolgirls in tow—a good thing, as it turned out, for the nuns saw nothing but sky while the tykes saw exactly what the young Barbedette brothers were seeing. Unprompted, they described the same Lady, the same golden crown, the same star-spangled blue robe.

This corroboration of the earlier testimony was convincing enough that Father Guérin, the local pastor, was called in. Though he too drew a celestial blank, the children's continuing excitement persuaded him that something unearthly was indeed going on, and so, even as other villagers came hurrying to the scene, he judiciously began a prayer vigil. People knelt either in the snow or in the barn, whose small door was kept open that those inside might hear the firsthand reports of the young witnesses. Indeed, even as Sister Mary Edward led the faithful in the rosary, the children kept up a running commentary, both enthusiastic and vivaciously detailed.

GUADALUPE CATHOLIC BOOKS
1815 THOMASVILLE RD
TALLAHASSEE / FL 32303

DATE: 11/29/03   TIME: 13:34
MER#: 00032505700   TER#: 0001
S-A-L-E-S D-R-A-F-T

REF: 0006   BCH: 610
CD TYPE: MC
TR TYPE: PR
INV#:
AMOUNT: $18.76

ACCT: ************6319   EXP: ****
AP: 007937

CARDMEMBER ACKNOWLEDGES RECEIPT OF
GOODS AND/OR SERVICES IN THE AMOUNT OF
THE TOTAL SHOWN HEREON AND AGREES TO
PERFORM THE OBLIGATIONS SET FORTH BY THE
CARDMEMBER'S AGREEMENT WITH THE ISSUER

X _____
TOP COPY-MERCHANT BOTTOM COPY-CUSTOMER

GUADALUPE CATHOLIC BOOKS
1815 THOMASVILLE RD
TALLAHASSEE FL 32303

DATE: 11/29/03   TIME: 13:34
MERH: 000000000000   TERMC: 0001
S-A-1-E-S 0-R-H-E-1

REF: 0006   BCH: 616
CD TYPE: MC
TR TYPE: PR
INV#:
AMOUNT: $18.76

ACCT: XXXXXXXXXXXX6317   EXP: XXXX
AP: 007437

CARDMEMBER ACKNOWLEDGES RECEIPT OF
GOODS AND/OR SERVICES IN THE AMOUNT OF
THE TOTAL SHOWN HEREON AND AGREES TO
PERFORM THE OBLIGATIONS SET FORTH BY THE
CARDMEMBER'S AGREEMENT WITH THE ISSUER

TOP COPY-MERCHANT/BOTTOM COPY-CUSTOMER

Soon, the children were reporting even more astonishing things in the night sky. As the villagers prayed, the apparition—seemingly in response—grew in size and was soon enclosed within a large blue oval background with four burning candles attached. All the while the stars on the Virgin's robe were multiplying, and, delight of delights, its dark blue was growing progressively lighter and brighter. One imagines the "oohs" and "aahs" from four little treble voices unable to contain their excitement, and one also imagines their elders straining for any glimpse at all of robe, crown, or candle.

But the adults were no less grateful despite being visually excluded, because they could not help but be excited by the apparent acknowledgment from on high to whatever they offered in speech or song. When the villagers sang in their rich Breton a devout Magnificat, the creator of this remarkable heavenly light-show responded by suddenly introducing one more brilliant element—a white banner on which letters of gold slowly began to form. Even as the singing continued, the young Barbedette boys kept earnestly trying to decipher the printing. At last, they could clearly read—and did so, aloud, with great excitement—the mighty message:

PRAY, MY CHILDREN, GOD WILL ANSWER BEFORE LONG
MY SON LETS HIMSELF BE MOVED

Not surprisingly, the villagers responded with a profound reverence on hearing of this Sinai-like tablet in the sky speaking to them alone in that eternal moment. It is one thing for priests and prophets to insist that God answers prayer, but it is quite another for heaven to confirm it in gold letters on a celestial banner. After an awed silence, the pastor led the singing of a resoundingly jubilant hymn, and so evidently pleasing was this to the court of heaven that the children abruptly exclaimed, "See how she smiles!" While the banner vanished once the hymn was over, it was promptly succeeded by another heart-stopping sight.

This time, a penitential hymn—"Gentle Jesus, pardon now our repentant hearts"—apparently set the tone above as well as below, for as the villagers intoned their mournful Breton, the children described an accompanying sadness in the Lady's expression. No doubt it was the sadness unto death, for now there appeared a large red crucifix, over which a placard proclaimed in beautiful red letters: JESUS CHRIST. The Lady then "presented" (held out) the crucifix to the children, her face registering an intense sorrow.

After a time, the red crucifix also vanished, and the Virgin resumed her initial position, arms extended downward. As she did so, she smiled once more, and a small white cross appeared on each of her shoulders: a silent epilogue to a dramatically silent evening. And now it was time for the farewell. As the pastor led his flock in evening prayer, a large white veil appeared at the feet of the Virgin, slowly rose, and gradually enshrouded her. The moment the evening prayer ended, the apparition faded from sight, and as it did the young Barbedettes dutifully announced the fact: "It's all over."

It was nine o'clock in the evening—or about three hours after the Virgin had first come into view. Three hours, and yet rare would be that soul who thereafter could look into the night sky of Pontmain and not feel the greatest comfort on remembering the gloriously reassuring words of the "silent" apparition that spoke—MY SON LETS HIMSELF BE MOVED.

⁂

Eight years and seven months later, four hundred miles away, and among yet another Celtic people in yet another small village, the Virgin made her fifth public appearance of the century. This time she chose a hilltop village in the southeast section of Ireland's County Mayo, that land of oats, potatoes, livestock, and lakes, which borders the Atlantic and occupies the two thousand square miles of green space between the counties of Galway and Sligo.

Those bright little kingdoms were once briefly the poetic property of the great William Butler Yeats, who wrote about everything in them from fairies and waterhorses to Connemara lace to ancient monarchs and the wild swans at Coole. Yet he was also to speak powerfully for County Mayo and the Virgin's appearance there in a way he probably was not even aware of. In 1893, fourteen years after the Knock apparition, the twenty-eight-year-old bard wrote "The Rose of the World", with a last stanza hauntingly applicable to the Lady who had found her way to a little country church one rainy summer evening:

> Bow down, archangels, in your dim abode:
> Before you were, or any hearts to beat,
> Weary and kind one lingered by His seat;
> He made the world to be a grassy road
> Before her wandering feet.

The grassy road that led Mary to Knock ("Cnoc" is Gaelic for hill) had also led Saint Patrick there in ancient days, and local legend insisted that the great missionary had blessed the place and foretold that it would one day be a magnet of devotion drawing pilgrims from Bantry Bay to Malin Head. Few in August 1879 would have thought the prophecy would be fulfilled any time soon: the effects of the gruesome potato famine of the 1840s were still being felt in a dispirited and dwindling population, and the heart-sickening rent evictions were still going on: even in the year of the apparition, eighteen families in the Knock area alone were cast out of house and home by the ham-fisted agents of an economic Moloch.

Faith was the one abiding consolation, and at its center was the church of Knock, tiny but tenacious-looking under its resolutely square tower. It had been built fifty years before, in

1829, and, appropriately, was named for a saint who knew all about hardscrabble life in the wilderness—John the Baptist. The pastor was a Father Cavanaugh, a soul of such ungrudging generosity he had sold even his horse and watch to help his poor, and who may well have inspired the great heavenly gesture to come because of his fondness for referring to the Virgin as "the ever Immaculate Mother of God". When a storm battered the church in 1878 and destroyed two of its statues, Father Cavanaugh somehow raised the money to replace them—and one of the replacements, significantly, was a statue of Our Lady of Lourdes, with her white robe and bright blue sash. It was to prove a remarkable harbinger.

August 21, 1879, was a working day like any other in Knock —which for some meant haying, for others digging turf, tending livestock, cooking cabbage, or washing overalls. If there was one thing that seemed to set that day apart, it was the relentless downpour that began late in the afternoon and that by seven o'clock was drenching everyone and everything and showing no signs of going into remission.

Yet what would truly make that day singular was a very different kind of "downpour"—a spiritual one. It came soon after the tireless Father Cavanaugh returned from a visit to parishioners in an outlying district. Still dripping like a spaniel, he was more than a little grateful for the fire his young housekeeper got blazing before hurrying off to visit a neighbor—a visit that was to set the stage for the greatest show seen in Ireland since Saint Patrick debated the Druid love-god Oisin.

The housekeeper was Mary McLoughlin, and she it was who would first see what all of Knock would soon be talking about forever. On her way back from the visit—to a Mrs. Beirne—she was accompanied by the latter's sixteen-year-old daughter, also named Mary, and passing by the church in the drilling rain, the two young women suddenly had their names added to that glorious roster of those who had seen the Virgin during her nineteenth-century visitations—Catherine Labouré, Mélanie Mathieu, Maximin Giraud, Bernadette Soubirous, and the young children of Pontmain. Between the low wall enclosing the church grounds and the church itself was an uncut meadow, and there the astonished pair looked out from under their black umbrellas to behold the Virgin herself, flanked by two male figures, all three seemingly standing on top of the tall grass, about a foot or two in front of the church's now dazzlingly illuminated gable wall. Though it was still raining pitchforks, it was also still daylight, and in the afterglow of one of those long Irish summer evenings the two passersby could plainly see that the three figures were not statues—as Mary McLoughlin had at first briefly thought—for their feet were above, not pressing down on, the tall meadow grass.

Nor did the two Marys have any difficulty identifying the male figures in the tableau. The figure on the Virgin's right, head bent toward her as though bowed in respect and devotion, his hair and beard gray, and the man himself clearly "old", was Saint Joseph. The figure on the Virgin's left, vested as a bishop, wearing a short miter and holding a large open book in his left hand, so closely resembled a statue Mary Beirne had seen in a nearby church that she quickly identified him as Saint John the Evangelist—Mary's Cross-appointed stepson.

And there was yet one more vital presence in this richly detailed spiritual fresco. To the rear of the three figures was an altar surmounted by a large cross in front of which rested a young lamb—an unmistakable symbol for the sacrifice of the Mass. Lamb of God, Mass, Cross, Gospel, Virgin, apostolic tradition as personified by Saint John, Marian devotion as personified by Saint Joseph—here, it seemed, was a magnificent heaven-sent hieroglyph depicting the essence of the Catholic faith down the ages. And at the same time it left no doubt that the fullness of that glory could be found as easily in a tiny church in Ireland as in the splendor of Chartres Cathedral.

It was of course too good a vision not to share, and the two Marys, no doubt crossing themselves furiously and crying out something like "Holy saints and shamrocks!" dashed off through the deluge to spread the word. Soon, another sixteen witnesses were staring in wonder, and while most fell immediately to their knees or began saying the rosary, one, thirteen-year-old Patrick Hill, ventured so close to the figures he could see the lines and letters in the book the Evangelist was holding.

But the sight of all sights was the Virgin—wearing, like her male companions, a robe of righteousness, dazzlingly white, and covered by an equally bright cloak that fastened at her throat and fell to her ankles. On her head was a crown topped by crosses, and on her forehead was a rose—a symbol that seemed literally to affirm her title of "Mystical Rose", the designation long since given her because she had "pondered in her heart" the words of the angel. (In fact, Pope John Paul II, when he visited the shrine at Knock in 1979 to celebrate the centenary of Mary's appearance, offered in memoriam a rose of gold.) Meanwhile, as with visitors to an art gallery, some of the witnesses were busy picking out particular details that others tended to overlook. Three of them noted that Mary's feet were bare, and two of those who went closest to the figures observed that both the wall and the uncut grass in front of it remained miraculously dry even as the rain splashed down without let or hindrance.

Alas, not among the witnesses was Father Cavanaugh. Weary from his journey, rained-on enough for one day, and aware that his housekeeper, though far from an alcoholic, nevertheless "liked her drop", he had been less than galvanized by her breathless assurance that a great sight was there to be seen on the gable wall. Theorizing it was probably only the reflection of one of the church's stained-glass windows, he stayed put by the fire, thereby missing the sight of a lifetime: the Lady of roses, fountains, and gold with her rose on her forehead, her fountain the sky, and her gold apparent both in the crown she wore and the golden light that mounted up from the gable (people saw it for miles around).

Though Father Cavanaugh was not in the number, the number of those who were there for all or part of those two hours of light in the rain was convincingly large—a jury of twelve with six alternates. Indeed, Knock might almost have been called the "people's apparition". Rue du Bac, La Salette, and Lourdes had all been essentially "private" affairs, and even at Pontmain, with the community gathered as one, the Virgin had suffered only the little children to behold her. But Knock was for all who would come to the waters, regardless of age, sex, social status, or depth of devotion. Even those nowhere near saw the light—one, Patrick Walsh, who lived half a mile from Knock, thought someone had built a great fire on the church grounds—and, had they but taken themselves thither, could have seen what all those others saw: the Church of the Lamb, presented in all its divine truth and Marian mercy, terrible as an army with banners.

In the days and weeks that followed, the pilgrims started coming in force—both to see the people who had seen the vision and to pray in the church that had been its backdrop. Many came seeking cures—and cures were waiting. Ten days after the apparitions, a deaf child had his hearing restored. Not long after that, a man born blind made a pilgrimage to Knock—and returned home a *seeing* pilgrim. A dying man, so violently ill that he vomited blood most of the way while being carried to the church, was restored instantly—merely by drinking some water in which a scrap of cement from the gable wall had been dissolved. Before long, seven or eight cures were being reported each week. Not surprisingly, then, that little Irish village is today one of the world's great pilgrimage sites—a powerful reminder that whether on the hill of Tepeyac or the hill of Knock, before one witness or eighteen, where the Virgin appears, good things follow.

Pontmain and Knock, those two silent but eloquent appearances, were the last of the century's five Marian apparitions. It
may be only fanciful, yet those five visits seem almost to parallel
the rosary's five joyful mysteries. The first, the visit to Catherine
Labouré, with its revelation about Mary's mediating of all grace,
recalls the Annunciation, when the angel revealed to Mary
("full of grace") that she had been chosen to be the Mother of
God. The second, the visit to the mountain of La Salette, recalls
the Visitation, when Mary journeyed to the hill country of
Judea to visit her cousin Elizabeth. The third, the visit to
Bernadette, with its dramatic confirmation that Mary was the
eternally immaculate creature alone worthy to bear the Christ
Child, suggests the Nativity. The fourth, with Mary "presenting" a crucifix to the children of Pontmain, powerfully brings
to mind the Presentation of the Child Jesus. And the fifth, with
Mary appearing near the gable wall of the Knock church, reminds us of the Finding of the Child Jesus in the temple—for
on the Knock temple, if not *in* it, the villagers found him in the
form of a young lamb.

Be all of that as it may, a century of revelations and annuncia-
tions was at an end—though, to be sure, the century still had
twenty-one years to run. Those two remaining decades, though,
would be little enough time in which to contemplate realities as
deep as the rings of grace at the Rue du Bac, the healing
streams at La Salette and Lourdes, the beautiful sky show at
Pontmain, and the great tableau at Knock. *Sic semper Maria, gra-
tia plena.*

16

FATIMA: THE SONG OF MARY AND THE DANCE OF THE SUN

And a great sign appeared in heaven: a woman clothed with the sun, and the moon under her feet, and on her head a crown of twelve stars.

—Revelation 12:1

Who spread its canopy? Or curtains spun? Who in this bowling alley bowled the sun?

—Edward Taylor (1644–1729)

During the noise and anger of 1917, while poison gas and machine guns were making the world safe for democracy and dangerous for people, the Blessed Virgin quietly appeared to three young children near the Portuguese village of Fatima and said and did stupendous things aimed at getting the tribes of earth back on the narrow path. In fact, she appeared once a month for six months beginning with May, among other things exhorting the children—and through them, the entire Catholic world—to pray, do penance, and say the rosary for the conversion of a Russia about to banish cross and ikon in favor of hammer and sickle. And she spoke as one having authority. She spoke of a heaven two of the children would soon enter, of a purgatory where a departed teenage neighbor of theirs would be suffering till the world closes up shop, and of an apocalyptic hell, showing them a harrowing vision of the damned tumbling about like so many red-hot coals in a sea of fire. She promised signs and wonders, and in her last visit appeared to the children in the October sky in a series of majestic tableaus even as heaven confirmed all these things to the rest of mankind with an awesome display of solar fireworks.

Of all the Virgin's appearances, Fatima was the one that spoke with the loudest voice—and in the most urgent tone. There were good reasons for that. Not only was Leninist darkness masquerading as humanist light about to swallow up Russia, but a young German corporal was even then dreaming dreams of his thousand-year Reich, and the red horseman of the Apocalypse was brandishing not one sword but two—for the world war then going on and the world war yet to come. Time was speeding up, hell was breaking loose, and heaven, wanting earth to be warned that it might repent and be delivered, sent the Virgin. Indeed, so important was this new undertaking of Mary's that the angel of peace went forth to prepare her way as John the Baptist had once gone forth to prepare the way of the Lord. And that she might have messengers who would worthily and fittingly proclaim the great truths to be imparted, it chose three very young but highly suitable children—innocent, devout, and astonishingly brave.

The story began one warm early afternoon in the summer of 1916, when nine-year-old Lucia Abóbora and her cousins, eight-year-old Francisco and six-year-old Jacinta (Hyacinth) Marto, were roaming a countryside much like a landscape by Cézanne—languid pines, rocky soil, sun-withered grass, and a scattering of bright blue wild flowers. In fact, they were tending their families' sheep near the hilltop cave of Cabeco, not far from the village of Aljustrel, having shortly before finished lunch and followed up with a swift rosary. Now, while the sheep grazed in the shade of some nearby trees, the children relaxed, taking turns lobbing stones into the echoing valley below.

Suddenly a strong wind—much like the Virgin-heralding

wind Bernadette Soubirous experienced at Massabielle and almost certainly the "mighty rushing wind" of the Holy Spirit—
suddenly that wind began to whip through the pinetops, and as
the startled children looked around, they saw what it seemed to
be announcing: a dazzling light that was clearly racing in their
direction. By the time it halted near the entrance of the cave,
the children, more fascinated than afraid, could see that it was an
angel, a "transparent young man", no more than fourteen or
fifteen years of age. Lucia later described him as "more brilliant
than a crystal penetrated by the rays of the sun" and incompara-
bly beautiful.

His greeting was the standard reassuring one of so many
heavenly messengers in the Bible: "Be not afraid." Then he
added the words that in all likelihood indicated that he was
Michael, the angel traditionally associated with both concord
and battle: "I am the Angel of Peace. Pray with me." With that,
he knelt—as did the children—prostrated himself until his forehead touched the rock-strewn ground, and said words as simple
and straightforward as a child's: "My God, I believe, I adore, I
hope, and I love You. I beg pardon of You for those who do not
believe, do not adore, do not hope, and do not love You!" (In
Portuguese, with its musical vowel endings, the prayer is even
more striking: "Meu Deus! Eu creio, adoro, espero, e amo-
vos . . .".) Three times the angel prayed these words, and three
times the children repeated them. Then he arose and, before
vanishing as if he had been "dissolved in sunlight", uttered these
final words: "Pray thus. The hearts of Jesus and Mary are atten-
tive to the voice of your supplications."

Though so transported by what had happened they found it
hard to sleep in the days following, the children wisely said
nothing of their earnest visitor. Nor did they report anything of
what happened several weeks later, when the angel again appeared to them. This time he dropped by while they were at
play not far from the Abóbora cottage and urged them on to

sterner things: "Offer prayers and sacrifices constantly to the Most High. . . . Thus draw peace upon your country. I am its Guardian Angel, the Angel of Portugal [Eu sou o Anjo da sua guarda, o Anjo de Portugal]. Above all, accept and endure with submission the suffering the Lord will send you." The advice was zealously heeded: the children not only gave up small pleasures to help smooth the path of grace into the hearts of hard-shell sinners but spent hours at a time lying prostrate on the ground, lisping out again and again the prayer the angel had taught them: "Meu Deus! Eu creio, adoro, espero, e amo-vos."

The angel's third and final appearance took place when they were once again at the Cabeco cave. As before, the sheep were grazing nearby, and as before, the children had just prayed the rosary. But now, instead of showering rocks on the valley below, they were reciting the brief phrases of the angel's prayer. Suddenly once again there was the light racing toward them and soon, there in front of them, dazzling and beautiful, was once again the angel himself. But this time, like some celestial Melchizedek come to earth, he held in his left hand the chalice of salvation and in his right, poised above it, a consecrated Host, drops of Blood falling from it into the chalice. Wonder followed wonder. As Lucia was to describe it in her memoirs many years later:

> Leaving the chalice suspended in the air, the angel knelt down beside us and made us repeat three times: "Most Holy Trinity, Father, Son, Holy Spirit, I adore You profoundly and offer You the most precious Body, Blood, Soul and Divinity of Jesus Christ, present in all the tabernacles of the earth, in reparation for the outrages, sacrileges, and indifference with which He Himself is offended. And through the infinite merits of His Most Sacred Heart and of the Immaculate Heart of Mary, I beg of You the conversion of poor sinners."

Then, rising, he took the chalice and the Host in his hands. He gave the sacred Host to me, and shared the Blood from the chalice between Jacinta and Francisco (they had not yet received their First Communion), saying as he did so: "Take and

drink the Body and Blood of Jesus Christ, horribly outraged by
ungrateful men! Make reparation for their crimes and console
your God."

Once again he prostrated himself on the ground and repeated
with us three times more the same prayer, "Most Holy Trinity . . ." and then disappeared. We remained a long time in this
position, repeating the same words over and over again. When
at last we stood up we noticed that it was already dark, and
therefore time to return home.

The mighty prelude was over. Heaven had opened the great
door separating the celestial from the terrestrial, and through it
had descended, with its own greater magic and miracle, a kind
of daytime *Midsummer Night's Dream*, not with fairies hanging a
pearl in every cowslip's ear, but with heaven's own wind, light,
and angel giving to airy nothing a local habitation and a name.
The children had heard the voice of one crying in the wilderness, beheld the Lamb of God under the sacramental veils, and
experienced the eternal moment of the Last Supper. Meanwhile, they had also been prepared—by vision, sacrifice, and
prayer—for the great new work that would begin eight months
later. Fittingly, that would be in May, the month of roses and
rebirth, the month that as far back as the thirteenth century had
been dedicated to Mary.

May 13, 1917, was a Sunday, but sheep have to graze even on the
sabbath, and so it was that around noon that day, the now ten-
year-old Lucia and her two young cousins took their flock to
the meadows owned by Lucia's father at the soon-to-be-leg-
endary Cova da Iria. The sheep were busily nibbling at the furze
on the hill overlooking the Cova, and the children were impro-
vising a kind of "house" in a nearby thicket, when suddenly
they saw a brilliant flash of what they took to be lightning—the
harmless-looking blue sky notwithstanding. Alarmed, they
sprinted downhill and took shelter under an oak tree—only to

be panicked anew by a second flash of light. This time they had raced a hundred yards or so when they found themselves witnesses of a new wonder. There, directly in front of them, was a ball of light, and in its center stood a dazzlingly bright Lady, suspended in the air just above a three-foot-high shrub called the azinheira (at Lourdes, it will be recalled, our Lady had similarly appeared above a rosebush).

Perhaps because the Fatima apparitions were meant to demonstrate, among other things, the authenticity of Mary's scriptural designation as "a woman clothed with the sun", she appeared to the children in her full solar glory. Lucia would later describe her as "a Lady all of white . . . clearer and more intense than a crystal cup full of crystalline water penetrated by the rays of the most glaring sun". Both countenance and garments seemed composed of the same dazzling light, and her white mantle was edged by a sunlike gold. Glittering rosary beads hung down from her prayerfully clasped hands, and the "indescribably beautiful" face, meanwhile, could not be looked at steadily because it hurt the eyes and obliged the children either to blink or look away. Even had this been another silent apparition like Knock or Pontmain, it would have been eloquent in the highest, but to use cinema parlance, Fatima was very much a "talkie". The conversation began with the Virgin speaking in what Lucia described as a low musical voice, telling the children they had nothing to fear. Lucia's first question, startlingly direct, initiated a sequence whose combination of matter-of-fact language with exalted spiritual reality is a bit like reading Dante in an Ernest Hemingway translation:

"Where does your Excellency come from?"

"I am from heaven."

"And what is it you want of me?"

"I come to ask you to come here for six months in succession, on the thirteenth day at this same hour. Then I will tell you who I am, and what I want . . ."

"And shall I go to heaven too?"

"Yes, you will."

"And Jacinta?"

"Also."

"And Francisco?"

"Also. But he will have to say many rosaries!"

This little matter of where the children would be spending their eternity resolved, Lucia became curious about the fate of two village girls who had recently died.

"Is Maria da Neves now in heaven?"

"Yes, she is.

"And Amelia?"

"She will be in purgatory till the end of the world."

One can imagine the gasps and gulps that must have been heard in three little throats at hearing words like "purgatory" and "the end of the world" in one sentence, but the Lady was wasting no time getting to the point of her visit:

"Do you wish to offer yourselves to God, to endure all the suffering that he may please to send you, as an act of reparation for the sins by which he is offended, and to ask for the conversion of sinners?"

That sounded good to the children. "Yes, we do."

"Then you will have much to suffer. But the grace of God will be your comfort."

At the words "*a graça de Deus*", the Lady opened her hands, and from the palms issued the grace of God made visible—two streams of brilliant light that both surrounded and penetrated the children, "making us", as Lucia later expressed it, "see ourselves in God". Eighty-seven years before, in 1830, the Virgin had explained to Catherine Labouré that the rings she wore in that great vision were symbols of the graces she shed upon those who asked for them; now, here, under the sun of Portugal, sight confirmed what symbol had suggested. Soon afterward, the Lady gave her little trio a final injunction: "Say the rosary every day to obtain peace for the world and the end of the war." She then slowly rose, leaving the azinheira far below, and, instead of simply vanishing, as in her previous apparitions, glided away toward the east, until as Lucia expressed it, "she disappeared in the immensity of the distance."

Now, the biggest immediate question was whether the younger children would follow the prudent advice of Lucia, ignore the exhilaration they felt, resist the temptation to speak of what had exhilarated them, and, as in the case of the angel's visits the year before, say nothing. For Jacinta, who kept repeating, "*Ai, que Senhora tão bonita!*" ("Oh, what a pretty lady!"), it would prove more than seven-year-old flesh and blood could bear. That very day she told her mother, who, half amused and half appalled, told Jacinta's father. Soon after, in the middle of Sunday dinner in the Marto household, Manuel Pedro Marto, father, faithful churchgoer, and veteran character analyst, insisted on hearing the story in full from both his children. Since he knew them to be truthful, what they proceeded to tell him with such obvious enthusiasm, such believability in detail and gesture, and with such a startling capacity to recite long words they would never have heard before, left him more than a little impressed.

"The power of God is great", he said. "We don't know what this is, but it'll turn out to be something real." That terse expression of prudent faith would prove to be one of the great understatements ever. Meanwhile, word reached the Abóbora household, and when it did, Lucia, though totally blameless, met with utter disbelief and contempt from both her parents and her sisters, thereby getting her first taste of the unpleasantness she had been promised.

Family reactions notwithstanding, the young shepherds went about carrying out their assignment of making sacrifices for sinners with astounding zeal—praying and fasting, giving their lunches away to beggar children, and frequently making a meal

for themselves out of pine cones, mulberries, and wild mush-
rooms. A month passed, and it was time for the Lady's second
appearance. Alas for that, it seemed that Lucia's father, after one
too many one evening, let slip to his drinking comrades the
story of the first apparition. As a result, that June 13, when the
children went to the Cova to wait for the Lady, a ragged troupe
of fifty or so pilgrims, cure-seekers, and professional onlookers
tagged along—and not altogether in vain, as it turned out.
Though they did not truly see and hear Mary (as of course the
children clearly did), there were crumbs.

Some heard the sound of a voice so faint that one witness
compared it to the buzzing of a bee; and all saw the effect created by the Lady's departure—the new leaves on top of the
azinheira drawn in her direction as if her garments had trailed
across them. (And this, from all accounts, was not some vaguely
remembered, impressionistic detail; on the contrary, it took several hours for those leaves to return to their usual position.) At
the very least, both of these phenomena were fascinating re-
minders of Saint Paul's famous line in First Corinthians 13:12:
"For now we see through a glass darkly."

The children, meanwhile, were seeing "face to face"—and
also hearing remarkable things: a certain sick person whose cure
Lucia requested would be healed "if he is converted"; Jacinta
and Francisco would soon be going to heaven; Lucia would remain on earth—among other things learning to read; and as to
the grand design behind all these marvels, that had to do with
Jesus' wish to make use of the children to establish the devotion
to Mary's Immaculate Heart. As if all this were not enough, the
Lady opened her hands as before, and the rays of grace again
streamed forth; suspended in front of the palm of the Lady's
right hand was "a heart encircled by thorns". The children at
once understood that "it was the Immaculate Heart of Mary
outraged by the sins of humanity, for which there must be
reparation." At the same time they saw a vision of the Trinity

enfolding them, with Jesus wearing an expression of "infinite sadness".

These heart-stopping details came across only as fantasy and fame-seeking to Lucia's mother, a doubting Thomas of the first magnitude. Furious that her daughter had created a commotion involving not merely her two young cousins but a pack of gossiping villagers as well, she marched her tearful ten-year-old to the Fatima rectory and turned her over to the pastor, a Father Ferreira, with the brutal words: "Tell the prior now that you lied, so that on Sunday he can say in the church that it was a lie and end the whole thing before all the people go running to Cova da Iria to pray in front of a bush!" But it seemed the priest was generally impressed with Lucia's truthfulness. The problem was that it did not seem to him like a revelation from heaven. "In fact," he said, reserving his opinion for a later time even as he sent a chill into the heart of Lucia, "it may be a deception of the devil."

Lucia's mother, meanwhile, was not about to reserve *her* opinion and enthusiastically confirmed the Virgin's prophecy of Lucia's earthly tribulation by continuing to savage her daughter verbally, adding, for good measure, occasional blows and kicks. Not surprisingly, caught between the grim possibility of a satanic impersonation at the Cova and the even grimmer reality of a persecuting mother at home, Lucia had scant desire to return to the azinheira when July 13 rolled around. But urged on by her little cousins, she conquered her reluctance and went with them that hot day at the usual hour to the usual place.

This time, instead of a mere fifty people looking on, some two thousand curious souls—including all four parents—had come to the Cova, there, according to their separate lights, to pray, ponder, gape, or sneer. Undismayed, the children took up their usual positions, began the rosary, and gazed toward the east, from where, appropriately, had come and would come again that Woman clothed with the sun. And come she did, heralded by Lucia's "Take off your hats!" Ti Marto, the only one of the visionaries' parents willing to suspend disbelief, saw through the dark glass of imperfect faith just enough to behold something on the order of a small white cloud descend on the azinheira. As time passed, he also heard a faint buzzing that he described as sounding like "a horsefly in an empty waterpot". But all that time the children, like Saint Paul, were coming to visions and revelations of the Lord.

These privileged glimpses into the mind of heaven and the future of the world were sometimes reassuring and sometimes terrifying. The first was that in October that year the Lady would reveal who she was and what she wished and that she would perform "a miracle that everyone will have to believe". The second was that beneath the earth, as penetrated by the radiance from her hands, was a "sea of fire and plunged in this fire the demons and the souls as if they were red-hot coals . . . falling on all sides without weight or equilibrium among shrieks and groans of sorrow and despair". And the children, to their shock and horror, witnessed the vision of hell they described. The third was that to save many from that unthinkable fate "God wishes to establish in the world the devotion to my Immaculate Heart."

The fourth made it clear that if souls did not stop offending God, another and worse war would begin in the reign of Pius XI (for the record, that Pope died in 1939, the same year World War II began). The fifth was a follow-up to the warning about the new war: "When you shall see a night illuminated by an unknown light, know that it is the great sign that God gives you that He is going to punish the world." (That grim luminescence would arrive on January 25, 1938, the feast of Saint Paul's conversion on being blinded by light from heaven—a mysterious and eerie red light all across Europe that would be dismissed as a sport of nature traceable to the Northern Lights.) Indeed, the warning was apparently repeated privately for the war's chief enthusiasts. In his book *Inside the Third Reich*, Albert Speer, Hitler's architect, revealed that he, Hitler, and Hitler's staff witnessed a strange light at 2 A.M. on the morning of August 22, 1939—exactly ten days before World War II began: "We stood on the terrace of the Berghof and marveled at a rare natural spectacle. Northern lights of unusual intensity threw red light on the legend-haunted Untersberg across the valley. . . . The last act of the *Götterdämmerung* could not have been more effectively staged. The same red light bathed our faces and our hands. . . . Abruptly turning to one of his military adjutants, Hitler said: 'Looks like a great deal of blood. This time we won't bring it off without violence.'"

In any case, after these five staggering revelations about hope, hell, salvation, and war, our Lady concluded with five additional disclosures, all considerably less soul-disturbing (with the conspicuous exception of the last): (1) that "I come to ask the consecration of Russia to my Immaculate Heart"; (2) that "in the end my Immaculate Heart will triumph"; (3) that "in Portugal, the dogma of the faith will always be kept"; (4) that after each mystery of the rosary, this request should be added: "O my Jesus, forgive us our sins, save us from the fires of hell; lead all souls to heaven, especially those in most need of Thy mercy"; and (5) a final, reportedly frightening secret that she wanted disclosed no later than 1960 but that is yet to pass beyond the walls of the Vatican.

The children were not only shaken by Mary's profound revelations out of the heart of light, but they were also beset by new troubles out of the world of this present darkness. Gossip inevitably sent the tale winging throughout all of Portugal, and from Lisbon's chief daily newspaper, the anticlerical and aptly named *O Seculo*, came the typical curled-lip response: "A Message from Heaven—Commercial Speculation?" Other lords of the pen suggested the Jesuits had fabricated the story to recover the prestige they had lost when republic had replaced monarchy in 1910. Meanwhile, the children were repeatedly being sought out by a motley tribe of sensation mongers, including numerous fore-runners of the jet set, dropping by in their pearls and picture hats to ask such probing theological questions as: "Did our Lady also have goats and sheep when she was a little girl? Did our Lady ever eat potatoes?" And for Lucia, at least, home was no sanctu-ary. Bitter because the crowds had destroyed the family's veg-etable gardens at the Cova da Iria, Lucia's mother and sisters counseled her to "Go eat what you find growing at the Cova." Often, afraid to ask for any food at all, she went to bed nourished only by faith, prayer, and pine cones.

And just when it seemed things could not get any darker, they turned pure charcoal. From the administrator of the Council of Ourem, the district's seat of government, came a summons for the children, "notorious disturbers of the public peace", to present themselves for trial on August 11—two days before the next apparition. The summoning official, Arturo de Oliveira Santos, was a villain straight out of central casting. This fire-breathing Mason and worshiper of the Goddess Reason, this father of children named Democracia, Republica, and Libertad, this blacksmith owner of a smithy called the Forge of Progress, was not only president of his Masonic lodge but presi-dent of the administration and deputy judge of commerce. By 1917, all of this had made him, at the interesting age of thirty-three, a kind of all-purpose local dictator, not to mention ruth-less enemy of the Church.

Of the three summoned children, only one, Lucia, appeared before the tyrant. Her father, thinking it prudent to comply with the administrator's wishes, had transported her the nine miles to Ourem on the back of his burro. The staunch Manuel Marto, by contrast, feeling the distance was too great a one for young children to undertake, had appeared at the town hall on their behalf and said just that. Santos accepted that explanation mildly enough and, after hearing Lucia out, let her go—but with a chilling farewell threat: "If you don't tell that secret, it'll cost you your life." And that evil-hearted comment was just the beginning.

On August 13, the day of the fourth apparition, the administrator showed up in Fatima, proclaimed that he was interested in seeing the miracle for himself, and, after taking the children for a question-and-answer session with Father Ferreira, calmly kidnaped them, driving off with them and locking them up in a room in his own house in Ourem. There, he piled outrage upon outrage. At ten o'clock the next morning, he marched the trio of waifs to the town hall and attempted to perform the secular equivalent of an exorcism. "Beautiful lady? All in white? Radiant? Preposterous! And that secret you speak of—tell me! If not, it's torture and death. Do you hear me?" No luck. Whereupon this champion of the rights of man had the children locked up in the town prison with an all-star cast of drunkards and pickpockets.

When that had no effect except to make the children pray more and worry less, the tyrant had them brought to his office. When they still refused to divulge their mysterious secret, he spoke with the perfect equanimity of perfect evil: "Very well. I've tried to save you. But since you won't obey the government, you shall be boiled alive in a cauldron of hot oil." With that, he had Jacinta taken away by a guard doing his best Boris Karloff imitation, who soon returned to announce, "That one's fried. Now for the next one!" And so it went, child by child. But since they were all too clearly willing martyr material, the exasperated fiend had no choice but to return them to Fatima, which he did two days after the kidnaping.

The young shepherds had of course missed the August 13 visit to the azinheira, but a make-up visit took place on the nineteenth in a new place—a hollow called Valinhos, where they had taken their sheep for Sunday grazing. And, interestingly enough, the Virgin again appeared over an azinheira. This time she reminded her young devotees that she wanted them to continue to go to the Cova da Iria on the thirteenth of each month, to continue to recite the rosary every day, and to continue to make sacrifices for sinners. All was back on schedule.

September 13 would be the next to last of the six Cova appearances and, knowing that, people poured in—clergy and laity, rich and poor, the devout and the curious. And that day, many got at least a taste of the miraculous, for they saw, even as they cried out in greeting, not the Virgin herself, to be sure, but the remarkable conveyance enclosing her. As Monsignor Joao Quarerma wrote in 1932, fifteen years after the event: "There was not a cloud in the azure sky. . . . To my great astonishment I saw clearly and distinctly a luminous globe that moved from the east toward the west, slowly and majestically gliding down across the distance. My friend also looked and had the good fortune to enjoy the same unexpected and enchanting apparition. . . . All who were near us observed what we did. . . . Many others, however, saw nothing."

The children, meanwhile, received their usual private vision of the Lady herself. She reported, among other things, that God was content with their sacrifices and that indeed they had been going a bit too far in their penitential practice of wearing a skin-abrading rope night and day: from now on, days only. She also gave them the electrifying news that in October, "Our Lord will come also." And there was more: "And Our Lady of the Sorrows, Our Lady of Mount Carmel, and Saint Joseph with the Child Jesus to bless the world." Finally, she reminded them of that earlier promise: "In October, I will perform the miracle so that all will believe."

The great day was October 13, 1917—just nine days before Lenin would reenter Russia from his hiding place in Finland to lead the revolution during the "ten days that shook the world". Fatima, though far less reported on by historians and journalists, would be something even more startling: the one day that shook the sun.

A torrential rain had fallen all morning, and the sky was still springing leaks over the now muddy landscape when the three young visionaries and their parents set off for the Cova. When they arrived, they saw what pure-eyed faith, white-handed hope, and even curiosity-seeking scepticism had wrought—seventy thousand wet and miserable people huddling under black umbrellas and soaked blankets. The central figures in the drama at last made their way through this madding crowd to the now denuded (because of relic-collectors) azinheira, touched up for the occasion by bright garlands of flowers. However, even as noontime, the traditional hour for the apparitions, drew near, the eastern sky remained unrelentingly leaden, and a visiting priest dampened spirits even further by checking his watch repeatedly and finally declaring: "Midday is past. Away with all this! It's all an illusion!" The children ignored this Sanballat-like comment and remained where they were, even as the minutes dragged by. Soon, shortly after Lucia cried out, "Put down your umbrellas!" their great visitor was once again standing above the flower-decked azinheira.

The Lady's message contained the familiar instructions about saying the rosary and offending God no more, but following that, she did something unprecedented. She opened her hands and disappeared into the radiance issuing from them, reappearing high above as part of a Holy Family tableau symbolizing the rosary's joyful mysteries: herself in white with a blue mantle, Saint Joseph all in white and holding the Child Jesus in his arms, the Infant in bright red. This heart-lifting sight was followed by a second great tableau, one symbolizing the sorrowful mysteries and presenting an unforgettable image: our Lady as the Mater Dolorosa, her divine Son standing beside her, grieving on his way to Calvary but pausing to make the sign of the cross over the multitude. Finally, in a third tableau, this one symbolizing the glorious mysteries, she appeared as Our Lady of Mount Carmel and crowned in all her quiet majesty as Queen of Heaven and Earth, her infant Son upon her knee.

And even as the children were staring in ecstasy at these breathtaking epiphanies, the crowd was receiving a vision in the suddenly blue sky that made it clear that if there was nothing new under the sun there was something very old and very powerful behind it. For twelve astonishing minutes, the sun did such things as take on the appearance of a silver disk, "dance", whirl like a fire-wheel, throw out streamers of flame, plunge in a terrifying zigzag motion toward the earth, zigzag upward again, then quietly return, like an obedient animal, to its perch in the hand of the invisible Ringmaster, there to resume its standard routine. Avelino de Almeida, a Freemason and the editor of Lisbon's largest newspaper, *O Seculo*, had gone in person to the Cova da Iria, and his dry and measured account of the event is wonderfully convincing—if only because of his painfully obvious attempt to remain matter of fact about the astounding things he saw:

> . . . a spectacle unique and incredible if one had not been a witness of it. . . . One can see the immense crowd turn toward the sun, which reveals itself free of the clouds in full noon. The great star of day makes one think of a silver plaque, and it is possible to look straight at it without the least discomfort. It does not burn, it does not blind. It might be like an eclipse. . . . Before the astonished eyes of the people, whose attitude carries us back to biblical times, and who, full of terror, heads uncovered, gaze into the blue of the sky, the sun has trembled, and the sun has made some brusque movements, unprecedented and outside of all cosmic laws. The sun has "danced," according to the typical expression of the peasants. . . . The people ask one another if they have seen anything and what they have seen. The greatest number avow that they have seen the trembling and dancing of the sun. Others, however, swear

that the sun turned around on itself like a wheel of fireworks; that it fell, almost to the point of burning the earth with its rays. . . . Another tells that he has seen it change color successively. . . . But what all aspired for—the Sign in the sky—has sufficed to satisfy them, to enroot them in their Breton-like faith.

To their credit, the anticlerical papers published full accounts, complete with pictures of the wet and gaping crowds. Still, they did bring up the usual theories of mass hysteria—theories that had to be jettisoned when reliable witnesses reported seeing the sun's *danse macabre* from substantial distances. The noted poet Alfonso Lopes Vieira, in fact, saw it from his house at San Pedro de Moel, some forty kilometers from Fatima.

One predictable dissenter was Arturo de Oliveira Santos, the administrator of Ourem, Freemason and terrorizer of children. Though he was not at Fatima on October 13, that did not stop him from insisting that nothing miraculous had taken place. The sun apart, his star was clearly falling, and alas for his promising career, he was removed from office following a coup d'état two months after the miracle. He was last heard of when he was injured by the premature explosion of a bomb he was making to throw at selected members of the new government.

Francisco and Jacinta Marto, as foretold by the Virgin, completed their earthly travail at a very early age and after great suffering—both dying of bronchial complications resulting from the influenza that swept through Europe like a latter-day Black Plague following World War I. Lucia Abóbora, after some preliminary schooling during which she acquired the literary skills that enabled her to tell her astonishing story to the world, entered the Sisters of Saint Dorothy and took the name Maria das Dores (Mary of the Sorrows). Today (1998), at the age of ninety-one, this ascetic nun remains a living reminder of the sacrifices required of those who would help make reparation for a sin-besotted world.

The devotion at the Cova da Iria, meanwhile, not only continued but grew. Until 1921, the Lady of roses, fountains, and gold had "spoken" only in the gold bordering her gown; that year she spoke through her two other great symbols as well. Dom José Alves Correira da Silva, the new bishop of Leiria (which includes the Cova da Iria, Aljustrel, and Fatima), reportedly was won over by a miraculous rain of flowers that he witnessed at the Cova, and later, when he ordered some workmen to make a cistern near the shrine whereby to collect rain for pilgrims, a spring of pure clear water burst through the dry, rocky soil—ultimately to become both the main supply of the local peasants and the source of numerous miracles. Perhaps the most striking was the June 1946 healing of Maria José da Silva, whose tuberculosis disappeared in the twinkling of an eye. The event caused a sensation almost as great as the events of 1917.

Also in 1946, the grim prophecy of war fulfilled and finally past, Sister Maria das Dores, then thirty-nine years old, was allowed to return to the Cova for the first time in a quarter of a century—and there she saw the Kingdom of Heaven's mustard seed grown to prodigious size and beauty: majestic gates leading down to the Virgin's fountain, a great white basilica on the northern hill, three chapels, a seminary, and a new convent. The little girl whose own mother had doubted her word had become a prophet not without honor. Nor had the faithful forgotten those saintly waifs with whom she had herded sheep and witnessed miracles under the blue Portuguese sky. Their bodies had been consigned to the earth of the old Fatima cemetery under the simple, eloquent monument Lucia visited that day in 1946:

HERE LIE THE MORTAL REMAINS
OF JACINTA AND FRANCISCO MARTO
TO WHOM OUR LADY APPEARED

The year 1925 was one in which everything seemed larger than life, not to mention wilder and stranger. In Germany, economic depression and moral depravity walked hand in hand through the ragpicker-filled streets and the cocaine-selling cafés. In Paris, more writers and painters than ever before drank their absinthe and cheerfully proclaimed themselves what an automobile mechanic had said of them to Gertrude Stein: *une génération perdue*—a lost generation. In America, the stock market climbed to new heights and so did flagpole sitters, aerial stuntmen, and such idols of sport as Babe Ruth, Jack Dempsey, and Red Grange. And it was also in 1925 that the brilliant young F. Scott Fitzgerald wrote the novel that seemed to sum up the madness better than any other work of art or social history, *The Great Gatsby*. In a famous passage, one that almost suggests a modern Dante at work, he found an unforgettable image for the sterility of an age addicted to good times and bad ideas:

> About halfway between West Egg and New York . . . is a valley of ashes—a fantastic farm where ashes grow like wheat into ridges and hills and grotesque gardens, where ashes take the forms of houses and chimneys and rising smoke and, finally, with a transcendent effort, of ash-grey men, who move dimly and already crumbling through the powdery air. . . . But above the grey land and the spasms of bleak dust that drift endlessly over it, you perceive, after a moment, the eyes of Doctor T. J. Eckleburg. The eyes of Doctor T. J. Eckleburg are blue and gigantic—their irises are one yard high. They look out of no face, but, instead, from a pair of enormous yellow spectacles that pass over a nonexistent nose. Evidently some wild wag of an oculist set them there to fatten his practice in the borough of Queens, and then sank down himself into eternal blindness, or forgot them and moved away. But his eyes, dimmed a little by many paintless days under sun and rain, brood on over the solemn dumping ground.

That was one vision in the year 1925. Another was the private vision given to Lucia Abóbora in her cloister cell by the Blessed Virgin on December 10 of that prophetic year: "Look, my daughter, at my Heart surrounded with the thorns with which ungrateful men wound it by their blasphemies and iniquities." Here, however, was not merely a vision but a revelation in which the Virgin promised "to assist at the hour of death, with the graces necessary for salvation" all those who for five consecutive first Saturdays of the month carry out a devotion that includes confession, Communion, rosary, and meditation.

For better or worse, those two very different 1925 visions are with us still. The eyes of Doctor T. J. Eckleburg continue to brood on over a valley of ashes that may yet engulf the world, while the heart pierced by a sword continues to speak to those who can believe in a Woman great enough to be clothed with the sun and in the God who tailored it that she might shine the more brightly.

17

LIGHT IN BELGIUM:
THE VIRGIN OF THE GOLDEN HEART
AND THE VIRGIN OF THE POOR

Far from the madding crowd's ignoble strife
Their sober wishes never learn'd to stray;
Along the cool sequester'd vale of life
They kept the noiseless tenor of their way.
— Thomas Gray, "Elegy Written in a Country Churchyard"

Fatima was an event so momentous in the apparitional life of
Mary as almost to make any further appearances seem an anti-
climax—rather as if, after electrifying his audience with the rage
and thunder of *King Lear*, Edwin Booth had returned to the
stage and meekly recited a couple of the Bard's sonnets. The
difference was that the Blessed Virgin's post-Fatima "sonnets"
were minor epics in their own right and, far from being anticli-
mactic, showed her in a brilliant new light.

Beauraing and Banneux—those were the little towns in Belgium that Mary visited with fresh visions and new hope in those
grim Depression years 1932 and 1933. And her tender mercies
were badly needed. In the fifteen years that had elapsed since
Fatima, Europe had seen an uncomfortable number of bread-
lines, street riots, and firing squads. Grimmest of all was the
Russia on whose behalf the Virgin had vainly sought the ransom
of prayer. There, the Bolsheviks had long since established the

religion of terror, with Siberia as purgatory and Lenin's tomb the shrine representing the only acceptable form of afterlife—quality embalming.

Even outside of Russia, the world that had been made safe for democracy seemed to have forgotten what democracy meant. By 1932, Italy was ruled by Mussolini and his blackshirts; France, by Socialist radicals; and Germany, by a swooning republic that was soon to anoint Adolf Hitler as its chief knight and deliverer. The rest of Europe, meanwhile, was suffering under the curse of the three great "un's"—unbelief, unreason, and unemployment. Belgium was no exception.

Times were hard in that nation of steel, coal, petrochemicals, and small farms, that nation that had given the world the glorious medieval architecture of Antwerp, the great paintings of Peter Paul Rubens, and the full-throated beauties of the Flemish language. Now, in the midst of economic misery and spiritual malaise, it was about to give it something more: two new names to join the great litany of the Rue du Bac, La Salette, Lourdes, Pontmain, Knock, and Fatima.

The Virgin appeared first in Beauraing, a farming village of two thousand in southern Belgium—the area called the Walloon, the French-speaking part of that language-divided nation. About sixty miles southeast of Brussels and only a few miles from the French border, Beauraing was peripheral in every sense—at least until the evening of November 29, 1932.

The key earthly figure in the events of that memorable day was thirteen-year-old Gilberte Voisin, a deeply religious girl who attended the academy run by the Sisters of Christian Doctrine and who was fortunate enough to have parents who could more than make ends meet in those cash-short times: her father was assistant manager of the railroad station; her mother ran a paint and linoleum shop in the front of their house. Part of the financial surplus went for Gilberte's tuition at the academy—and it was at the academy that this improbable tale properly begins.

A day pupil, Gilberte normally stayed at school until 6:30 in the evening, when her fifteen-year-old sister Fernande and nine-year-old brother Albert arrived to walk her home. That November 29 they were joined by two friends, the sisters Degeimbre, fourteen-year-old Andrée and nine-year-old (Little) Gilberte. The youthful escorts were just about to ring the doorbell, as it happened, when Albert, the only boy in the pack, turned and looked in the direction of a railroad viaduct about fifty yards away and saw something not of this world.

"Look!" he shouted, proceeding to supply some highly unnecessary detail. "I see the Blessed Virgin dressed in white and walking above the bridge!" The girls, not used to seeing the Blessed Virgin at all, let alone dressed in white and walking above a bridge, at once looked, also saw her, and, eager to share the news with Big Gilberte, insistently rang the bell.

A Sister Valeria came to the door and, seeing who it was, called out the French equivalent of "Gilberte Voisin, front and center." Meanwhile, it took no gift of spiritual discernment to see that the children were frantically excited about something. But when the good nun was told what it was, she could not for the life of her see any Lady in white. Big Gilberte soon arrived, however, and, like the other four young people, clearly beheld the bright visitor above the dark viaduct.

Indeed, it almost seemed as if the Lady had been waiting for Gilberte, because soon after the thirteen-year-old's arrival on the scene, the Lady promptly vanished. With that, Gilberte gathered up her books, said good-night to the mystified nun, and joined the little band for the walk home and the inevitable speculations as to what their viaduct visitor had in mind. Even more mystified than Sister Valeria by the tale of the apparition were Gilberte's parents, the Voisins, and Mrs. Degeimbre, the widowed mother of the other two girls. For all of these older and wiser veterans of life, not seeing was not believing. Nor did they believe the next evening, when the children returned home with the same wild story about once again having seen the Virgin casually strolling above the same railway viaduct.

On the third evening, however, at last convinced the children were seeing *something*, perhaps a skilled impressionist from hell, Mrs. Degeimbre, stick in hand and accompanied by a posse of neighbors, followed the children rear-guard style all the way to the convent. There, they became considerably more sympathetic to what the young people had been trying to tell them— if only because of the convincing reverence with which, on entering the convent grounds, all of them abruptly knelt as one and commenced reciting a Hail Mary.

They had done so, in fact, because they had suddenly beheld the Virgin, not walking above a viaduct this time, but standing under the arched branch of a hawthorn tree. (Once again, it seems, she was associating herself with creation's green and flowering world. At Lourdes it had been a rosebush, at Fatima an azinheira. Now she had chosen a tree powerfully symbolic in two different ways—as a member of the rose family, it was especially appropriate to herself, and, as a bearer of fierce thorns, it was dramatically reminiscent of the mocking crown pressed down on her Son's brow.)

The children's description of the Virgin of Beauraing was very much in keeping with the accounts of other apparition witnesses from the Rue du Bac to Fatima. They described her as blue-eyed, about eighteen or twenty years old, wearing a long, heavily pleated white gown, and holding her hands together as if in prayer. In this first close-up appearance, by the way, she said nothing. But two evenings later, on December 2, she made it clear this would not be another silent apparition, like Pontmain or Knock.

By then, Mother Théophile, the superior of the convent, had locked the gates to try to keep the inevitable crowds at bay, and the children were obliged to kneel on the cobblestones outside the fence when they again beheld the Lady under the hawthorn. This time, young Albert got right to the point. "Are you the Immaculate Virgin?" he called out. The Lady smiled and nodded. "What do you want?" he asked. For the first time the Lady spoke: "Always be good." Leaving the children to ponder *that* little counsel of perfection, she promptly disappeared.

The apparitions continued evening after evening, becoming as much a part of social life in Beauraing as high tea in London. Inevitably, the crowds of visionary-watchers grew larger, and just as inevitably, the authorities decided to look into the matter. Starting on December 6, the children were regularly taken inside the convent after each apparition and questioned by a kind of coroner's jury of doctors and town officials. Meanwhile, the Virgin had managed to get in a word or two of her own, making it clear to her visionaries that she especially wanted them to be present on December 8, the feast of the Immaculate Conception.

The word about that command performance raced with the speed of a Belgian hare across the farming communities of the Walloon, and when the feast day arrived, the true believers arrived with it. When the little knot of children, escorted by their still dubious parents and four solemn doctors as eager to check the children's reflexes as any dog-testing Pavlov—when these principals made their way to the usual spot at ten minutes past six, the ranks of the witnesses had swollen to an astonishing fifteen thousand.

Though the lookers-on would see nothing celestial, they would see the children pass into their usual unearthly trance, a state much like ecstasy, in which they remained oblivious to everything except the Lady in white. Even as they knelt transfixed, staring in the direction of the tree, a certain Dr. Maistriaux took it upon himself to check Albert's pulse. Albert did not so much as glance down.

Meanwhile, the other three doctors aggressively pinched, slapped, and pricked the children, even pointed the beams of flashlights into their fixated eyes—all to no effect. And—shades of Bernadette at Massabielle and the candle flame that proved powerless to scorch her hand—one earnest man of science held a lighted match under Gilberte Voisin's left palm, neither provoking cry nor causing burn. Clearly, once in the trance, the children were no longer in a dimension subject to the laws of earthly physics. For both the watchdogs of science and the pilgrims of faith, then, that feast of the Immaculate Conception left no doubt that any time Mary speaks, it is also the feast of the Immaculate Attention.

The appearances continued all that December, and little milestones of special significance were duly recorded. On December 17, the Lady asked for "a chapel". On December 21, she declared once and eternally, "I am the Immaculate Virgin." On December 23, when she was asked, "Why do you come?" she responded, "That people might come here on pilgrimages." But the revelation that gave Beauraing its enduring stamp was the vision of December 29. That evening when the Virgin opened her arms in her usual gesture of farewell, fifteen-year-old Fernande Voisin, the eldest of the children, saw in the region of the Virgin's chest a heart of gold surrounded by glittering rays. The next day, two more of the children saw it, and on the following day, which was in fact New Year's Eve, all five were witnesses.

The golden heart has since come to be seen as a link to Fatima and Mary's emphasis there on her Immaculate Heart and its desire for frequent prayer. But even if it is seen as merely a symbol for garden-variety golden-heartedness, an endearing symbol it is. Indeed, had the revelation occurred in Renaissance times, the Virgin of the Golden Heart would doubtless have been a favorite subject of Leonardo, Botticelli, and other great translators of the holy into the language of paint. After the final showing of that heart of gold on December 31, in any case, the Virgin would appear only three times more—on January 1, 2, and 3 of 1933. And on January 2, she told the children that the next day—which would also mark the last visit—she would speak to each of them separately.

That bit of dramatic news brought out a great crowd on the bitterly cold evening of January 3. Bundled up in hats, head-cloths, mufflers, and overcoats, the milling thousands looked more like war refugees than pilgrims, but for every shiver endured there was the consolation of being able to tell by the children's reactions that exciting things were happening in that private twilight zone near the hawthorn tree. In fact, the visionaries were calmly saying the rosary when abruptly, just after they had finished the second decade, four of the five youngsters—obviously seeing the Lady and feeling something special if only because it would be their last meeting—abruptly and passionately shouted for joy. The fifth, Fernande Voisin (the first to have seen the heart of gold), saw nothing, however, and promptly burst into tears at this apparent snub. But though she could not know it then, her time was coming.

Meanwhile, as promised, the Virgin was speaking to each separately. And to Fernande's younger sister, Gilberte, the day-pupil whose presence at the academy had been the occasion of the apparitions, Mary imparted the most significant of her individual messages, what has in fact come to be called the Great Promise of Beauraing: "I will convert sinners."

Finally, four of the five separate messages received, all the children except Fernande proceeded into the convent for the usual round of "Now just what did you see and what did you hear?" Fernande, still weeping and wondering, chose to remain kneeling in front of that tree of life—a wait, as it turned out, that was to prove well worth it. Suddenly, in what seemed an echo of both Fatima and the burning bush of Moses, she heard a loud noise and looked up to see a ball of fire resting on the bare winter branches of the hawthorn—a sight, incidentally, that many in the crowd also reported seeing. With that, the Virgin appeared, asked the relieved Fernande if she loved the

Virgin's Son and the Virgin herself, and when Fernande said yes, asked the young girl to sacrifice herself—by which, of course, she meant, not diving into a volcano, but following an earnest regime of prayer and fasting.

And that was that. The brief conversation with Fernande ended the apparitions—except, of course, for the afterglow and the afterthoughts. As Saint Paul wrote to the Philippians: "Finally, brethren, whatsoever things are true . . . whatsoever things are pure, whatsoever things are lovely . . . if there be any virtue, and if there be any praise, think on these things." The true, pure, and lovely things of Beauraing, it seems, would not only be very much thought about, they would be very widely talked about.

Surprisingly, the story did what the story of Fatima had not done—it caused a sensation all across Europe. Books and articles streamed forth, both praising and damning, and there were enough "exposés" of this alleged fraud as to make it seem the children had been involved more in table-rapping séances than heavenly conversation. But fortunately the doubting Thomases were resolutely ignored: in the year 1933 alone, two million pilgrims visited the hawthorn, many of them, including hard-bitten socialists, joining the ranks of the sinners Mary had promised to convert and many others receiving miraculous cures.

One such miracle recipient was Maria van Laer of Turnhout in northern Belgium. A bedridden invalid for sixteen of her thirty-three years, she suffered from an especially virulent form of tuberculosis that had deformed her spinal column, ravaged one of her lungs, and riddled her with tumors that had developed into hideous open sores. Needless to say, the doctors were not optimistic. Indeed, when Maria van Laer was taken to Beauraing in June 1933, she was clearly beyond the help of anything but the large economy-size miracle. Wonderful to relate, that is just what she got.

Transported by ambulance from Turnhout and carried on a

stretcher to the hawthorn tree, Maria said her prayers, hoped her hopes, and then was taken into the Degeimbre home to talk with the younger of the two Gilbertes. That seemed to act as a booster shot to Maria's faith, because when she was then brought back to the hawthorn for a second visit, she found herself able to move for the first time in years. More than a little hopeful, she reentered the ambulance for the return trip to Turnhout and soon fell into a deep sleep. When she reached her hometown, shortly after midnight, she awoke—no doubt to the accompaniment of wild and incredulous shouts—to find herself completely cured: no pains, no tumors, no sores, no deformities. Here was a prodigious physical fulfillment of the Apostle's great spiritual declaration (2 Cor 5:17): "Therefore if any man be in Christ he is a new creature." This new creature became Sister Pudentia of the Franciscan Sisters of the Holy Family and, fittingly, a visiting nurse.

In 1935, the bishop of Namur (the diocese in which Beauraing is located) appointed a commission to look soberly into all these signs and wonders. When he died, his successor, Bishop André-Marie Charue, continued the investigation, and on February 2, 1943, a little more than ten years after Mary had first been seen walking above that railroad viaduct, he authorized public devotions to Our Lady of Beauraing. And on August 21, 1954, in fulfillment of the Lady's request for a chapel, a chapel was consecrated. Meanwhile, the hawthorn, that symbol of suffering and grace, received a large statue of our Lady and was surrounded by bronze railings, the inevitable resting place of the votive candles that would be kept perpetually ablaze by once and future pilgrims.

Apart from all its other distinctions, Beauraing included a doctrinal statement of more than passing interest. At Lourdes, seventy-five years before, the Virgin had said, "I am the Immaculate Conception." Now, she had added, "I am the Immaculate Virgin." The conclusion is inescapable: the Virgin of Bethlehem and the Virgin of Beauraing are one, perpetually virginal and perpetually immaculate.

※

If it was unusual, it was by no means unprecedented for Mary to appear at two separate sites in the same nation within a short period of time. After all, she had appeared at the French locales of La Salette in 1846 and Lourdes in 1858, a difference of a mere twelve years. But when, following her last apparition at Beauraing, she appeared in Banneux, another little Belgian town fifty miles to the north, the interval was not twelve years but a breathtakingly brief twelve days. As a result, this second visit was at first looked on as no more than a kind of postscript, as if the Virgin were tacking on a message that could just as well have been delivered at Beauraing. That it was, in fact, something quite different and distinct took some time to appreciate.

No doubt many of us, on first hearing of this new "miracle", would have shared the sentiments of a witty Banneux chronicler: "Beauraing, second edition." Indeed, considering how swiftly the events in Banneux followed those in its southern neighbor, it was natural to conclude that the matter had less to do with heavenly revelation than with earthly fantasy. Even the village priest, the twenty-nine-year-old Father Louis Jamin, grumblingly ascribed it to the power of suggestion. Referring to Mariette Beco, the child to whom the Virgin had appeared one frosty January night, he commented: "We don't see the Blessed Virgin as easily as that. Mariette has heard talk of the children of Beauraing." Like many others, Father Jamin had a theory, and he did not want it tampered with by anything as perplexing as a fact.

Mariette Beco was the eldest of the eleven children of Julien Beco, an overworked farmer who somehow managed to till the desolate soil of that part of Belgium industriously enough to keep bread on the table for thirteen mouths. Mariette, a strong-willed twelve-year-old with an adult sense of responsibility, not only helped her mother with the housekeeping but looked after the younger children. In fact, it was because she was hoping to spot her far-ranging ten-year-old brother, Julien, that, on the early evening of January 15, 1933, she lifted up the bedsheet that served as a front-window curtain and got the surprise of her young life.

Instead of Julien, she saw a beautiful and graciously smiling Lady, enveloped in light and wearing a pleated, dazzlingly white gown, a sky-blue sash, and a transparent veil. On her right foot was a golden rose, and on her right arm was draped a rosary with golden chain and cross. (For the record, the description almost precisely matches that given by Bernadette at Lourdes seventy-five years earlier.)

Whether or not Mariette sensed the identity of her exalted visitor, she reported her sighting to her mother, seated nearby, in the blandest possible terms: "Mama, there's a woman in the garden." "Oh, indeed", came the response. "Perhaps it's the Blessed Virgin." Still, solitary women in the gardens of Belgian farmers are not an everyday sight, and Madame Beco was curious enough to go to the window to see for herself. To her considerable surprise she saw, if not a woman, at least a white light in the form of a person of normal size—wearing, it seemed, a sheet over its head. "It's a witch!" she shrieked, abruptly pulling down the makeshift curtain.

Despite her mother's protests, Mariette looked again and soon witnessed something not only human and heartwarming but unique in the annals of Marian apparitions: she saw the Lady lift her right hand to the level of her head and beckon with her index finger. The flattered girl at once took the hint and headed for the garden. But the staunch Madame Beco, not of a mind to have her eldest carried off by a luminescent witch, intercepted her and pointedly locked the door. And for one night at least, that was that.

Mariette's father, returning from the earthy reality of feeding cows and pigs to be met with this gossamer tale of a spiritual visitor who may have been either a heavenly visitor, a witch, or a light, did not know what to think. But at least he did not object to Mariette going forth to repeat her tale to the closest thing Banneux could offer in the way of a specialist in visions and revelations—Father Jamin. And that, as it turned out, resolved nothing. When Mariette came to see him the next day with her story of the visitor in white, the priest faithfully recorded her remarks, declared he was impressed by her directness and sincerity, and believed not a word of what he was hearing.

Fortunately for Mariette's peace of mind, another apparition, even more dramatic than the first, was soon to follow. At seven o'clock on the cold evening of January 18, three nights after the Lady first appeared in the garden, Mariette, moved by a mysterious impulse, abruptly sailed out the front door, walked a short distance along the path that led to the front gate, then suddenly knelt and began saying the rosary. Her watchful father was right behind, it seems, convinced now that it was more madness than miracle. Yet it seems that though he desperately meant to pick her up and carry her back inside, he found that something irresistibly prevented him from so much as touching her. Meanwhile, according to Mariette's account, the Virgin was even then descending toward her from a point between the tops of two pine trees—yet another plant of honor to go with the rosebush of Lourdes, the azinheira of Fatima, and the hawthorn of Beauraing.

Soon the Lady was only five feet away, standing on a small gray cloud a foot above the earth. Mariette continued the rosary while the Lady moved her lips in response, apparently joining in. After a time, though, she beckoned with her index finger as she had during her first appearance, and Mariette promptly followed. Floating on her little cloud, the Lady proceeded through the opening in the fence and onto the road beyond, while the flustered Julien Beco—in the meantime he had rounded up his cousin Michael Charleseche and the latter's eleven-year-old son—desperately shouted to his fast-stepping daughter: "Where are you going? Come back!" Mariette's answer must have seemed like the response of some incurably deluded mental patient: "She calls me!"

The frantic little farce continued for some three hundred feet down the road and through three additional kneeldowns by Mariette (she stopping whenever the lady stopped), with the two men and the boy following at a distance of twenty-five yards and one eternal gulf. Finally, M. Beco's perplexing off-spring turned sharply off the road and fell to her knees by the side of a ditch—which, not surprisingly for any follower of the Lady of roses, fountains, and gold—suddenly began brimming with a previously unknown spring.

Nor was it merely to be looked at. "Place your hands in the water", the lady commanded. Mariette did so, and the sound of splashing in a ditch where there had never previously been any liquid other than rainwater startled the trio of watchers, even then looking on in great Belgian-farmer bafflement under the cold moon. There was to be yet another surprise. The three suddenly heard Mariette, repeating the Virgin's words, say aloud, "This stream is reserved for me", and, finally, "*Au revoir.*"

Whether because of the miraculous calling forth of a spring where no spring had been or the conviction apparent in his daughter's manner, Julien Beco, less a fallen-away Catholic than an exhausted one, found his faith beginning to revive. He not only saw to it that Father Jamin was informed of these piquant happenings, he made an appointment the next day to confess and receive Communion.

Be that as it may, there was more to come in the way of building faith and changing hearts. On January 19, at the same magic hour of seven o'clock, Mariette set the stage for a new and highly reassuring revelation when she quickly pulled on her coat, shot out the front door, whisked down the steps, abruptly fell to her knees a few paces beyond, and resumed her wintry vigil. When her visitor once more appeared, at long last the young girl decided it was time to ask the vital question, and did: "Who are you, lovely Lady?" The response was both immediate and arresting: "I am the Virgin of the Poor."

"The Virgin of the Poor." In time, this was to become the signature phrase of Banneux, the statement of identity setting that apparition apart from the previous seven and signaling the world at large that a figure far greater than Marx or Lenin was concerned with the sufferings of the have-nots. Following this dramatic revelation, the Virgin again led Mariette to the spring and declared it "reserved for all nations—to relieve the sick".

Meanwhile, word was beginning to spread, and the next night, some thirty people were there saying their rosaries with icy fingers in the Beco garden when Mariette looked up and, once more seeing the Lady coming down between the tall pines, called out, "Here she is!" Though it would turn out "she" was there only for a brief visit, it would be a memorable one.

No doubt the most important thing the Lady did that night was to request that a chapel be built. But the most *interesting* thing she did belonged to the architecture of gesture. In a kind of supernatural laying on of hands, the Lady unclasped her prayerfully joined palms, placed them on Mariette's shoulders, and then raised her right hand and blessed the young girl with the sign of the cross—an honor beyond the dreams of knighthood or the confirmations of bishops. It was a blessing Mariette would have all the more reason to treasure when the jibes and jeers of schoolmates became all but unbearable in the weeks following—weeks when the Virgin no more appeared.

All that while, Mariette continued her nightly seven o'clock vigils, and at last, after a hiatus of twenty-two nights, the Virgin once more visited Banneux. Significantly, she chose February 11, the seventy-fifth anniversary of her first appearance to Bernadette at Massabielle. She appeared again on February 13, with the message, "Believe in me. I will believe in you. Pray much." That was to prove the penultimate visit. The eighth and last took place on the rainy night of March 2, when the skies abruptly cleared and the Virgin came down through the pine trees one final time—in order, it would seem, simply to say good-bye. After uttering the gracious words, "*Adieu*—till we meet in God", the Lady departed by her familiar aerial path and Mariette saw her no more.

In his great elegy, Thomas Gray had written, "Let not Ambition mock their useful toil . . ./ Nor Grandeur hear with a disdainful smile/ The short and simple annals of the poor." Was Banneux, this great new addition to those annals, perhaps meant to reinforce by its wintry austerity and humble setting the great dignity of human existence as lived without the comforts of the rich? Whether or not, this renewed declaration of heavenly concern for those on the short end was a powerful reminder of other and greater events in those other poor and remote communities, Bethlehem and Nazareth.

Banneux's obscurity, in any case, did not last long, for soon pilgrims were streaming in by the battalion—rich, poor, and middle class—and treating the hundred yards separating the Beco home from the Mary fountain like holy ground. Twenty doctor-certified miraculous cures took place between 1933 and 1938 alone, and by 1942, the evidence was impressive enough that the case of Banneux received clearance in Rome. That meant all further approval was in the hands of the bishop of Liège, and the bishop of Liège liked what he heard. On the feast of the Immaculate Heart of Mary in 1949, that bishop, Louis Joseph Kerkhofs, made it official.

Before long, five hundred thousand pilgrims a year were retracing, mostly in summer, the winter footsteps of Mariette Beco or stopping by to join the seven o'clock rosary or to visit the Virgin-inspired hospital and home for children. The chapel she had asked for was of course built, and so have been three hundred other chapels and twenty-five churches throughout the world that have also been dedicated to the Virgin of the Poor. "The poor you always have with you"—and the poor always have with *them*, Banneux tells us, the divine speaker of those words, who comes to us through his golden-hearted Mother, bearing roses on her feet as she glides down through the tall pines toward the waters of mercy.

18

THE WOMAN CLOTHED WITH THE SUN
IN AN AGE OF DARKNESS

And I will show wonders in the heavens and in the earth,
blood, and fire, and pillars of smoke. The sun shall be turned
into darkness, and the moon into blood, before the great and
the terrible day of the Lord come.

—Joel 2:30–31

And ye shall hear of wars and rumors of wars. . . . For nation
shall rise against nation, and kingdom against kingdom, and
there shall be famines, and pestilences, and earthquakes in
divers places. All these are the beginning of sorrows.

—Matthew 14:6–8

In the center of Hell I saw a dark and horrible-looking abyss,
and into this Lucifer was cast, after first being strongly secured
with chains; thick clouds of sulphurous black smoke arose from
its fearful depths, and enveloped his frightful form in the dismal
folds, thus effectively concealing him from every beholder.
God himself had decreed this; and I was likewise told, if I remember it rightly, that he will be unchained for a time fifty or
sixty years before the year of Christ 2000.

—Anne Catherine Emmerich (1774–1824),
nun and visionary,
The Dolorous Passion of Our Lord Jesus Christ

As our shell-shocked millennium moves nervously to its close,
with wars and rumors of wars, floods, famines, hurricanes, and

earthquakes battering the planet in unprecedented numbers, more and more earthlings are pondering the Bible's doomsday passages, among them, for Mary-watchers, that one pitting the Great Red Dragon against the Woman Clothed with the Sun. The larger question, of course, is whether the climactic struggle between good and evil is just around the corner, has already begun, or has some time yet to bide.

Yet even if the Four Horsemen of the Apocalypse have not yet arrived on the scene, Anne Catherine Emmerich's vision of Lucifer unchained fifty or sixty years before the year 2000 would seem to have been right on target. In no other period in history has more hell broken loose than in the years since 1940—not only an exponential increase in natural disasters but the biggest and most lethal war of all time, along with Hitler, Stalin, Mao, Idi Amin, Pol Pot, Auschwitz, Buchenwald, Dresden, Hiroshima, Beirut, Chernobyl, Brave New World genetics, epidemic abortion, AIDS, child pornography, pederast priests, nuns joining covens, and ten thousand other horrors ranging from genocide in Bosnia to slavery in Sudan.

Another indication that the Great Red Dragon is breathing out record amounts of smoke, fire, and all-weather temptation is the stupefying increase in moral and religious frivolity, with, sad to say, vast numbers of befogged Catholic shepherds and their spiritually undernourished sheep joining in the revels. In the third chapter of his Second Letter to Timothy, the great Apostle zeroed in on social horseplay and self-indulgence as a sure-fire sign of the end: "In the last days . . . men shall be lovers of their own selves, unthankful, unholy, lovers of pleasures . . . having a form of godliness, but denying the power thereof . . . ever learning and never able to come to the knowledge of the truth."

The world of the late twentieth century would almost seem to be a full-color illustration of that prophetic text, a world of self-gratification so widespread and so democratically insisted on that the late Malcolm Muggeridge was to dub it People's Hedonism. Indeed, simply to look around in any of today's Western democracies is to see things that would have been un-imaginable as recently as 1960—a vast network of abortion mills, condom distribution to schoolchildren, homosexuality not only rampant but respectable, divorce routine, the zodiac and the "psychic hotline" treated as oracles, the music nasty, and even the crime undertaken as much for vicious pleasure as for simple gain.

With so many signs pointing in the direction of the abyss, then, and so many millions eager to pass "Go" and collect what-ever lies ahead, the time would seem to be growing ever riper for the appearance of that mysterious apocalyptic figure whose number is 666 and whose earthly reign will assuredly one day begin with all the power and horror of a black sun. As Cardinal Newman so convincingly put it a century and a half ago: "That Antichrist is to come is as categorical a heading to a chapter of history as that Nero or Julian was emperor of Rome."

In fact, the great Oxford scholar wrote those words in *The Idea of a University* only six years after the Blessed Virgin, at La Salette in 1846, warned of the Antichrist in the secret she con-fided to Mélanie Mathieu. And obviously that was not some playful comment on Mary's part aimed at getting a rise out of the stuffy Vatican bureaucracy but a serious reminder that his-tory has an end and Satan has an agent. We may well ask, then, after solemn warnings going back to the prophet Joel seven cen-turies before Christ, the words of Jesus himself, and 150 years of advance notice from the Blessed Virgin, are we now in the bell lap with the finish line in sight? And if so, are Mary's post–La Salette warnings the last shouts in the ear to the always hard-of-hearing human race?

One of those warnings, which took place in Akita, Japan, during the 1970s, may not have had quite the immediacy of the handwriting on the wall at Belshazzar's feast, but it sent a chill nonetheless. The chief witness was the then forty-two-year-old Agnes Sasagawa Katsuko, a Catholic nun at the convent of the Servants of the Eucharist in this Japanese city some two hundred miles north of Tokyo, and what she experienced made it clear that even the fixed routine of life inside a modern convent can have its wild surprises.

In June 1973 Sister Agnes was praying before a wooden statue of the Virgin when she became aware of a mysterious light. That was just the beginning. On August 3, the statue not only spoke but spoke of an ominous future chastisement from God the Father in which "fire" would "fall from the sky" unless there followed "a dramatic increase in prayer, penance, and sacrifice". At another point, the statue bled. Then, beginning September 29 and continuing for a considerable period, it intermittently perspired, gave off a scent of lilies and roses, and, finally, wept. Between January 1975 and September 1981, there were 101 separate such incidents and a cloud of witnesses to confirm them.

Altogether, the events so impressed John Shogiro Ito, bishop of Niigata, that on April 22, 1984, and despite the opposition of a national commission appointed by the other Japanese bishops, he declared them "undeniable" and authorized the veneration of Our Lady of Akita. The threat of fire falling from the sky, fortunately not yet carried out, continues to seem all the more ominous for having been made in the nation of Hiroshima and Nagasaki.

While there have been a number of other unsettling apparitions in recent decades, none have so far received the resident bishop's accreditation—though that of course does not necessarily mean they are invalid, simply that sentence has not so far been passed. As it happens, the one recent apparition apart from Akita to have been given an episcopal seal of approval (1987) took place in Betania, Venezuela, and contained no ominous messages whatsoever. Still, authenticated or not, a number of these recent apparitions have offered impressive, if not quite conclusive, evidence and are definitely worth looking at. As the saying goes, if they are not true, they are well invented. Here are three examples:

Kibeho (Rwanda). On November 28, 1981, the Blessed Virgin reportedly began appearing (individually) to six young Rwandans, urging them, as she had done with others so many times elsewhere, to act as her messengers and beseech their nation and their world to pray, fast, and be converted. The apparitions were said to have inspired a lively spiritual renewal in that part of Africa along with a remarkable increase in priestly vocations.

On August 19, 1982, the apparition supposedly wept, and appropriately so, for on that day the Virgin showed the young people horrifying images of the future: fierce combat, a river of blood, great heaps of abandoned corpses. A decade or so later, during the Rwanda-Burundi conflict, the visions had a chillingly graphic confirmation—front-page photographs of a blood-stained river into which had been dumped vast numbers of bodies, some half-eaten by dogs.

Garabandal (Spain). This is perhaps the most fascinating of all reported Marian apparitions since Fatima. Between June 18, 1961, and June 18, 1965, four young girls (all either eleven or twelve years old when the apparitions began) from this tiny mountainside village in northern Spain claimed to have seen and talked with both Saint Michael the Archangel and the Blessed Virgin, the latter more than two thousand times. Since there was no evidence of coaching or co-opting on the part of priests, parents, or other adults, and truly astonishing things happened (for example, all of the girls were tested when in trance with results every bit as convincing as those registered by the young visionaries at Beauraing), "Garabandal" seemed destined to join the roll call of authentic grand-scale Marian appearances. But there were problems.

First, there was the startlingly uncharacteristic number of Marian appearances—some five hundred or so every year for four years. By comparison, even at such vitally important apparition sites as Guadalupe, Lourdes, and Fatima, the number of appearances were, respectively, only four, eighteen, and seven. And at La Salette, of course, there was only one.

Second, there has so far been no physical sign approaching the dramatic concreteness of the signs given by the Blessed Virgin to confirm the validity of her earlier appearances. At Guadalupe, there was the tilma; at Lourdes, the healing stream; at Fatima, the dance of the sun—and further, all these great miracles occurred no later than six months after the first apparition. At Garabandal, there was only the so-called "little miracle", reportedly announced at the bidding of Saint Michael fifteen days in advance by Conchita Gonzalez, one of the young seers. On that occasion (the 1:40 A.M. darkness of July 19, 1962), a visible host suddenly appeared on Conchita's tongue; among the many people on hand for the event was a photographer who captured it on film. But the "great miracle", unlike those at the famous apparition sites just mentioned, has not only not come swiftly, it has not come at all—and it was promised well over thirty years ago.

Third, and perhaps most troubling of all, the four young visionaries were allegedly told by the Virgin that as a kind of parallel to the confusion soon to beset the Catholic Church herself, they would undergo a period of perplexity when they would doubt that the apparitions had ever happened—and that indeed came to pass. In fact, one of the visionaries—Mari Cruz Gonzalez—has doubts to this day.

Fourth, a detail that a number of critics have found unsettling was that during the Virgin's first appearance, a peculiar symbol appeared on her right side and parallel with her head—a square of red fire framing a triangle containing a large eye. Some commentators saw in it a symbol of the Trinity; others, a disturbing resemblance to the Masonic symbol that appears on the American dollar bill over the Latin words signifying New World Order. Also, as opposed to her traditional practice, the Virgin wore a crown but no headdress—her long dark hair, reaching to her waist, was fully visible.

Fifth, Mari Loli, another of the visionaries, was reportedly told by the Virgin that the Great Tribulation "could" be coming, that if it did, its name would be Communism, it would become worldwide, and it would precede the three chief events prophesied at Garabandal—the warning, the miracle, and the chastisement. Since Communism is not presently in the ascendant and since the Great Tribulation mentioned in the Apocalypse is to last forty-two months, all of these things would seem to be very far off. It is also unclear as to why, after the horrors of the Great Tribulation, anyone would require either a warning or a chastisement.

Finally, there was the case of Father Luis Andreu, a young Garabandal-believing Jesuit priest whose early death was followed by the promise his body would be found incorrupt on the day after the great miracle. Yet when his remains were dug up in 1976 at the Jesuit cemetery at Ona, they were found to be already partially corrupt. Garabandal's defenders responded that the prophecy had specified incorruption after the miracle, not before, but the doubting Thomases could only smile.

Yet despite these difficulties, there are compelling reasons to take Garabandal seriously. Here are some of them:

- In 1962, the Virgin told Conchita there would be only two more popes after Paul VI and that one would have a very short reign. Since John Paul I died after occupying the chair of Peter for only thirty-three days, at least half that prophecy was uncannily accurate.

- On June 18, 1965, the last day of the apparitions, Saint Michael reportedly told Conchita, "Many cardinals, many bishops, and many priests are on the road to perdition and are taking many souls with them", adding ominously, "Less and less importance is being given to the Eucharist." Since these prophetic words were spoken during the optimistic glow of the soon-to-conclude Second Vatican Council and just before the Church went into her tailspin, they have the force that goes with truth expressed at a time when truth seems at odds with reality. (By the way, it seems more than coincidental that the years of Garabandal, 1961–1965, and the years of Vatican II, 1962–1965, were so nearly identical.)

- Not only did Conchita keep a diary during the four years, but what she set down in it is consistent in all respects with Catholic doctrine. Also, the emphasis was on maintaining belief in the very things the modernist element in the Church would soon be trying to discard, diminish, or ignore: the Blessed Sacrament, the rosary, the scapular and sacramentals, penance, sorrow for sins and conversion of life, prayer for priests, respect for Church authority, and modesty in dress. Indeed, the Virgin went so far as to instruct the girls in how to say the rosary.

- There were any number of extraordinary physical phenomena that were witnessed, reliably reported, and even photographed. For example, in what were described as "ecstatic marches", undertaken on the way to or from an apparition, the girls were able to look up continuously and yet negotiate steep and rockly slopes either backward or forward at high speed without stumbling.

- Again, during one so-called "ecstatic fall", there was the observation of a witnessing priest that, given the backward tilting of her torso, Man Loli's dress should have been pulled up well above her knees. Instead, he saw this: "Her clothes moved downward in an anti-natural movement, as though an invisible hand were assuring the girl's perfect modesty." It would seem unlikely, given his well-known dislike for moral fastidiousness, that the invisible hand was the devil's.

- Finally, though no bishop of nearby Santander (and there have been six since 1961) has so far given official sanction, Rome was sufficiently interested to summon two of the young visionaries there to testify, and officials in the Congregation for the Doctrine of the Faith were reportedly impressed. And significantly, Padre Pio, the only Franciscan to receive the stigmata since Saint Francis himself and a soul gifted with an astonishing power of clairvoyance, met privately with Conchita and was by no means sceptical. Indeed, one of his last requests was that the veil that covered his face when he was laid in his coffin be given to Conchita.

Padre Pio, Garabandal's chief character witness, died in 1968. Thirty years have passed, and still the world awaits confirmation of the major Garabandal prophecies: (1) a divine interior warning to be given simultaneously to every person on earth during which the person will see not only all his sins, but all their consequences, (2) a public miracle that will be performed in Garabandal not more than a year after the warning, and that will remain, so to speak, on permanent exhibition, and (3) a terrible chastisement conditional on mankind's response for good or evil following the warning and the miracle. All of this will supposedly occur within the lifetimes of the visionaries (all of them now married women in their late forties), and further, Conchita, who was long ago told the date of the miracle, will announce it eight days in advance. Thus the faithful and those seeking cures can make plans to be in Garabandal on that promised Thursday evening in March, April, or May of the mystery year. Las Vegas is not yet quoting odds on any or all of this happening, but it looks like a long shot.

Gortnadreha (Ireland). Christina Gallagher, then thirty-four years old, of sound mind with no record of having consorted with ghosts, faeries, or leprechauns, and the happily married mother of two, received, on January 21, 1988, and in almost every sense out of the blue, a Marian apparition. This refreshingly ordinary woman, just five feet tall and as Irish as the harp of Tara, has since received many more—not to mention breathtaking visions of our Lord, the Holy Trinity, and heaven, hell, and purgatory. A so-called "chosen soul", she claims to have been asked by Jesus, "Will you allow me to suffer in you?" As a result of her agreeing to do so, she not only reportedly endures the stigmata every week at midweek but has received a vast and often harrowing series of visions and revelations past and future.

Unless she is secretly a charlatan to rank with Lola Montez, Lord Gordon-Gordon, and Count Cagliostro, it would seem this largely unlettered housewife from a tiny village in County Mayo has been living out an existence of remarkable spiritual depth and range, one whose illuminations rank with those of figures as great and various as Saint John the Evangelist, Theresa Neumann, the Curé of Ars, and the aforementioned Padre Pio and Anne Catherine Emmerich. Among other things, she has become a magnet for Catholic priests in need of spiritual renewal—this at least in part because of her powers of clairvoyance. Asked for an example of her ability to see through the human surface, she once related this little fireside tale out of Nathaniel Hawthorne by way of *The Exorcist*:

> This particular priest, who was losing his sight, asked me to pray for him and ask our Blessed Mother to help him. All of a sudden I was aware of things about him. . . . I saw where the Lord had led a lady to him in a foreign country. I could see this lady; she was in her fifties. She was dark-skinned and possessed by an evil spirit. Jesus led her there to this particular priest . . . and (he) was meant to help her. When she came to this priest, he became frightened. He said to me, "Christina, when I looked into her eyes, I thought I was looking into the eyes of the Devil." He said, "I thought I'd never get her out of the door fast enough." . . . Then I told him what happened,

how God sent this lady to him. I told him she was guided to
him by God even with an evil spirit in her. I also told him that
it had been up to him to help her and I said, "You didn't." I
said, "You showed her the door and when she went out, this is
what cost you your sight. She cursed you for not helping her
and God permitted the loss of your sight to be part of your
purification."

The ability to read hearts represents only a small part of this
privileged woman's spiritual field of sight. At a far greater level,
she was granted a step-by-step vision of our Lord's Passion, an
epiphany to rank with anything in Theresa Neumann's private
witness. She has also seen what she would rather not—enduring, à la the Curé of Ars, a terrifying two-hour visit from the
Prince of Darkness as well as a dozen of his briefer courtesy
calls. She has also been shown his celebrated protectorate,
which she describes in language strikingly similar to that of the
young Fatima visionaries: "All I could see was an endless sea of
fire, and somehow I could look down through it. . . . And there
were the shapes of bodies in it, as if in a sea, swimming in this
fire. . . . There were an enormous amount of bodies. I felt an
awful sense of terror. I could do nothing but quiver."

Since prophets traditionally speak to the condition of the
earthly house of God, it is not surprising that Christina's visions sometimes deal with the current Catholic practice of
throwing out ten babies with every drop of bath water. In one
such vision she saw a roofless church with Michael the Archangel repeatedly descending into it to rescue a number of tab-
ernacles. Later, asking what it had meant, she was told that the
church with the roof off represented the state of the Church
today—"that the authorities within the Church were throwing
away the treasures of God"—even as Michael strove to protect
the Holy Eucharist.

Protecting the Eucharist was also stressed by Jesus when he
reportedly asked Christina to relay his request (but not com-

mand) that Catholics make an act of reparation for the abuse of the Eucharist by receiving on the tongue only. "Someone . . . later said that I was going against the Church's teaching, but . . . when I told Jesus of my plight regarding this person, Jesus then replied, 'My little one, *I* am the Church.' "

Perhaps the most ominous of all her visions and warnings are those involving the mysteries of the Apocalypse—the Seven Seals, the Angel of Wrath, and, here on earth, what may well represent the laying of the foundation for the Antichrist's world economic system—the Maastricht Treaty. The small city of Maastricht, Holland, was the treaty's site, but the treaty's scope was and is vast: European monetary union with a single currency to be put in place sometime in 1999, an autonomous central bank, a common foreign policy, and "social cohesion". Here could be a major step on the road to fulfilling that harrowing passage in chapter 13 of the Apocalypse: "And . . . no man might buy or sell, save he that had the mark, or the name of the beast, or the number of his name"—which, of course, is the mysterious 666. (One interpretation of that unhappy number is a man acting as God: since 6 is the number of a man—man having been created on the sixth day—the man heaven calls Antichrist will attempt to elevate himself to trinitarian status by using the number thrice.)

Be all that as it may, in November 1991, in words that should have brought plaster falling from the ceiling in every home on earth, the Blessed Virgin reportedly told Christina to observe what happened in the world on three dates: December 9, 1991, and January 3 and June 15, 1992. On December 9, meeting in Maastricht, the European Council reached conclusions on all the outstanding points in the treaty. When, on December 10, our Lady appeared to Christina and was asked about the previous day's significance, she replied, "That meeting was a sign of the power of the Antichrist. Few realize how soon he will raise himself up."

January 3, meanwhile, proved to be the date on which Eastern European countries were invited to join this growing economic superpower (eleven months later, agreements with Poland, Hungary, and Czechoslovakia would be signed). Finally, June 15 was the day on which the Irish government "bribed" its people with a promise to farmers of a 30 percent grant increase if Irish voters ratified the Maastricht Treaty. The bribe may not even have been necessary—the June 18 vote, despite the awareness that the European Community's insistence on freedom to provide "services" would undermine Ireland's ban on abortion, was a pro-treaty landslide: 69 percent to 31 percent in favor.

For those tempted to think that all these revelations represent the crazed visions of an Irish bulimia victim who has wolfed down too much soda bread, it should be mentioned that Christina has received at least a degree of official endorsement from Archbishop Joseph Cassidy of Tuam. In 1993, he blessed and dedicated the chapel closest to her heart—Our Lady Queen of Peace House of Prayer, located on Achill, Ireland's largest island.

And yet, while there are strong indications that Christina Gallagher is a true seer seeing true things, it should be remembered that the world has never been short of convincing counterfeit mystics, including those Jesus warned about in Matthew 24:24: "For there shall arise false Christs and false prophets, and shall show great signs and wonders, insomuch that, if it were possible, they shall deceive the very elect." And impressive as they are in many particulars, Kibeho, Garabandal, and Gortnadreha are yet to cross the threshold of confirmation. In any case, these three represent only a handful of the vast number of apparitions reported worldwide over the last twenty years or so, among which at least three others—San Nicolas (Argentina), Cuapa (Nicaragua), and Naju (Korea)—are superficially just as impressive.

Then there are those that seem to have come out of left field with all the fans in the bleachers following. One such case was that of the movement begun by the late Mrs. Veronica Leuken of Bayside, Queens, who built a devoted following starting in 1976 after announcing that she had begun receiving Marian messages loud and clear. Whatever the source may have been, one of the pronouncements that subsequently came out of Bayside contained perhaps the most bizarre theory ever put forth about a sitting pope: "An impostor rules in the place of Paul VI. He is a creature of the mind of Satan's agents. One of the best plastic surgeons has been employed to create this impostor. . . . My child, shout this from the rooftops." Shouted from the rooftops in response was episcopal disapproval on the part of the Archdiocese of New York.

Then there are those apparitions that, while they have encountered similarly loud and clear opposition by the local bishop, have nevertheless been accorded a wait-and-see response on the part of Rome. One such example is Medjugorje in present-day Bosnia, where a series of Marian apparitions allegedly witnessed by a group of teenaged seers were supposed to have begun in 1981 and to have continued thereafter for some thirteen years. And yet, for all the miraculous claims and apparent good fruits that have made it the most popular apparition site since Fatima, Medjugorje has inspired as much scepticism as it has devotion.

The episcopal figure charged with oversight of Medjugorje in the first years of the "miracles", Bishop Pavao Zanic of Mostar, was reportedly at first impressed. But after interviewing the children and receiving what he considered unsatisfactory answers, he came to suspect behind-the-scenes manipulation and—though it in no way slowed the flood of pilgrims—uttered a resounding "No." So, too, did his successor, Bishop Ratko Peric. Meanwhile, the Yugoslavian Bishops' Conference, after nine years of Medjugorje-watching, declined to pronounce the events there in any way supernatural. And apart from official nonacceptance, there have been three book-length exposés—by the noted Catholic journalists Michael Davies and E. Michael

Jones and by the Reverend Vittorio Guerrera. For its part, however, Rome has in no way discouraged visits to Medjugorje, and great numbers of people continue to go there.

With Medjugorje, as with all other alleged apparitions that have not received offical approval, it is wise to bear in mind that an apparition can be any one of four things: genuine, hallucinatory, deliberately invented, or satanic. Father Guerrera issued an instructive warning about the last of those possibilities in his 1993 book, *Medjugorje: A Closer Look*:

> An example of the devil's work is evident in the story of Sister Magdalen of the Cross, a Franciscan nun who was born in Spain in 1487. She experienced visions from the age of five. When she was thirteen years old, the source of her revelations was made manifest to her. It was the devil. Despite this declaration, she made a pact with the devil in exchange for a reputation of holiness, which she possessed for over thirty years. At the age of seventeen, she entered the convent. During that time she was made abbess of her monastery three times, experienced ecstasies and levitations, made prophecies that came true, and had the stigmata. . . . As a result, she was frequently visited by ecclesiastics and other prominent figures who succumbed to her charade. When she lay at death's door, however, she made a public confession that she had been in concert with Satan. After having been exorcised by the Church, she was sent to another convent for the remainder of her days.

It is thus not always an easy matter to determine what is genuine in cases where the spiritually extraordinary is on display, which is why the Church traditionally takes her time before pronouncing yea or nay. Yet no matter who really has been seeing the Blessed Virgin and who has not, we can trust that her true message will eventually be heard and felt. That, after all, has been the rule ever since Mary first uttered the words of the Magnificat. Meanwhile, be the future what it may, to follow her path in history is to receive a continuing lesson in holiness and a permanent education in wonder:

Saluted by an angel, Mother of the Messiah, given to the Church at Calvary, assumed into Paradise, declared the second Eve, prayed to by Christians as early as the third century, declared *Theotokos* in 431, her image carried by Gregory the Great through the streets of Rome in 590, credited by the Greeks with saving Constantinople in 626, honored by Charlemagne's Mary Church in 794, inspirer of Chartres Cathedral, revered in rosary, scapular, and Angelus, patroness of Mount Carmel, exalted subject of Dante and Michelangelo, conqueror of Quetzalcoatl, deliverer at the Battle of Lepanto in 1571, comforter in the trials at Siluva in 1608, help of Christians in the French Revolution, and glorious sight to the pure in heart beginning with Catherine Labouré at the Rue du Bac in 1830 and continuing through La Salette, Lourdes, Pontmain, Knock, Fatima, Beauraing, and Banneux in 1933, she is that majestic mother of all living and mediatrix of all graces, that queen of heaven and rose of the world, that eternally young woman who lives and reigns in Paradise even as she comforts the earth with the beauty of roses, the mercy of fountains, and the permanence of gold.

ART CREDITS